Lac de Moiry (Stage 9b)

KNIFE EDGE
Outdoor Guidebooks

Publisher: Knife Edge Outdoor Limited (NI648568)
12 Torrent Business Centre, Donaghmore, County Tyrone, BT70 3BF, UK
www.knifeedgeoutdoor.com

Second edition 2025
ISBN: 978-1-912933-62-4

First edition 2019

Mapping produced by Knife Edge Outdoor Limited:

A catalogue record for this book is available from the British Library.

Front cover: The Matterhorn viewed on Zermatt's Walk 23 (see p175)

Back cover: The wonderful Europaweg (Stage 13b)

Title page: Views of Mont Blanc on the route to Croix de Fer (Stage v1e)

This page: Sunset view from Cabane de Mille (Stage v3b)

All routes described in this book have been recently walked by the author and both the author and publisher have made all reasonable efforts to ensure that all information is as accurate as possible. However, while a printed book remains constant for the life of an edition, things in the wild often change. Trails are subject to forces outside our control. For example, landslides, avalanches, tree-falls or other matters can result in damage to paths or route changes; waymarks and signposts may fade or be destroyed by wind, snow or the passage of time; or trails may not be maintained by the relevant authorities. If you notice any discrepancies between the information in this guide and the facts on the ground, then please let us know by email (info@knifeedgeoutdoor.com).

Contents

Getting Help 1
Introduction 3
Using this book 5
When to go 6
How hard is the trek? 8
Direction and start/finish point 9
Hiking shorter sections of the trek 9
Guided tours, self-guided tours or independent walking? 10
Itinerary Planner 11
Suggested Itineraries 12
Variant Stages 15
Accommodation 16
Camping 18
Accommodation Listings 20
Campsite Listings 27
Food 28
Travel to/from the trail-heads 30
Primary trail-heads 30
Secondary trail-heads 31
Transport map 35
On the Trail 36
Costs & budgeting 36
Weather 36
Maps 37
Paths and waymarking 38
Water 39
Storing bags 40
Baggage transfer 41
Fuel for camping stoves 41
Outdoor shops 42
Ticks 42
Pastous 42
Equipment 43
Recommended basic kit 44
Additional gear for campers 46
Safety 48
General Information 49
Wildlife 50
Plants & Flowers 52
Route Descriptions 53
1. Chamonix to Trient 54
v1d. Col de Balme to Chalet du Glacier (via les Grands) 62
v1e. Col de Balme to le Peuty (via Croix de Fer) 64
2. Trient to Champex 66
v2b. Col de la Forclaz to Champex (via Bovine) 72
3. Champex to le Châble 76
4. Le Châble to Cabane du Mont Fort 82
5. Cabane du Mont Fort to Cabane de Prafleuri 86
v5a. Cabane du Mont Fort to Cabane de Prafleuri (via Col de la Chaux) 90

v5b. Col Termin to Cabane de Louvie 93
v5c. Louvie Link Route 94
Champex to Cabane de Prafleuri (High Altitude Variant) 95
v3. Champex to Col de Mille (via Orsières) 96
v4. Cabane de Mille to Cabane de Louvie 100
6. Cabane de Prafleuri to Arolla 104
v6a. Cabane de Prafleuri to Refuge de la Barmaz (via Barrage de la Dixence) 110
v6b. Refuge de la Barmaz to Arolla (via Cabane des Dix) 112
v6c. Hotel du Barrage to les Haudères (via Col de la Meina) 114
7. Arolla to la Sage 118
8. La Sage to Cabane de Moiry 122
v8. La Sage to Barrage de Moiry 126
v9a. Barrage de Moiry to Grimentz 129
9. Cabane de Moiry to Zinal 134
10. Zinal to Gruben 138
v10. Zinal to Gruben (via Meidpass) 142
11. Gruben to St-Niklaus 148
Routes between St-Niklaus and Zermatt 152
12. St-Niklaus to the Europahütte 154
v12a. St-Niklaus to Randa (valley route) 160
v12b. St-Niklaus to Grächen 164
v12c. Grächen to Gasenried 165
13. The Europahütte to Zermatt 166
v13a. Randa to Zermatt (valley route) 172
v13b. Randa to the Europahütte (Link Route) 173
Zermatt Day Hikes 174
Facilities along the route 178

Getting Help

Emergency services number: **dial 112**

Distress signal

The signal that you are in distress is 6 blasts on a whistle spaced over a minute, followed by a minute's silence. Then repeat. The acknowledgment that your signal has been received is 3 blasts of a whistle over a minute followed by a minute's silence. At night, flashes of a torch can also be used in the same sequences. Always carry a torch and whistle.

Signalling to a helicopter from the ground

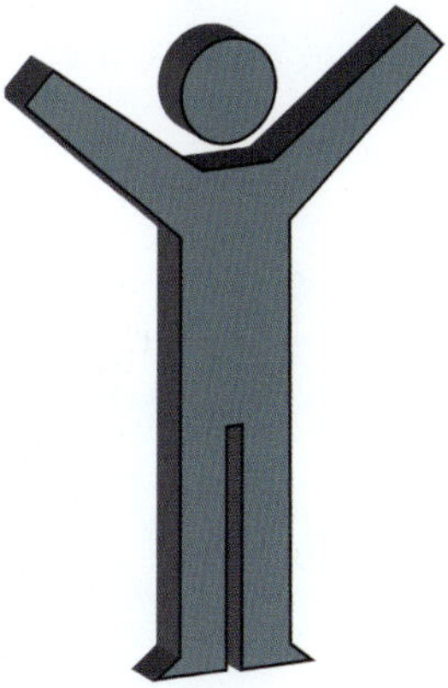

Help Required

Raise both arms in the shape of a 'Y'

Help Not Required

Raise one arm and extend the other arm down and outwards

WARNING

Hills, cliffs and mountains can be dangerous places and walking is a potentially dangerous activity. Some of the routes described in this guide cross potentially hazardous terrain. You walk entirely at your own risk. It is solely your responsibility to ensure that you and all members of your group have adequate experience, fitness and equipment. Neither the author nor the publisher accepts any responsibility or liability whatsoever for death, injury, loss, damage or inconvenience resulting from use of this book, participation in the activity of mountain walking or otherwise.

Some land may be privately owned and we cannot guarantee that there is a legal right of entry to the land. Occasionally, routes change as a result of land disputes.

Sunset at Cabane de Mille (Stage v3b)

Introduction

If the Tour du Mont Blanc (TMB) is the most famous trek in the Alps, the Walker's Haute Route (WHR) is surely a close runner-up. Because both start in the Chamonix valley, the two treks are considered to be sisters and many who have completed the TMB look to the WHR for their next trekking challenge: the WHR is slightly tougher than the TMB so it is the logical next step. To be spoken about in the same breath as the exquisite TMB is in itself a huge compliment, however, for many trekkers, the WHR is superior both in terms of scenery and experience.

Whilst the TMB is a circular route, the WHR is linear. It is an uninterrupted journey between the two most famous mountaineering locations in the Alps, and between the two most famous Alpine mountains: travelling from Chamonix in France to Zermatt in Switzerland, you will start at Mont Blanc and finish at the Matterhorn. Fair weather views of either of these peaks would rank as highlights of anybody's walking career but the WHR also exhibits a dizzying array of other Alpine giants. In fact, the route leads you past the largest collection of 4000m summits in the Alps: Mont Blanc, Grand Combin, the Weisshorn, the Zinalrothorn, the Dom, the Täschhorn, the Breithorn and the Matterhorn, to name a few. To facilitate passage through this incredible wonderland of high peaks, there is a succession of exhilarating mountain passes (known as 'cols'), helping you cross from one magnificent valley to another. And there are exquisite alpine pastures, sparkling azure lakes and carpets of wild-flowers, the like of which you will never have seen before.

Lac de l'Armina (Stage v10b)

But there are perhaps two other key characteristics of the WHR. Firstly, its wildness: parts of the trek are fabulously remote and rugged, delivering a more intense and adventurous mountain experience than the TMB. Secondly, the magnificent glaciers: they are seemingly everywhere and the route brings you extremely close to some of them.

You will live and breathe these scenic delights, night and day, because you need never leave the mountains: fabulous accommodation is available in beautiful alpine villages and remote mountain huts, spaced out along the route. Places with views that most people dream of but few will ever see. Places that you will never forget. Places that will leave you with remarkable memories. This is a trek that easily justifies its place on your bucket list.

Although the WHR is a popular trek, it rarely feels crowded. After the first few sections (which are shared with the busy TMB), peace and solitude are not difficult to find: this huge swathe of the Alps is easily large enough to swallow the many hikers that descend upon it each summer. Get a reasonably early start and you will find yourself largely alone for much of the day. You will occasionally pass, or be passed by, other trekkers but these meetings can be as fleeting as you wish. And at the end of the day, on arrival at your resting place, often high above the valleys, you will likely meet some of the people that you bumped into earlier. Then bonds can be formed over dinner or a drink: like the TMB, the WHR has a fine reputation as a sociable trek.

Unlike the TMB, the WHR has no official route: it is merely a crossing of the Alps between Chamonix and Zermatt, using the most convenient and scenic routes. However, over time, the route has largely become settled and the main paths that we describe are the ones followed by most trekkers. Nevertheless, in our opinion, the generally accepted routing is not always the best or most scenic option: there are many variant routes that you could follow which use different high passes to those crossed on the main route. To give you more choice, we include in this book a wide range of these variants: sometimes they are more adventurous than the main route but, in other cases, they offer a safer alternative in periods of bad weather. Although many of the variants are widely known and well-documented, for this second edition, we have developed some new alternatives which you are unlikely to find elsewhere and which will take you further off the beaten track. In fact, we have included so many different options that you could return for a second crossing and, for the most part, hike different routes from those used first time around.

Our main WHR route is 218km in length with 14,100 metres of ascent and 13,500 metres of descent. You will cross 12 magnificent mountain passes. In addition, we describe 24 incredible variants, totalling 205km: they are summarised in the table on p15.

Those statistics may sound intimidating but it is reassuring to note that plenty of normal people complete the trail each year: with the right preparation, planning and approach, it is manageable for most people of reasonable fitness. Yes, it is a challenge but it is an achievable one. And that is where this book comes in: most of what you need to know to plan, and prepare for, the WHR is here within these pages and the entire route is described in detail to guide you on the trail itself. Furthermore, unlike some other books, this one contains real topographical maps: for each stage, there are 1:40,000 scale maps to go with the accurate and concise route descriptions. Because we were unable to find commercially available maps which suited our purposes, we commissioned our own maps and they are perfect for navigating the trail. As well as including those maps in this book, we have also published a sheet map for the WHR which is extremely helpful for planning and navigation: ***Trekking Map: Walker's Haute Route: Chamonix to Zermatt*** (ISBN 9781912933518).

We aim to ensure that you have the best chance possible of completing the trek. We place great importance on the correct preparation and we focus in detail on modern lightweight equipment (p43). We also believe that it is crucial to match your itinerary to your experience, fitness and ability. Accordingly, we have included here an extraordinary level of detail on itinerary planning: our unique itinerary planner (p11) has 6 different itineraries to choose from. For each itinerary, we have completed for you all the difficult calculations of time, distance and altitude gain/loss. This makes it easy for you to design a manageable itinerary that suits your specific needs. Once on the trail, you will be able to relax and fully enjoy one of the world's great treks.

Using this book

This book is designed to be used by trekkers of differing abilities. Many guidebooks for long-distance treks rigidly divide the route into a fixed number of long day-stages, leaving it up to the hiker to break down those stages to design daily routes which suit his/her abilities. This book, however, has been laid out differently to give the trekker flexibility: it divides the route into 26 shorter stages which you can combine to design daily routes that meet your own specific needs.

Each stage covers the distance between one accommodation option and the subsequent one. Every accommodation option on the route is the start/finish point of a stage. You can choose how many of these stages you wish to walk each day. Each stage has its own walk description, route map and elevation profile.

The labelling of the stages uses a combination of numbers and letters. It is a simple system but requires a little bit of explanation. Firstly, we have divided the route into 13 'Sections' (numbered from 1 to 13 from W to E): each Section represents one day of our standard 13-day itinerary. Within some Sections, the route is further broken down into two or more 'Stages': these stages are also labelled with a number between 1 and 13, representing the relevant Section that the Stage is part of. These Stages are also labelled with a letter. So, for example, the first stage in Section 7 is 'Stage 7a', the second stage is 'Stage 7b' and so on. Take a look at the detailed Itinerary Planner on p11 and all should become clear.

The Itinerary Planner includes a range of tables outlining six suggested itineraries of 10, 11, 12, 13 and 14 days. In each table, we have crunched the numbers for you so there is no need for you to waste time (and mental strength) working out daily distances, timings and altitude gain/loss.

Of course, the suggested itineraries are only suggestions. You can shorten or lengthen your day to suit yourself: just decide how many stages you want to walk that day. It is up to you. As there is accommodation at the end of every stage, it is easy to design your own bespoke itinerary and adjust it on the ground as you go (subject to accommodation availability).

For example, day 6 of the standard 13-day itinerary involves walking Stages 6a and 6b. However, you could decide to extend your day by walking Stages 6a, 6b and 7a, all on the same day. Or you might be tired and decide to shorten your day by walking only Stage 6a. With some other guidebooks, you would have to work out how to split stages yourself, involving some complicated maths to plan distances and times going forward. This guide, however, does all the hard mental work for you.

We also provide a comprehensive range of variants which you can choose instead of the main route. The labelling for variants is similar to that used for the main stages except variant stages also have the prefix 'v'. The variants are summarised in the table on p15.

In this book:

Timings indicate the approximate time required by a reasonably fit walker to complete a stage. They do not include stoppage time. Do not get frustrated if your own times do not match ours: everyone walks at different speeds. As you progress through the trek, you will soon learn how your own times compare with those given here and you will adjust your plans accordingly.

Walking distances are given in kilometres (km) to match maps and signposts in Europe. One mile equates to approximately 1.6km.

Place names in brackets in the route descriptions indicate the direction to be followed on signposts. For example, "('Arolla')" would mean that you follow a sign for Arolla.

Ascent/descent numbers are the aggregate of all the altitude gain or loss (measured in feet and metres) on the uphill or downhill sections of a stage. As a rule of thumb, a fit walker climbs 1000 to 1300 feet (300 to 400m) in an hour. The statistics tables in the route descriptions are based on W-E itineraries: E-W trekkers should simply swap the ascent and descent figures.

Elevation profiles are provided for each Section, indicating where the climbs and descents fall on the route. The profiles are based on W-E itineraries: E-W hikers should simply read them in reverse.

Real maps are provided. These are extracts from 1:40,000 scale maps produced by Knife Edge Outdoor Guidebooks. On the maps, we have marked the route of the trek (red for the main route; purple for variants), the start/finish points of stages (yellow markers), significant waypoints (red markers for the main route; purple for variants) and the accommodation/campsites along the WHR. On each map, N is at the top of the page (except for the map on p158 where N is to the left). As well as printing these maps in this book, we have also published a sheet map for the WHR which is extremely helpful for planning and navigation: ***Trekking Map: Walker's Haute Route: Chamonix to Zermatt*** (ISBN 9781912933518).

The following abbreviations are used:

BCE	Before the Common Era (a secular alternative to 'BC')
CE	The Common Era (a secular alternative to 'AD')
CKSB	Charles Kuonen Suspension Bridge (see p162)
CMF	Cabane du Mont Fort (see p82)
GC Massif	Massif of the Grand Combin
MB	Mont Blanc
MBE	Mont Blanc Express train (see p30)
OR	Off-route
UTMB	Ultra Trail du Mont Blanc
WW1/WW2	World War 1/World War 2
TL	Turn left
TR	Turn right
SH	Straight ahead
N, S, E and W, etc.	North, South, East and West, etc.
W-E	West to East
E-W	East to West

When to go

The weather window for hiking the WHR is quite short: the trekking season usually starts towards the end of June and finishes around the third week of September. Even in this period, high winds, heavy rain, and low cloud (which reduces visibility), can occur: occasionally, it can even snow on the trail. You will probably hike in fine weather but you should prepare for the worst. Throughout the main trekking season, there is plenty of daylight. The relative merits of each season are discussed in detail below but, taking all the factors into consideration, we prefer to hike the WHR in the first two weeks of September.

Late June: this can be the most beautiful time for walking. The weather is often sunny and warm. The peaks are frequently at their most photogenic, still frosted with snow. Summer haze has not yet arrived so visibility is generally excellent, with wide-ranging views. This is peak season for wild-flowers too. Fewer visitors means that accommodation is easier to find and significantly, the mountains are more peaceful. However, as with all Alpine treks, snow sometimes remains on the high cols until early July, making parts of the route difficult and/or dangerous: in such conditions, crampons/spikes and/or an ice axe might be helpful. There are now some very light, compact crampons available which weigh a mere 300g so carrying them just in case is not the burden it once was. For those planning an early season trek, the weeks prior to the start date can be stressful because it might not become clear until the very last minute whether the snow has cleared sufficiently to hike the route safely: changing bookings at the last minute can be challenging, time consuming and costly (because you may not get all your money back).

July/August: this is the main summer season when the high cols are normally passable. During July/August, accommodation is harder to find and advance booking is recommended unless you are camping. It can be hot, reaching more than 30°C. Mornings often start with clear, sunny skies and heat up as the sun gains height. If there is to be cloud or haze, often this will arrive in the afternoon when thunderstorms are more likely. Start walking early in the morning to complete the main climb while the temperature is cooler and before storms arrive. As July progresses, the trails gradually become busier. The busiest time is probably the first two weeks of August, when many of the Swiss, Italians and French will be taking annual vacations. Towards the end of August, the number of trekkers starts to decrease.

September: this is our favourite month for hiking as the weather is often more settled than in summer. Skies are usually clear and visibility excellent. Daytime temperatures are still warm but evenings get cooler and the days get shorter. As the month progresses, the risk of light snowfall on the cols increases but any snow usually clears quickly. Occasionally, there are more significant dumps of snow in September that adversely impact the safety of trekking for a few days or more: this occurred in both 2023 and 2024. During September, visitor numbers gradually reduce: the mountains are quieter and there is less demand for accommodation. However, towards the end of the month, some accommodation closes for the season so check availability in advance.

October: this can be a very beautiful time, with spectacular autumn colours. However, careful planning is needed to undertake the route in October. As the month progresses, the possibility of snowfall on the cols increases which could make them impassable or dangerous. Check the weather forecasts carefully along the way to avoid getting trapped by snow between cols. If fresh snow is forecast, do not set out. Some accommodation will be closed. You will need to be prepared to carry more food as there will be fewer places to eat or buy supplies. Trekking in October is for experienced and well-equipped hikers only.

Month	Pros	Cons
Late June	Pleasant temperatures **Frequent sunny skies** Good visibility **Wild-flower season** Fewer trekkers **Hut beds easier to find** Longest days	Snow on the high parts of the trail: cols and peaks occasionally inaccessible
July/August	Generally reliably fine weather **High cols normally passable** Long days	The hottest period **Sometimes hazy** Afternoon thunderstorms **Visitor numbers highest** Hut beds harder to find **Some snow remains in early July**
September	Pleasant temperatures **Frequent sunny skies** Excellent visibility **Fewer visitors** Hut beds become easier to find **Autumn colours** Still sufficient daylight	Accommodation closes as the month progresses **Cooler evenings** Increasing possibility of snow
October	Autumn colours **Frequent sunny skies** Excellent visibility **Fewer visitors**	Greater possibility of snow **Much accommodation closed** Short days **Cold mornings and evenings**

How hard is the trek?

The WHR is a multi-day trek with significant distances to travel each day. It crosses remote landscapes of mountains and valleys: each day, you will need to climb and descend significantly to negotiate the undulating terrain. Sometimes, the climbs and descents are steep and challenging. As the days go by, such exertions take their toll on your body, both physically and mentally. Accordingly, a reasonable level of fitness is required and the fitter you are at the start of the trek, the better your chances of success and the more you will enjoy the experience.

The demand on your body is intensified by the requirement to carry a pack. However, because there is plenty of accommodation along the route, you do not need to carry camping equipment or food (other than basic rations) and therefore your bag can be kept light. Even so, it is fair to say that many trekkers set off carrying some equipment which is unnecessary or simply too heavy: this can contribute to injury and/or exhaustion, leading to abandonment. Accordingly, you should give equipment choice careful consideration (see p43): it will be crucial to your enjoyment of the trek and the likelihood of success.

Sometimes paths are steep, rocky and challenging underfoot. Occasionally, you might have to climb up or down sections of boulders but you will not require any technical scrambling/climbing skills. Often, the route is exposed with large, steep drops.

For the most part, the paths/tracks are clear, well-marked and simple to follow in good conditions. However, occasionally, the route is less obvious and more difficult to navigate: some sections of the route have no paths and you will have to rely on cairns and waymarks. That said, most people have no major difficulties staying on course. However, take care in poor conditions or low visibility when navigation on the highest sections of the trail can be tricky. Furthermore, on the high points of the route, snow can remain into July, covering paths and making progress/route-finding more difficult.

Many who have completed the TMB (the most famous Alpine trek) look to the WHR for their next trekking challenge. Accordingly, it can be useful to compare these two treks. The WHR is the harder of the two: it is longer (218km compared to 174km) and has much more climbing (14,100m compared to 9,700m). Furthermore, the remoteness and high altitude of much of the terrain means that there are fewer facilities along the route of the WHR than you will find on the TMB. Because there are fewer locations where you can spend the night, there are fewer ways to break up the trek to suit your own fitness and experience. Consequently, you are locked into a few fairly long stages: some of these are harder than the TMB's most difficult sections. The terrain on the WHR can be tougher too: the paths are sometimes rougher, less-frequented and harder to follow than those on the TMB.

However, notwithstanding the challenges, thousands of hikers walk the WHR each year. It is therefore an achievable endeavour. To improve fitness, it is sensible to train in advance: there is no substitute for training hikes, carrying a pack. Although not absolutely necessary, previous experience of trekking will help. And, of course, the level of difficulty depends upon how quickly, and how far, you travel each day: faster itineraries are obviously more challenging than slower ones and the WHR will be more manageable if you choose an itinerary that matches your fitness and experience. Most people walk the WHR in 12-13 days. However, fit and experienced hikers could finish it faster. Others prefer to walk more slowly, adding more days to soak up all the delights on offer. Our Itinerary Planner will help you decide what is best for you.

GC Massif (Stage 5)

Direction and start/finish point

Traditionally, the WHR is walked W to E (starting in Chamonix) and, because most trekkers travel that way, this book describes it in that direction. Although it could also be tackled in the other direction, there are some good reasons why most people travel W-E. Firstly, by walking W-E, you head towards the rising sun which falls first on E-facing slopes: this means that you benefit from shade (during the morning) on most of the steep climbs (which are often W-facing). It can be hot in the summer so this helps preserve your strength and stamina. Secondly, the views of the Matterhorn are arguably the highlight of the whole trek so it is wonderful to save the best for last; also, it is preferable to hike the Europaweg facing towards the Matterhorn. Furthermore, Zermatt is a wonderful place in which to spend a few days at the end of the trek. It is also worth bearing in mind that, because most hikers travel W-E, that is probably the more sociable approach: you are more likely to bump into the same people each day, making it easier to develop trail friendships.

Nevertheless, occasionally people do hike E-W and that approach is not without merit: some prefer not to meet the same people every day and walking against the flow achieves this. The real maps in this book, with numbered waypoints, make the route descriptions simple to follow in either direction.

Hiking shorter sections of the trek

Hiking the WHR in one go is a wonderful experience but there are other ways to enjoy this incredible trail. It is also possible to walk shorter sections of the route because there are many access points along the way which have public transport: for example, Champex, Trient, Sembrancher, le Châble, Barrage de la Dixence, Arolla, les Haudères, Zinal, Gruben, St-Niklaus and Herbriggen. In this book, we refer to these access points as 'secondary trail-heads'. You could start at any of these places and walk a few sections. Or you could skip sections by leaving the route at one of these secondary trail-heads and using public transport to resume at another point. For public transport options at secondary trail-heads, see p31.

Alternatively, you could use secondary trail-heads to walk certain parts of the WHR as day-hikes or you could hike to one of the wonderful mountain huts, stay the night and then return the next day.

If you only wish to walk some of the highlights of the trek then we would suggest the following options (all of which are served by public transport):

- **Cabane de Mille (1 or 2 days):** hike from Orsières to Cabane de Mille (Stage v3b). Then retrace your steps the same day or the following morning (after a night at the cabane).
- **Cabane de Mille & Cabane Brunet (2 days):** on day 1, hike from Orsières to Cabane de Mille (Stage v3b). Spend the night at Cabane de Mille. On day 2, hike to Cabane Brunet (Stage v4a) and then descend into Val de Bagnes (Stage v4b). From there, you can catch a bus to le Châble train station.
- **Le Grand Désert (2 days):** take the cable car from le Châble to les Ruinettes. Then hike to Cabane du Mont Fort (Stage 4) and spend the night there. The following day, hike to Barrage de la Dixence (Stages 5/v6a) where you can catch a bus to Sion (which has a train station).
- **Col de Riedmatten/Pas de Chèvres (1 or 2 days):** take the bus from Sion to Barrage de la Dixence. Then hike to Arolla via Col de Riedmatten/Pas de Chèvres (Stage v6a/6b). From Arolla, take the bus, or hike Stages 7a/7b, to les Haudères (where there is a bus connection back to Sion).
- **Europahütte/Europaweg (2 days):** hike from Randa to Europahütte (Section v13b) where you can spend the night. The following day, hike to Zermatt along the magnificent Europaweg (Section 13). Both Randa and Zermatt have train stations.

Guided tours, self-guided tours or independent walking?

A frequently asked question is whether to walk independently or with an organised group. The answer is a personal one and depends upon your own particular circumstances and requirements. For many, the decision to organise the trek themselves, and to walk independently, can be almost life-changing, opening the door for other challenges in the future. There is much satisfaction to be gained from planning and navigating a trek yourself and the sense of achievement on completion is to be savoured.

However, the independent trekker usually carries a full pack and is responsible for all daily decisions such as pacing, which way to go at junctions, when to stock up with food and water, and choice of route in bad weather. For some, this will be too great a burden on top of the physical effort required simply to walk the route. For those walkers, a guided group is a great solution: the tour company typically organises food and accommodation and the guide makes all the decisions, enabling the hiker to concentrate on the hiking. Tour companies can also usually organise transfer of luggage to your accommodation (see p41). However, the remoteness of a few of the huts on the WHR means that baggage transfer is not possible at every location: even guided trekkers need to carry their own gear for nights at the more remote huts such as Cabane de Prafleuri, Cabane de Moiry and the Europahütte. There are many tour companies operating guided trips on the WHR but you should check whether they cover the full official route or just some of the highlights.

Self-guided tours are much more popular and are a sensible middle-ground. As with guided tours, the tour company books all the accommodation and provides advice and information on walking the route. However, you will walk the trail without a guide, navigating with the help of this guidebook and/or any instructions provided by the tour company. Normally, breakfast and evening meals will be provided and you can request packed lunches. As with guided tours, self-guided tour companies can also usually organise transfer of luggage to many accommodation locations.

In recent years, there has been a rise in the number of businesses offering guided/self-guided tours. Consequently, some of the accommodation along the WHR is block-booked in advance by the tour companies. At peak times, this makes it harder for the independent trekker to secure accommodation unless booked well in advance. As a result, many confident trekkers (who would be perfectly capable of walking independently) book a self-guided trip simply to avail of the accommodation booking service. By booking a tour, much of the hassle of planning the trek is alleviated, albeit at a price.

Col de Balme (Stage v1d)

Itinerary Planner

All our itineraries start in Chamonix and finish in Zermatt. However, if you would prefer to begin your trek at one of the secondary trail-heads (see p31), then simply start reading from that location in the tables below.

Stage	Start	Finish	Time (hr)	Distance km	Distance miles	Ascent m	Ascent ft	Descent m	Descent ft	Max Alt m	Max Alt ft
1a	Chamonix	Argentière	2:45	9.3	5.8	274	899	67	220	1252	4108
1b	Argentière	Le Tour	1:30	4.0	2.5	252	827	43	141	1475	4839
1c	Le Tour	Col de Balme	2:20	4.3	2.7	738	2421	0	0	2191	7188
1d	Col de Balme	Le Peuty	1:40	5.2	3.2	0	0	865	2838	2191	7188
1e	Le Peuty	Trient	0:20	1.2	0.7	0	0	26	85	1326	4350
2a	Trient	Col de la Forclaz	0:45	1.5	0.9	239	784	13	43	1526	5007
2b	Col de la Forclaz	Arpette	6:00	12.9	8.0	1149	3770	1048	3438	2665	8743
2c	Arpette	Champex	0:40	2.6	1.6	0	0	160	525	1627	5338
3	Champex	Le Châble	4:00	14.1	8.8	192	630	838	2749	1490	4888
4	Le Châble	Cabane du Mont Fort	6:45	12.3	7.6	1665	5463	30	98	2456	8058
5	Cabane du Mont Fort	Cabane de Prafleuri	6:45	14.7	9.1	954	3130	754	2474	2987	9800
6a	Cabane de Prafleuri	Cabane de la Barmaz	1:30	3.2	2.0	195	640	393	1289	2803	9196
6b	Cabane de la Barmaz	Arolla	5:30	15.8	9.8	640	2100	1090	3576	2918	9573
7a	Arolla	La Gouille	1:50	4.8	3.0	252	827	426	1398	2130	6988
7b	La Gouille	Les Haudères	1:10	4.0	2.5	20	66	404	1325	1834	6017
7c	Les Haudères	La Sage	0:50	2.9	1.8	230	755	13	43	1667	5469
8	La Sage	Cabane de Moiry	5:55	11.8	7.3	1676	5499	518	1699	2868	9409
9a	Cabane de Moiry	Barrage de Moiry Junction	2:15	7.2	4.5	96	315	548	1798	2825	9268
9b	Barrage de Moiry Junction	Zinal	3:30	9.4	5.8	478	1568	1177	3862	2837	9308
10	Zinal	Gruben	6:40	17.7	11.0	1270	4167	1126	3694	2875	9432
11	Gruben	St-Niklaus	7:00	18.4	11.4	1096	3596	1787	5863	2892	9488
12a	St-Niklaus	Gasenried	2:00	3.9	2.4	548	1798	15	49	1660	5446
12b	Gasenried	Herbriggen	2:30	8.1	5.0	265	869	665	2182	1713	5620
12c	Herbriggen	Europahütte	3:50	7.2	4.5	1094	3589	90	295	2345	7694
13a	Europahütte	Täschalp	3:30	9.5	5.9	512	1680	619	2031	2264	7428
13b	Täschalp	Zermatt	3:45	12.4	7.7	298	978	850	2789	2347	7700

Suggested Itineraries

14 Days Option 1: this option is useful for those arriving in Chamonix later in the day as you can warm up with a half-day walk of 9km and overnight in Argentière. Days 2 and 3 are more difficult but then the easy Day 4 allows recovery before the harder stages to come.

Day	Stages	Start	Finish	Time (hr)	Distance km	Distance miles	Ascent m	Ascent ft	Descent m	Descent ft
1	1a	Chamonix	Argentière	2:45	9.3	5.8	274	899	67	220
2	1b, 1c, 1d, 1e, 2a	Argentière	Col de la Forclaz	6:35	16.2	10.0	1229	4032	947	3107
3	2b, 2c	Col de la Forclaz	Champex	6:40	15.5	9.6	1149	3770	1208	3963
4	3	Champex	Le Châble	4:00	14.1	8.8	192	630	838	2749
5	4	Le Châble	Cabane du Mont Fort	6:45	12.3	7.6	1665	5463	30	98
6	5	Cabane du Mont Fort	Cabane de Prafleuri	6:45	14.7	9.1	954	3130	754	2474
7	6a, 6b	Cabane de Prafleuri	Arolla	7:00	19.0	11.8	835	2740	1483	4865
8	7a, 7b, 7c	Arolla	La Sage	3:50	11.7	7.3	502	1647	843	2766
9	8	La Sage	Cabane de Moiry	5:55	11.8	7.3	1676	5499	518	1699
10	9a, 9b	Cabane de Moiry	Zinal	5:45	16.6	10.3	574	1883	1725	5659
11	10	Zinal	Gruben	6:40	17.7	11.0	1270	4167	1126	3694
12	11	Gruben	St-Niklaus	7:00	18.4	11.4	1096	3596	1787	5863
13	12a, 12b, 12c	St-Niklaus	Europahütte	8:20	19.2	12.0	1907	6257	770	2526
14	13a, 13b	Europahütte	Zermatt	7:15	21.9	13.6	810	2657	1469	4820

14 Days Option 2: similar to 14 Days Option 1 except that days 1-4 are structured differently so that the hiking is more evenly spread out over the four days.

Day	Stages	Start	Finish	Time (hr)	Distance km	Distance miles	Ascent m	Ascent ft	Descent m	Descent ft
1	1a, 1b	Chamonix	Le Tour	4:15	13.3	8.3	526	1726	110	361
2	1c, 1d, 1e, 2a	Le Tour	Col de la Forclaz	5:05	12.2	7.6	977	3205	904	2966
3	2b	Col de la Forclaz	Arpette	6:00	12.9	8.0	1149	3770	1048	3438
4	2c, 3	Arpette	Le Châble	4:40	16.7	10.4	192	630	998	3274
5	4	Le Châble	Cabane du Mont Fort	6:45	12.3	7.6	1665	5463	30	98
6	5	Cabane du Mont Fort	Cabane de Prafleuri	6:45	14.7	9.1	954	3130	754	2474
7	6a, 6b	Cabane de Prafleuri	Arolla	7:00	19.0	11.8	835	2740	1483	4865
8	7a, 7b, 7c	Arolla	La Sage	3:50	11.7	7.3	502	1647	843	2766
9	8	La Sage	Cabane de Moiry	5:55	11.8	7.3	1676	5499	518	1699
10	9a, 9b	Cabane de Moiry	Zinal	5:45	16.6	10.3	574	1883	1725	5659
11	10	Zinal	Gruben	6:40	17.7	11.0	1270	4167	1126	3694
12	11	Gruben	St-Niklaus	7:00	18.4	11.4	1096	3596	1787	5863
13	12a, 12b, 12c	St-Niklaus	Europahütte	8:20	19.2	12.0	1907	6257	770	2526
14	13a, 13b	Europahütte	Zermatt	7:15	21.9	13.6	810	2657	1469	4820

Col Termin (Stage 5)

13 Days: our standard schedule which successfully divides the trek up into manageable stages. It is a tried and tested approach which is perfect for many walkers.

Day	Stages	Start	Finish	Time (hr)	Distance km	Distance miles	Ascent m	Ascent ft	Descent m	Descent ft
1	1a, 1b, 1c, 1d, 1e	Chamonix	Trient	8:35	24.0	14.9	1264	4147	1001	3284
2	2a, 2b, 2c	Trient	Champex	7:25	17.0	10.6	1388	4554	1221	4006
3	3	Champex	Le Châble	4:00	14.1	8.8	192	630	838	2749
4	4	Le Châble	Cabane du Mont Fort	6:45	12.3	7.6	1665	5463	30	98
5	5	Cabane du Mont Fort	Cabane de Prafleuri	6:45	14.7	9.1	954	3130	754	2474
6	6a, 6b	Cabane de Prafleuri	Arolla	7:00	19.0	11.8	835	2740	1483	4865
7	7a, 7b, 7c	Arolla	La Sage	3:50	11.7	7.3	502	1647	843	2766
8	8	La Sage	Cabane de Moiry	5:55	11.8	7.3	1676	5499	518	1699
9	9a, 9b	Cabane de Moiry	Zinal	5:45	16.6	10.3	574	1883	1725	5659
10	10	Zinal	Gruben	6:40	17.7	11.0	1270	4167	1126	3694
11	11	Gruben	St-Niklaus	7:00	18.4	11.4	1096	3596	1787	5863
12	12a, 12b, 12c	St-Niklaus	Europahütte	8:20	19.2	12.0	1907	6257	770	2526
13	13a, 13b	Europahütte	Zermatt	7:15	21.9	13.6	810	2657	1469	4820

12 Days: similar to the 13-day itinerary except that Sections 2-7 are structured slightly differently. The key difference is that Sections 5, 6 and 7 are hiked in two days instead of three, with an overnight stay at the wonderfully serene Refuge de la Barmaz (which is unmanned): these two days are hard but your legs should be well walked in by then.

Day	Stages	Start	Finish	Time (hr)	Distance km	Distance miles	Ascent m	Ascent ft	Descent m	Descent ft
1	1a, 1b, 1c, 1d, 1e	Chamonix	Trient	8:35	24.0	14.9	1264	4147	1001	3284
2	2a, 2b	Trient	Arpette	6:45	14.4	8.9	1388	4554	1061	3481
3	2c, 3	Arpette	Le Châble	4:40	16.7	10.4	192	630	998	3274
4	4	Le Châble	Cabane du Mont Fort	6:45	12.3	7.6	1665	5463	30	98
5	5, 6a	Cabane du Mont Fort	Cabane de la Barmaz	8:15	17.9	11.1	1149	3770	1147	3763
6	6b, 7a, 7b, 7c	Cabane de la Barmaz	La Sage	9:20	27.5	17.1	1142	3747	1933	6342
7	8	La Sage	Cabane de Moiry	5:55	11.8	7.3	1676	5499	518	1699
8	9a, 9b	Cabane de Moiry	Zinal	5:45	16.6	10.3	574	1883	1725	5659
9	10	Zinal	Gruben	6:40	17.7	11.0	1270	4167	1126	3694
10	11	Gruben	St-Niklaus	7:00	18.4	11.4	1096	3596	1787	5863
11	12a, 12b, 12c	St-Niklaus	Europahütte	8:20	19.2	12.0	1907	6257	770	2526
12	13a, 13b	Europahütte	Zermatt	7:15	21.9	13.6	810	2657	1469	4820

Hotel Weisshorn (Stage v10a)

11 Days: for fit walkers used to trekking. You will need to be in shape before starting as days 1 and 2 are very tough.

Day	Stages	Start	Finish	Time (hr)	Distance km	Distance miles	Ascent m	Ascent ft	Descent m	Descent ft
1	1a, 1b, 1c, 1d, 1e, 2a	Chamonix	Col de la Forclaz	9:20	25.5	15.8	1503	4931	1014	3327
2	2b, 2c, 3	Col de la Forclaz	Le Châble	10:40	29.6	18.4	1341	4400	2046	6713
3	4	Le Châble	Cabane du Mont Fort	6:45	12.3	7.6	1665	5463	30	98
4	5, 6a	Cabane du Mont Fort	Cabane de la Barmaz	8:15	17.9	11.1	1149	3770	1147	3763
5	6b, 7a, 7b, 7c	Cabane de la Barmaz	La Sage	9:20	27.5	17.1	1142	3747	1933	6342
6	8	La Sage	Cabane de Moiry	5:55	11.8	7.3	1676	5499	518	1699
7	9a, 9b	Cabane de Moiry	Zinal	5:45	16.6	10.3	574	1883	1725	5659
8	10	Zinal	Gruben	6:40	17.7	11.0	1270	4167	1126	3694
9	11	Gruben	St-Niklaus	7:00	18.4	11.4	1096	3596	1787	5863
10	12a, 12b, 12c	St-Niklaus	Europahütte	8:20	19.2	12.0	1907	6257	770	2526
11	13a, 13b	Europahütte	Zermatt	7:15	21.9	13.6	810	2657	1469	4820

10 Days: these ten relentless and challenging days are for very fit walkers only. It starts hard and stays hard all the way to the end. Day 7 is a monster!

Day	Stages	Start	Finish	Time (hr)	Distance km	Distance miles	Ascent m	Ascent ft	Descent m	Descent ft
1	1a, 1b, 1c, 1d, 1e, 2a	Chamonix	Col de la Forclaz	9:20	25.5	15.8	1503	4931	1014	3327
2	2b, 2c, 3	Col de la Forclaz	Le Châble	10:40	29.6	18.4	1341	4400	2046	6713
3	4	Le Châble	Cabane du Mont Fort	6:45	12.3	7.6	1665	5463	30	98
4	5, 6a	Cabane du Mont Fort	Cabane de la Barmaz	8:15	17.9	11.1	1149	3770	1147	3763
5	6b, 7a, 7b, 7c	Cabane de la Barmaz	La Sage	9:20	27.5	17.1	1142	3747	1933	6342
6	8, 9a	La Sage	Barrage de Moiry Junction	8:10	19.0	11.8	1772	5814	1066	3497
7	9b, 10	Barrage de Moiry Junction	Gruben	10:10	27.1	16.8	1748	5735	2303	7556
8	11	Gruben	St-Niklaus	7:00	18.4	11.4	1096	3596	1787	5863
9	12a, 12b, 12c	St-Niklaus	Europahütte	8:20	19.2	12.0	1907	6257	770	2526
10	13a, 13b	Europahütte	Zermatt	7:15	21.9	13.6	810	2657	1469	4820

Descending to St-Niklaus (Stage 11)

Variant Stages

Stage	Start	Finish	Time (hr)	Distance km	Distance miles	Ascent m	Ascent ft	Descent m	Descent ft	Max Alt m	Max Alt ft
v1d	Col de Balme	Chalet du Glacier (via les Grands)	2:55	6.7	4.2	104	341	718	2356	2203	7228
v1e	Col de Balme	Le Peuty (via Croix de Fer)	2:40	6.6	4.1	190	623	1055	3461	2343	7687
v2b	Col de la Forclaz	Champex (via Bovine)	5:15	14.6	9.1	738	2421	798	2618	2049	6722
v3a	Champex	Orsières	1:00	4.0	2.5	19	62	586	1923	1490	4888
v3b	Orsières	Cabane de Mille	6:00	12.5	7.8	1689	5541	118	387	2571	8435
v4a	Cabane de Mille	Cabane Brunet	3:00	7.9	4.9	341	1119	709	2326	2473	8114
v4b	Cabane Brunet	Fionnay	1:40	5.5	3.4	165	541	776	2546	2103	6900
v4c	Fionnay	Cabane de Louvie	2:30	3.8	2.4	757	2484	10	33	2239	7346
v5a	Cabane du Mont Fort	Cabane de Prafleuri (via Col de la Chaux)	6:00	11.6	7.2	987	3238	781	2562	2987	9800
v5b	Col Termin	Cabane de Louvie	0:50	2.5	1.6	11	36	420	1378	2648	8688
v5c	Cabane de Louvie	48 (Louvie Link Route)	1:25	2.7	1.7	417	1368	30	98	2626	8615
v6a	Cabane de Prafleuri	Cabane de la Barmaz (via Barrage de la Dixence)	1:45	5.3	3.3	200	656	398	1306	2656	8714
v6b	Cabane de la Barmaz	Arolla (via Cabane des Dix)	7:25	20.0	12.4	956	3136	1405	4610	2928	9606
v6c	Hotel du Barrage	Les Haudères (via Col de la Meina)	7:30	21.6	13.4	959	3146	1647	5404	2702	8865
v8a	La Sage	Barrage de Moiry (via Col de Torrent)	5:40	13.0	8.1	1251	4104	688	2257	2916	9567
v8b	Barrage de Moiry	Barrage de Moiry Junction	0:30	1.5	0.9	124	407	0	0	2374	7789
v9a	Barrage de Moiry	Grimentz	1:30	5.9	3.7	14	46	676	2218	2250	7382
v10a	Zinal	Hotel Weisshorn	4:15	11.5	7.1	819	2687	156	512	2423	7949
v10b	Hotel Weisshorn	Gruben (via Cabane Bella Tola & Meidpass)	5:30	16.3	10.1	715	2346	1234	4049	2789	9150
v12a	St-Niklaus	Randa (valley route)	2:40	9.6	6.0	329	1079	47	154	1409	4623
v12b	St-Niklaus	Grächen	2:00	4.6	2.9	540	1772	48	157	1619	5312
v12c	Grächen	Gasenried	0:35	2.3	1.4	67	220	26	85	1660	5446
v13a	Randa	Zermatt (valley route)	3:00	11.1	6.9	281	922	85	279	1645	5397
v13b	Randa	Europahütte (link route)	2:30	4.1	2.5	866	2841	11	36	2264	7428

Accommodation

Cabane de Moiry

The WHR is a popular trek and, these days, most people have their entire trip booked before they depart. In July/August, forward booking is essential. Even outside of July/August, it is wise to book ahead, particularly at weekends and on stages where there is only one place to stay. That said, in June and September, fewer people walk the route and there is less demand for accommodation: in these periods, you can sometimes get away with only booking a day or two in advance; however, because the WHR becomes more popular each year, this is becoming more difficult; furthermore, you can get caught out if, for example, a large group has booked up a lot of beds. Before mid-June, and from late-September onwards, some accommodation may be closed so check in advance. Also, be aware that Stages 1c, 1d, 1e, 2a, 2b, 2c and v2b share the trail with the increasingly popular TMB so demand for accommodation there is even greater. And the Ultra Trail du Mont Blanc (UTMB), a long-distance trail running race, takes place each year at the end of August/start of September: although it does not prevent you from hiking the trails (which are only slightly busier), accommodation around Chamonix can be scarce during the race.

Accommodation can be particularly hard to secure at the following hot-spots:

- **Chamonix:** during the UTMB.
- **Col de la Forclaz:** the hotel is the only place to stay and is sometimes booked up by groups.
- **Cabane du Mont Fort:** it is a very long way to the next hut (Cabane de Prafleuri) and the only other place to stay is Cabane de Louvie (which is OR).
- **Cabane de Prafleuri:** this hut sits at the E end of the challenging Stage 5 and most trekkers will want to finish the day there. If you cannot secure a booking, you can continue to the unmanned Refuge de la Barmaz (Stage 6a) or descend to Hotel du Barrage (v6a).
- **La Sage:** there is only a gîte and a hotel.
- **Cabane de Moiry:** this is a highlight of the trip so book ahead.
- **Barrage de Moiry:** the gîte is the only place to stay. It is small and books up quickly. If you cannot secure a place, you will have to continue along Stage 9b to Zinal or descend to Grimentz on Stage v9a.

- **Gruben:** Hotel Schwarzhorn is often full, particularly at weekends. Although there is now additional accommodation at Grindjisand Mountain Inn, it is 2.3km OR.
- **St-Niklaus:** the two hotels book up quickly. If you cannot secure a booking then you may have to continue to Grächen, Gasenried, Herbriggen or Randa.
- **Europahütte:** this hut is a highlight of the trip and is also used by trekkers doing the Tour of Monte Rosa so book ahead.

All accommodation is numbered and marked on the maps in this book. Detailed accommodation listings are provided on p20. All contact details were correct at the date of press but this information frequently changes: please let us know about any changes you notice.

Hotels: the majority of hotels are in the one to three star categories and quality varies. There are, however, some more luxurious options available in the larger villages/towns (such as Chamonix, Champex and Zermatt). Most hotels offer 'half-board' (bed, breakfast and dinner) which can be good value. Most hotels have their own websites.

Chambres d'hôte/B&Bs: simple bed and breakfast accommodation. Normally, you will have a private room with an ensuite bathroom.

Gîtes d'étape: Traditionally, a gîte would have been comparable to a youth hostel, offering beds in dormitories and evening meals. These days, gîtes are often more upmarket: private rooms are often available and they can be better than some hotels. Most gîtes have their own websites.

Cabane/Refuge/Hütte: these are mountain huts which offer dormitory accommodation, meals and drinks (including alcohol). Occasionally, it is possible to book a private room. The huts are situated in the heart of the mountains where they are often accessible only to hikers: the settings are spectacular. A stay in a hut can be one of the highlights of a mountain adventure such as the WHR. Although prices have risen in recent years, the huts are still good value: see p36.

Dormitories are mixed-sex. Mattresses, pillows and duvets/blankets are provided but you will need a sleeping sheet: this is a thin bag made of silk/cotton which can be purchased cheaply at most outdoor shops; in French, it is called a 'drap de couchage' or 'sac à viande'. Most huts offer showers but you may need to pay extra for this luxury (€3-5). There are usually facilities for charging electronic devices but you may have to wait in line.

The opening/closing dates for each hut are different and change from year to year: they are usually set out on the huts' websites. Usually, huts open sometime in June and close sometime in September/October. You can book some huts online (using their individual websites), however, others are booked by phone/email: although most huts have English speaking staff these days, it can be a good idea to send emails in French (or German, for accommodation between Gruben and Zermatt), using Google Translate if you do not speak the language. Huts which are affiliated to Club Alpin Français or Club Alpin Suisse offer a discount to members of other international alpine clubs.

Mountain hut etiquette

- On arrival, check in at the warden's office.
- Take off your boots and wet clothing at the front door and store them in the places provided at the entrance.
- Do not make noise after 10pm as most walkers go to bed early.
- If you change your plans, cancel your reservation as soon as possible to allow someone else to take your place.

Camping

Between Chamonix and Champex, camping is straightforward as there are plenty of campsites. However, E of Champex, there are fewer official campsites and in Switzerland, it is rarely permitted to camp at mountain huts. A list of official campsites is set out on p27.

Along the WHR, the rules on wild camping (known as 'bivouac' in France and Switzerland) are complicated. The trek enters two countries and different rules apply in each (which we explain in detail below). However, a few common principles apply in both countries: firstly, emergency bivouac (where you have no choice due to injury, exhaustion, etc.) is usually tolerated and is unlikely to be penalised. Secondly, bivouac on private land is not permitted without landowner consent: accordingly, if you wish to camp near huts, ski resorts or 'alpages' (pastures used for grazing), then you should first ask for permission; fortunately, much of the land above the tree-line in France and Switzerland is communal land (not privately owned). All rules and laws are subject to change so check in advance: if you get caught breaking the rules, you could get a stiff fine.

Irrespective of the formal rules, wherever you pitch up, ensure that you leave no trace: for wild camping guidelines, see p19. You should also bear in mind that camping along the WHR is a tougher option because you will need to carry more gear: tent, sleeping bag, sleeping mat, cooker, food, etc. For information on travelling light, see p43.

France: around the Chamonix valley, local laws provide that you are only permitted to bivouac 'at high altitude' from sunset to sunrise. It is not clear what 'high altitude' means exactly but presumably these rules exist to facilitate mountaineers who often sleep out on long routes. If you camp discreetly above 2500m and leave no trace, then you are unlikely to have any issues.

Switzerland: under Article 699 of the Swiss Civil Code, forests, pastures and meadows are generally accessible by everyone. The code does not prohibit wild camping, however, it does state that this general access right is subject to any specific restrictions imposed by a competent authority in the interests of conservation: accordingly, local authorities in the relevant canton/municipality can override Article 699. Putting it simply, the general rule is that wild camping is permitted unless it has been expressly prohibited/limited by another more specific law which has been implemented locally.

In the parts of Switzerland crossed by the WHR, specific laws have indeed been enacted which limit the general access right: wild camping is expressly prohibited in certain protected areas including hunting ban reserves, designated wildlife protection areas and nature reserves. This means that you are not permitted to wild camp in any parts of the WHR which lie within these types of areas. You can see the extent of these areas on a map at **www.map.geo.admin.ch**, however, the web page is difficult to use: you must select from various data sets so that the map displays only the information you need. Fortunately, the Swiss Alpine Club has done the hard work for you and displays the map (with the correct filters applied) on its own website: **www.sac-cas.ch/de/umwelt/bergsport-und-umwelt/campieren-und-biwakieren**.

The map shows that the reserves/protection areas along the WHR (where wild camping is not permitted) include the following:

- **Stages 1e/v1e:** the slopes W of le Peuty and Trient.
- **Stage v3b:** the restriction covers large sections of the v3b route (but does not cover the zone around Col de Mille).
- **Stage v4a:** the forest of le Mortay which is on the N side of the WHR route between Col de Mille and Cabane Brunet.
- **Stage 4:** the forest between Clambin and les Ruinettes.
- **Stage 5:** a hunting ban reserve (where bivouac is not permitted) covers most of this section. It starts about 1km NW of Col Termin and stretches all the way to Cabane de

Prafleuri. However, the small section between Col de Louvie and Col de Prafleuri is outside the reserve.

- **Stage v5a:** a hunting ban reserve (where bivouac is not permitted) covers most of this section. It starts about 0.5km W of Col de la Chaux and stretches all the way to Cabane de Prafleuri. However, the small section between Col de Louvie and Col de Prafleuri is outside the reserve.
- **Stages v4c/v5b/v5c/6a/v6a/v6b:** bivouac is not permitted anywhere on these sections.
- **Stage 6b:** bivouac is not permitted W of Col de Riedmatten.
- **Stage v6c:** there is a wildlife protection area (where bivouac is not permitted) covering the slopes W of the valley between Molignon and les Haudères.
- **Stage 7a:** a wildlife protection area (where bivouac is not permitted) covers much of the stage.
- **Stage v9a:** part of the route crosses a wildlife protection area (where bivouac is not permitted).
- **Stage 9b:** about 1km W of Zinal the route enters a wildlife protection area (where bivouac is not permitted).
- **Stage 10/v10a:** the zone W of the route is a wildlife protection area (where bivouac is not permitted).
- **Stage v10b:** E of the Meidpass, all land N of the WHR path is a hunting ban reserve (where bivouac is not permitted).
- **Stage 13b:** between Täsch and Zermatt, most of the land W of the WHR path is a wildlife protection area (where bivouac is not permitted).

If you are intending to wild camp in Switzerland, you should check this map carefully to make sure that you will not be camping in a prohibited area. Bear in mind that rules can change and the list above may not outline all the restricted areas: carry out your own research before your trip. Outside of the prohibited areas, bivouac is rarely a problem above the tree-line as long as you are discreet, pitching up after 7pm and breaking camp before 9am.

Wild camping guidelines

- **Leave no trace:** you should leave the environment in exactly the same condition as you found it. Leave nothing behind and take nothing away with you. When you have packed up and are ready to leave, look back on your campsite and make sure that another person would not be able to tell that you have been there (except for the flattened grass where your tent was pitched).
- **Do not light open fires:** bush-fires are becoming more common. Parts of the trail are close to wooded areas so the lighting of open fires carries risk. Do not be that person who accidentally destroys acres of pristine countryside.
- **Perform toilet duties responsibly:** this means that you should use a trowel to dig a hole in which to 'do your business'. There are some incredibly lightweight backpacking trowels available these days. Your hole should be at least 30m from water-courses. Fill the hole in afterwards and carry away your used toilet paper in a bag that you have brought along specifically for that purpose. Defecating and placing a stone on top is not acceptable: animals can move stones and imagine how you would feel if you sat down next to such a place! Also carry out tampons and sanitary towels.
- **Be discreet and have respect for others:** try to camp where others cannot see you. Keep your group small: it is supposed to be a 'wild' experience. Do not make a lot of noise at night.
- **Stay for only one night** at a particular spot and then move on.
- **Pitch up late and break camp early:** it is good practice to pitch up after 7pm and break camp before 7am.

Accommodation Listings

(Key on back cover flap)

Stage		Name	Facilities	Contact Details
1a Chamonix	1	Hotel Vallée Blanche		+33 (0)4 50 53 04 50 info@vallee-blanche.com www.vallee-blanche.com
1a Chamonix	2	Hotel le Chamonix		+33 (0)4 50 53 11 07 www.hotel-le-chamonix.com
1a Chamonix	3	La Folie Douce		+33 (0)4 50 55 10 00 infos@lafoliedoucehotels.com www.lafoliedoucehotels.com
1a Chamonix	4	Auberge du Manoir		+33 (0)4 50 53 10 77 contact@aubergedumanoir.com www.chalethotelchamonix.fr
1a Chamonix	5	Hotel le Morgane		+33(0)4 50 53 57 15 reservation@hotelmorganechamonix.com www.morgane-hotel-chamonix.com
1a Chamonix	6	Auberge de Jeunesse Chamonix		+33(0)4 50 53 14 52 chamonix@hifrance.org www.hifrance.org
1a les Praz	7	Hotel Eden		+33 (0)4 50 53 18 43 relax@hoteleden-chamonix.com www.edenchamonix.com
1a les Praz	8	Chalet Hotel le Castel		+33 (0)4 50 21 12 12 www.lecastel-chamonix.com
1a les Praz	9	Hotel les Lanchers		+33 (0)4 50 53 47 19 booking@lanchers.com www.lanchers.com
1a les Praz	10	Hotel le Labrador		+33 (0)4 50 55 90 09 info@hotel-labrador.com www.hotel-labrador.com
1a les Tines	11	Excelsior Chamonix Hôtel & Spa		+33 (0)4 50 53 18 36 reception@hotelexcelsior-chamonix.com www.hotelexcelsior-chamonix.com
1a Argentière	12	Hôtel de la Couronne		+33 (0)4 50 54 00 02 www.hotelcouronne.com
1a Argentière	13	Les Grands Montets Hotel		+33 (0)4 50 54 06 66 info@hotel-grands-montets.com www.hotel-grands-montets.com
1b Montroc le Planet	14	Gîte le Moulin		+33 (0)6 82 33 34 54 contact@gite-chamonix.com www.gite-chamonix.com
1b Tré-le-champ	14a	Auberge la Boerne		+33 (0) 4 50 54 05 14 www.la-boerne.fr
1b le Tour	15	Hotel l'Olympique		+33 (0)7 88 77 56 15 hotel.olympique@orange.fr www.hotel-olympique-chamonix.com

Stage		Name	Facilities	Contact Details
1b le Tour	16	Chalet Alpin du Tour		+33 (0)4 50 54 04 16/(0)6 16 24 50 71 www.chaletdutour.ffcam.fr
1c Charamillon	17	Les Écuries de Charamillon	**Equipped tents also available**	+33 (0)4 50 54 17 07 info@charamillon.fr www.charamillon.fr
1c Col de Balme	18	Refuge du Col de Balme		+33 (0)6 07 06 16 30 refugeducoldebalme@gmail.com www.refugeducoldebalme.com
1d/v1e le Peuty	19	Refuge le Peuty		+41 (0)78 719 29 83 info@refugelepeuty.ch www.refugelepeuty.ch
v1d	20a	Chalet les Grands		+41 (0)79 928 65 38 nic@azymuthe.ch
1e Trient	20	Auberge du Mont Blanc		+41 (0)77 420 08 14 info@aubergemontblanc.com www.aubergemontblanc.com
1e Trient	21	Hôtel La Grande Ourse		+41 (0)27 722 17 54 contact@la-grande-ourse.ch www.la-grande-ourse.ch
2a Col de la Forclaz	22	Hôtel du Col de la Forclaz		+41 (0)27 722 26 88 colforclazhotel@bluewin.ch www.coldelaforclaz.ch
2b Arpette	23	Relais d'Arpette		+41 (0)27 783 12 21 info@arpette.ch www.arpette.ch
v2b Champex d'en Haut	24	Gîte Bon Abri		+41 (0)27 783 14 23 contact@gite-bon-abri.com www.gite-bon-abri.com
2c/v2b Champex	25	Au Club Alpin		+41 (0)27 780 14 14 contact@auclubalpin www.auclubalpin.ch
2c/v2b Champex	26	Le Cabanon		+41 (0)27 783 11 72 info@le-cabanon.ch www.le-cabanon.ch
2c/v2b Champex	27	Hôtel du Glacier		+41 (0)27 782 61 51 info@hotelglacier.ch www.hotelglacier.ch
2c/v2b Champex	28	La Gentiana		+41 (0)27 783 12 58 leonlovey@netplus.ch
2c/v2b Champex	29	Pension en Plein Air		+41 (0)79 858 78 54 contact@pensionenpleinair.com www.pensionenpleinair.ch

Stage		Name	Facilities	Contact Details
2c/v2b Champex	30	Hotel Mont Lac		+41 (0)26 565 66 00 hotelmontlac@gmail.com www.hotel-montlac.com
2c/v2b Champex	31	Le Belvédère		+41 (0)27 783 11 14 belvedere@dransnet.ch www.le-belvedere.ch
2c/v2b Champex	32	Hôtel Splendide		+41 (0)27 783 11 45 hotel-splendide@bluemail.ch www.hotel-splendide.ch
2c/v2b Champex	33	Hôtel Alpina		+41 (0)27 783 18 92 www.alpinachampex.ch
v3a Orsières	34	Hotel Terminus		+41 (0 27 552 11 00 info@terminus-orsieres.ch www.terminus-orsieres.ch
3 le Châble	35	Le Giétroz		+41 (0)27 776 11 84 info@hotel-gietroz.ch www.hotel-gietroz.ch
3 le Châble	36	Motel l'Escale		+41 (0)27 776 27 07 info@hotel-lescale.ch www.hotel-lescale.ch
3 le Châble	37	A Larze		info@alarze.ch www.alarze.ch
3 le Châble	38	Mont-Fort Swiss Lodge		www.montfortswisslodge.ch
3 le Châble	39	Hotel de la Poste		Closed at date of press +41 (0)27 777 13 00
v3b Col de Mille	40	Cabane de Mille		+41 (0)27 783 11 82 info@cabanedemille.ch www.cabanedemille.ch
v4a	41	Cabane Brunet		+41 (0)27 778 18 10 info@cabanebrunet.ch www.cabanebrunet.ch
v4b Fionnay	42	Dortoir de Fionnay		+41 (0)79 277 72 87 www.fermedesglariers.ch
v4b Fionnay	43	Hotel Grand Combin		+41 (0)27 778 11 22 www.grand-combin-fionnay.ch
v4b Fionnay	44	Le Mazot Chambres d'Hôtes		+41 (0)27 778 11 47 le_mazot@outlook.com www.lemazot-fionnay.com
v4c/v5b	45	Cabane de Louvie		+ 41 (0)27 778 17 40 claudia@louvie.ch www.louvie.ch
4	46	Cabane du Mont Fort		+41 (0)79 197 47 53 booking@cabanemontfort.com www.cabanemontfort.com

Stage		Name	Facilities	Contact Details
5	47	Cabane de Prafleuri		+41 (0)27 281 17 80 cabane.prafleuri@gmail.com www.visit-grande-dixence.ch
6a	48	Cabane les Ecoulaies		info@lespyramides.ch www.lespyramides.ch
6a	49	Cabane de la Barmaz		+41 (0)79 847 11 18 www.cabanedelabarmaz.ch
v6a Barrage de la Grande Dixence	50	Hotel du Barrage		+41 (0)27 281 13 22 www.hotel-barrage.ch
v6b	51	Cabane des Dix		+41 (0)79 197 31 14 www.cabanedesdix.com
6b Arolla	52	Hotel du Pigne		+41 (0)27 283 71 00 hotel.pigne@bluewin.ch www.hoteldupigne.ch
6b Arolla	53	Hotel du Glacier		+41 (0)27 283 12 18 hotel.glacier@bluewin.ch www.hotelduglacier.ch
6b Arolla	54	Hotel Aiguille de la Tza		+41 (0)27 283 14 06 info@latza.ch www.latza.ch
6b Arolla	55	Grand Hotel & Kurhaus		+41 (0)27 283 70 00 www.grandhotelkurhaus.com
7a La Gouille	56	Pension du Lac Bleu		+41 (0)27 283 11 66 contact@lagouille.com www.lagouille.com
7b les Haudères	57	Hôtel-Gîte des Alpes		+41 (0)27 283 16 77 alpes.hauderes@bluewin.ch www.hotel-gite-alpes-hauderes.com
7b les Haudères	58	Hôtel les Haudères		+41(0)27 283 15 41 hoteldeshauderes@bluewin.ch www.hoteldeshauderes.ch
7b les Haudères	59	Hôtel Dents de Veisivi		+41 (0)27 283 11 01 info@veisivi.ch www.veisivi.ch
7b les Haudères	60	Hotel les Mélèzes		+41 (0)27 283 11 55 info@hotel-melezes.ch www.hotel-melezes.ch
7c la Sage	61	Hotel de la Sage		+41 (0)27 283 24 20 info@hoteldelasage.ch www.lasage-boutiquehotel.com
7c la Sage	62	Café-Restaurant L'Ecureuil		+41 (0)27 283 24 55 +41 (0)79 401 55 53 info@gite-ecureuil.ch
v8a Villa	63	Gîte-BnB de Caractère au Val d'Hérens		+41 (0)79 359 80 12 patricia@balconduvaldherens.com www.balconduvaldherens.com

Stage		Name	Facilities	Contact Details
8	64	Cabane de Moiry		www.cabane-moiry.ch
v8a/v8b Barrage de Moiry	65	Gîte de Moiry		+41 (0)27 475 15 48/(0)78 621 04 00 virmoiry@gmail.com www.clemsfabs.ch
v9a Grimentz	66	Hôtel Cristal		+41 (0)27 475 43 06 info@cristal-grimentz.ch www.cristal-grimentz.ch
v9a Grimentz	67	Hotel Alpina		+41 (0)27 476 16 16 info@alpina-grimentz.com www.alpina-grimentz.com
v9a Grimentz	68	Hôtel de Moiry		+41 (0)27 475 11 44 info@hotel-grimentz.ch www.hotel-grimentz.ch
v9a Grimentz	69	Becs de Bosson		+41 (0)27 475 19 79 becs-de-bosson@netplus.ch www.becsdebosson.ch
9b Zinal	70	Pension de la Poste		+41 (0)27 475 11 87 www.lapostezinal.ch
9b Zinal	71	Hôtel le Trift		+41 (0)27 475 14 66 info@zinaltrift.ch
9b Zinal	72	Hotel le Besso		+41 (0)27 475 31 65 info@lebesso.com www.le-besso.ch
9b Zinal	73	Hotel Europe		+41 (0)27 475 44 04 info@europezinal.ch www.europezinal.ch
9b Zinal	74	Hotel la Pointe		+41 (0)27 475 11 64 info@lapointedezinal.ch www.lapointedezinal.ch
9b Zinal	75	Hotel Garni des Bouquetins		+41 (0)79 276 43 00/(0)79 389 01 61 mireille.peter@netplus.ch
9b Zinal	76	Relais de la Tzoucdana		+41 (0)27 475 12 19 info@tzoucdana.ch www.tzoucdana.ch
9b Zinal	77	Auberge Alpina		+41 (0)27 475 12 24 info@auberge-alpina.ch www.auberge-alpina.ch
v10a	78	Hôtel Weisshorn		+41 (0)27 475 11 06 info@weisshorn.ch www.weisshorn.ch
v10b	79	Cabane Bella Tola		+41 (0)27 476 15 67 cabane@funiluc.ch www.cabanebellatola.ch
10/v10b Gruben	80	Hotel Schwarzhorn		+41 (0)27 932 14 14 info@hotelschwarzhorn.ch www.hotelschwarzhorn.ch

Stage		Name	Facilities	Contact Details
10/v10b Gruben (2.3km OR)	81	Grindjisand Mountain Inn		www.mountaininn.ch (Currently reservations are made by contacting Hotel Schwarzhorn: see p24)
11 St-Niklaus	82	Heimatlodge		+ 41 (0)27 966 26 96 info@heimatlodge.ch www.heimatlodge.ch
11 St-Niklaus	83	Hotel la Réserve		+41 (0)27 955 22 55 info@la-reserve.ch www.la-reserve.ch
12a/v12c Gasenried	84	Hotel Alpenrösli		+41 (0)27 956 17 81 info@bnb-alpenroesli.ch www.bnb-alpenroesli.ch
v12b Grächen	85	Camping Grächbiel		info@camping-graechbiel.ch www.camping-graechbiel.ch
v12b Grächen	86	Aktiv Hotel & Spa Hannigalp		+41 (0)27 955 10 00 info@hannigalp.ch www.hannigalp.ch
v12b Grächen	87	Hotel Eden		+41 (0)27 956 26 66 info@eden-hotel.ch www.eden-hotel.ch
v12b Grächen	88	Chez BeNi B&B		+41 (0)77 403 81 81 www.chez-beni.ch
v12b Grächen	89	Hotel Walliserhof		+41 (0)27 956 11 22 www.hotel-walliserhof.ch
v12b Grächen	90	Mountain Lodge		+41 (0)79 342 51 19 www.mountain-lodge-grächen.ch
v12b Grächen	91	Family Hotel & Spa Desirée		+41 (0)27 956 30 60 info@hoteldesiree.ch www.hoteldesiree.ch
v12b Grächen	92	Hotel Gädi		+41 (0)27 956 18 28 info@hotel-gaedi.ch www.hotel-gaedi.ch
v12b Grächen	93	Hotel Alpha		+41 (0)27 956 13 01 www.alpha-graechen.ch
12b/v12a Herbriggen	94	Hotel Bergfreund		+41 (0)27 955 23 23 info@hotel-bergfreund.ch www.hotel-bergfreund.ch
12c/v13b	95	Europahütte		+41 (0)27 967 82 47/079 291 33 22 europahuette@sunrise.ch
12c (1.7km OR)	96	Domhütte		+41 (0)27 967 26 34 info@domhuette.ch www.domhuette.ch
v12a Randa	97	Hole in One Hostel		+41 (0)27 967 13 79 info@restaurant-holeinone.ch www.restaurant-holeinone.ch

Stage		Name	Facilities	Contact Details
v12a Randa	98	Aparthotel Klein Matterhorn		+41 (0)79 418 07 86 hotelranda@gmail.com www.hotelkleinmatterhorn.com
13a	99	Kinhütte		+41 (0)79 766 47 07 info@kinhuette.ch www.kinhuette.ch
13a Täschalp	100	Täschalp Restaurant & Lodge		+41 (0)27 967 23 01 info@taeschalp.ch www.taeschalp.ch
v13a Täsch	101	Welcome Hotel by Täscherhof		+41 (0)27 966 62 62 info@taescherhof.ch www.taescherhof.ch
v13a Täsch	102	Hotel City		+41 (0)27 967 36 06 www.hotel-city.ch
v13a Täsch	103	Matterhorn Inn		+41 (0)27 966 26 44 info@matterhorn-inn.com www.matterhorn-inn.com
v13a Täsch	104	Hotel Täscherhof		+41 (0)27 966 62 62 info@taescherhof.ch www.taescherhof.ch
v13a Täsch	105	Mountime Hotel		+41 (0)27 967 12 26 info@mountime.ch www.mountime.ch
v13a Täsch	106	Hotel Walliserhof		+41 (0)27 966 39 66 info@taesch-walliserhof.ch www.taesch-walliserhof.ch
13b/v13a Zermatt	107	Zermatt Youth Hostel		+41 2(0)7 967 23 20 zermatt@youthhostel.ch www.youthhostel.ch
13b/v13a Zermatt	108	Hotel Bahnhof		+41 (0)27 967 24 06 welcome@hotelbahnhofzermatt.com www.hotelbahnhofzermatt.com
13b/v13a Zermatt	109	Chalet Hotel Schönegg		+41 (0)27 966 34 34 info@schonegg.ch www.schonegg.ch
13b/v13a Zermatt	110	Hotel Bristol		+41 27 966 33 66 info@hotel-bristol.ch www.hotel-bristol.ch
13b/v13a Zermatt	111	Hotel Astoria		+41 (0)27 967 52 22 info@astoria-zermatt.ch www.astoria-zermatt.ch
13b/v13a Zermatt	112	Hotel Walliserhof		+41 (0)27 530 20 20 hotel@walliserhof-zermatt.ch www.walliserhof-zermatt.ch
13b/v13a Zermatt	113	Hotel Pollux		+41 (0)27 966 40 00 info@hotelpollux.ch www.hotelpollux.ch
13b/v13a Zermatt	114	Hotel Helvetia		+41 27 967 10 20 mail@helvetia-zermatt.ch www.hotel-helvetia-zermatt.ch
13b/v13a Zermatt	115	Hotel Weisshorn		+41 (0)27 967 11 12 www.weisshorn-zermatt.ch

Campsite Listings

Stage		Name	Contact Details
1a Chamonix	1	Camping les Arolles	+33 (0)6 75 02 26 44/47 60 92 21 infocamping@lesarolles.com www.lesarolles.com
1a les Praz	2	Camping de la Mer de Glace	www.chamonix-camping.com
1a Argentière	3	Camping du Glacier d'Argentière	+33 (0)4 50 54 17 36 camping.glacier.argentiere@gmail.com www.campingchamonix.com
1d le Peuty	4	Bivouac site	Managed by Commune de Trient (+41 (0)27 722 21 05); first come, first served; toilets; covered eating area
1e Trient	5	Bivouac site	Managed by Commune de Trient (+41 (0)27 722 21 05); first come, first served; toilets; covered eating area
2a Col de la Forclaz	6	Hôtel du Col de la Forclaz	+41 (0)27 722 26 88 colforclazhotel@bluewin.ch www.coldelaforclaz.ch
2b Arpette	7	Relais d'Arpette	+41 (0)27 783 12 21 info@arpette.ch www.arpette.ch
2c/v2b Champex	8	Camping les Rocailles	+41 (0)27 783 19 79 www.champex-camping.ch
6b Arolla	9	Camping Arolla	info@camping-arolla.ch www.en.camping-arolla.ch
7b les Haudères	10	Camping Molignon	+41 (0)27 283 12 40 info@molignon.ch www.camping-molignon.ch
v9a Grimentz	11	Camping Ilot Bosquet	www.valdanniviers.ch (pay online)
9b Zinal	12	La Tzoucdana Campsite	+41 (0)27 475 12 19 info@tzoucdana.ch www.tzoucdana.ch
v12b Grächen	13	Camping Grächbiel	info@camping-graechbiel.ch www.camping-graechbiel.ch
v12a Randa	14	Camping Randa	+41 (0)27 967 25 55 sommercamping@oberwallis.ch www.campingranda.ch
v13a Täsch	15	Camping Alphubel	+41 (0)27 967 36 35 www.campingtaesch.ch
13b/v13a Zermatt	16	Camping Zermatt	+41 (0)79 536 46 30 info@campingzermatt.ch www.campingzermatt.ch

Food

Ibex statue at Sorebois (Stage 9b)

Breakfast: most accommodation (including mountain huts) will provide breakfast. In hotels, there is usually a breakfast buffet with a wide selection of foods: cereals, bread, fruit, cheese, cold meats, jams and boiled eggs are common. In mountain huts, the choice is more limited and quality varies widely. In some huts, there is little more than a continental breakfast of cereal, bread and jam but in others, this may be supplemented with cold meats and cheese. Coffee and tea are provided: in huts, breakfast coffee may be instant/granulated.

Lunch: on many stages, there are villages, towns or mountain huts along the route which have restaurants serving local cuisine at lunchtime (normally 12-2pm). However, on some more remote sections of the trek, there is nowhere to buy a meal mid-route and you will need to bring a picnic lunch. Fortunately, excellent bread, fantastic cheeses and cold meats are available in bakeries and grocery shops/supermarkets in the villages: however, a little forward planning is required as there are some stages where there are no shops. Furthermore, shop opening hours can be a little irregular: usually, they open in the morning around 8-9am; often they close for a long lunch (12-3pm) and then re-open for a few hours in the late afternoon/evening. If you arrive in a town/village late then the shops may be closed. Alternatively, you can buy picnic lunches from most hotels and huts along the route: order them the night before. In French and Swiss mountain huts, it is not generally acceptable to make up a sandwich for lunch using the breakfast food.

Rösti

Dinner: most accommodation (including mountain huts) will provide evening meals which are usually hearty three course affairs suitable for weary hikers. A starter, often soup, is normally followed by a main course of meat with vegetables, rice, pasta or salad. This will be rounded off with dessert or cheese. Vegetarian/vegan options will normally be available: request this when you book and remind them when you arrive.

Self-catering: because huts and hotels rarely have communal kitchen facilities, self-catering is only a practical option if you are camping. Food is heavy and therefore it is not wise to attempt to start the trek carrying all the food that you will require for the full distance. Fortunately, on many stages, there are villages/towns along the route which have grocery shops/supermarkets. However, some stages have no shops so you will need to plan ahead. For shop opening hours, see p28.

It is sensible to carry dried food (such as pasta/rice): water is food's heaviest component. Pre-packed freeze-dried meals for backpackers are an excellent choice because they are light and are prepared simply by adding boiling water: you can eat them directly out of the bag so there is no washing-up. These days, there are some very tasty meals available from companies like Real Turmat and Firepot. Canned food is not a good choice as it usually has a high water content and is therefore heavy.

How much food do I need?

According to the National Health Service (NHS) in the UK, the recommended daily calorie intake is 2,000 calories for women and 2,500 for men. As you will be expending a lot of energy, it seems sensible to increase this slightly: perhaps a minimum of 2,500 for women and 3,000 for men. Of course, every person has a different metabolism and will have different requirements but this is a good starting point. Also bear in mind that your daily requirement will depend on how far you are planning to hike each day: the further you hike, the more energy you will use and the more food you will need. Remember also to bring a little extra food (over and above your estimated daily requirements) for emergencies.

Suggested daily menu for campers

Breakfast: instant porridge is a good option because it is light and packed with calories. You can get a variety of different flavours. It is also cheap and, in many countries, it is available in supermarkets. You prepare it simply by adding hot water. You can also buy pre-packed freeze-dried breakfast meals: although they are convenient, they are more expensive.

Lunch & snacks during the day: nuts are hard to beat as they are light and packed with energy. Peanuts, for example, have more calories per gram than most other foods. Dried fruit is also good and will help keep your bodily functions regular. Energy bars and candy can help to provide some variety (and boost moral in tough moments).

Dinner: freeze-dried meals are a good choice. Although they can be expensive, the good quality brands make dinner on the trail something to look forward to. Dried pasta and rice are good too: you can eat these with packet sauces (prepared by adding water).

Glacier du Trient (Stage 2b)

Travel to/from the trail-heads

The Mattertal valley's train line

Primary trail-heads

The WHR starts in Chamonix and finishes in Zermatt. Because these are two of the most important towns in the Alps, they are well-served by public transport.

Getting to/from Chamonix

By train: the Mont Blanc Express (MBE) travels between St Gervais-le Fayet in France and Martigny in Switzerland, stopping in Chamonix along the way. From St Gervais-le Fayet, the train takes 45min to get to Chamonix; from Martigny, it takes 1.5 to 1.75hr to reach Chamonix (with a change at Vallorcine). Both St Gervais-le Fayet and Martigny are connected to the wider European rail network so you can travel there from numerous other European cities: you could even travel by train from London, using the Eurostar (between London and Paris).

By air: the closest international airport to Chamonix is Geneva in Switzerland. Geneva Airport has flights to/from many cities in Europe, North America and other parts of the world. There are a few different ways to travel from Geneva Airport to Chamonix:

- **Shuttle bus:** this is usually the fastest way of getting to Chamonix. Many businesses offer shared and private transfers throughout the day which are scheduled to depart shortly after flights land. They must be booked in advance and take 75-90min. Cheaper shared services only drop off at fixed points in Chamonix but other shared services can drop off directly at your hotel. Private transfers are the most expensive. Popular businesses include Mountain Drop-offs (**www.mountaindropoffs.com**) and Alpybus (**www.alpybus.com**).
- **Scheduled bus:** there are plenty of scheduled buses between Geneva Airport and Chamonix. Advance booking is recommended. Popular services include AlpyTransfers (**www.alpytransfers.com**), easyBus (every 75min; **www.easybus.com**) and Flixbus (**www.flixbus.com**).
- **Train:** both French and Swiss rail operators provide trains between Geneva Airport and Chamonix. The French service uses the Léman Express to St Gervais-le Fayet: from there, you change to the MBE (see above) to travel to Chamonix; the entire trip takes 3-4hr and you have to change three times. The Swiss service runs from Geneva Airport to Martigny: from there, change onto the MBE to Chamonix; the entire trip takes about 4hr (with two changes). Neither option is particularly fast or cost effective when compared to the shuttles or scheduled buses.

However, Geneva Airport is not the only option. You could also fly to another European airport and then take a train/bus to Chamonix. The following are good choices:

- **Turin Airport:** there is no train station at the airport. Take a bus/taxi from Turin Airport to one of the two main stations in Turin city centre: Turin Porta Susa or Turin Porta Nuova. From there, it is 3hr by bus to Chamonix (**www.flixbus.com**).

- **Milan Bergamo Orio al Serio Airport:** direct buses to Chamonix from the airport (5hr; **www.flixbus.com**).
- **Zurich Airport:** 5-6hr by train from the airport train station.
- **Lyon Airport:** 5-6hr by train from the airport train station; alternatively, there are direct buses to Chamonix from the airport (3hr; **www.flixbus.com**).
- **Paris Charles de Gaulle Airport:** 8-10hr by train from the airport train station.

By car: you could leave a car in Chamonix and use the train to return to it at the end of the trek (see 'Getting to/from Zermatt' below). However, there are few parking spaces in Chamonix which are free of charge and long-term parking can be hard to find at a reasonable price. Alternatively, you could park in one of the nearby villages (such as les Houches or Argentière) where free parking is easier to find: after parking, take the MBE train from les Houches/Argentière to Chamonix to start the trek. In les Houches, you can park free of charge for up to 15 days at the Prarion ski-lift car park. In Argentière, the Grand Montets ski-lift car park is also free: no official information is provided on the maximum duration but we have had no problems with parking long-term there. For further information on parking, see **www.chamonix.net**.

Getting to/from Zermatt

By train: Zermatt is connected to the European rail network so you can travel there from numerous other European cities. Trains between Zermatt and Chamonix take 4-5hr: change at Martigny and Vallorcine.

By air: the closest international airports to Zermatt are Geneva and Zurich. Regular trains connect Zermatt with Geneva Airport (4hr) and Zurich Airport (3.5 to 4hr). Milan is also a good option: trains between Zermatt and Milan Centrale train station take 3.5 to 5hr (via Domodossola); for Milan Linate Airport, take the Metro or a bus from Milan Centrale; for Milan Malpensa Airport, the Malpensa Express train runs from Milan Centrale every 30min (**www.malpensaexpress.it**); for Milan Bergamo Orio al Serio Airport, regular buses run from Milan Centrale.

Top Tip

You can buy Swiss train and bus tickets together (in a single transaction) at the airports or online at **www.sbb.ch** or using SBB's efficient smart-phone app.

Secondary trail-heads

In addition to Chamonix and Zermatt, there are many access points along the WHR which have public transport (including Champex, Sembrancher, le Châble, Barrage de la Dixence, Arolla, les Haudères, Zinal, Gruben, St-Niklaus and Herbriggen). In this book, we refer to these access points as 'secondary trail-heads'. You could start or finish the trek at any of these places. Or you could skip sections by leaving the route at one of these secondary trail-heads and using public transport to resume at another point: this can be a good option during bad weather.

Secondary trail-head	Public transport to/from trail-head
1a **Les Praz**	**Train:** MBE towards Martigny (N) or St Gervais-le Fayet (S). **Bus:** frequent daily buses run along the Chamonix valley between les Houches and le Tour (**www.chamonix.net**).
1a **Les Tines**	**Train:** MBE towards Martigny (N) or St Gervais-le Fayet (S). **Bus:** frequent daily buses run along the Chamonix valley between les Houches and le Tour (**www.chamonix.net**).

Secondary trail-head	Public transport to/from trail-head
1a **Argentière**	**Train:** MBE towards Martigny (N) or St Gervais-le Fayet (S). **Bus:** frequent daily buses run along the Chamonix valley between les Houches and le Tour (**www.chamonix.net**).
1b **Le Tour**	**Bus:** frequent daily buses run along the Chamonix valley between les Houches and le Tour (**www.chamonix.net**). **Cable car:** Charamillon ski-lift climbs to Charamillon. Then the Autannes ski-lift travels from Charamillon almost all the way up to Col de Balme: **www.chamonix.net**.
1c **Charamillon**	**Cable car:** see 'le Tour' above.
1c **Col de Balme**	**Cable car:** see 'le Tour' above.
1e **Trient**	**Bus 213:** heads E to Col de la Forclaz (2a) and Martigny. It also heads W to le Châtelard (where you can catch the MBE either N to Martigny or S towards Chamonix and St Gervais-le Fayet).
2a **Col de la Forclaz**	**Bus 213:** heads E to Martigny. It also heads W to Trient (1e) and le Châtelard (where you can catch the MBE either N to Martigny or S towards Chamonix and St Gervais-le Fayet).
2c/v2b **Champex**	**Bus 271:** heads E to Orsières (Stage v3a). Operated by TMR. For travel onwards from Orsières, see below.
v3a **Orsières**	**Train:** Orsières is at the S end of a branch line which travels to/from Sembrancher and Martigny. You can also travel by train between Orsières (v3a) and le Châble (Stage 3). **Bus 211:** travels between Orsières and Aosta; (Mon-Fri; operated by TMR). **Bus 271:** to Champex.
3 **Sembrancher**	**Train:** lines run to Martigny (N), Orsières (S) and le Châble (E). **Bus 211:** travels to Martigny, Orsières (v3a) and Aosta; (Mon-Fri; operated by TMR).
3 **le Châble**	**Train:** lines run W to Martigny and Sembrancher (Stage 3). From Sembrancher, a branch line runs S to Orsières (v3a). **Bus 253:** runs SE up Val de Bagnes to Fionnay (v4b). **Bus 251:** heads up to Verbier where there is accommodation. **Cable car:** from le Châble, a gondola runs to Verbier. From Verbier, another gondola climbs to les Ruinettes: from there, you can hike 4km to CMF (Stage 4). Alternatively, from les Ruinettes, a third lift can take you to la Chaux which is only 2km from CMF.
v4b **Fionnay**	**Bus 253:** runs NW down Val de Bagnes to le Châble (Stage 3).
v6a **Barrage de la Dixence**	**Bus 372:** runs between Hotel du Barrage and Sion.
6b **Arolla**	**Bus 382:** runs between Arolla, La Gouille (7a) and les Haudères (7b/v6c).
7a **la Gouille**	**Bus 382:** see 'Arolla' above.

Secondary trail-head	Public transport to/from trail-head
7b/v6c **les Haudères**	**Bus 382:** between Arolla (6b), La Gouille (7a) and les Haudères. **Bus 381:** between les Haudères and Sion. **Bus 383:** between les Haudères and la Sage (7c).
7c **la Sage**	**Bus 383:** between les Haudères (7b) and la Sage.
8 **Moiry Glacier** (Lac de Châteaupré)	**Bus 452:** between Moiry Glacier, Barrage de Moiry (v8a/v8b/9a), Grimentz (v9a) and Vissoie. For onward transport from Vissoie, see below. **Bus 455:** between Moiry Glacier, Barrage de Moiry (v8a/v8b/9a), Grimentz (v9a) and Zinal (9b).
9a/v8a/v8b **Barrage de Moiry**	**Bus 452:** between Moiry Glacier (Stage 8), Barrage de Moiry, Grimentz (v9a) and Vissoie. For onward transport from Vissoie, see below. **Bus 455:** between Moiry Glacier (Stage 8), Barrage de Moiry, Grimentz (v9a) and Zinal (9b).
v9a **Grimentz**	**Bus 452:** between Moiry Glacier (Stage 8), Barrage de Moiry (v8a/v8b/9a), Grimentz and Vissoie. For onward transport from Vissoie, see below. **Bus 455:** between Moiry Glacier (Stage 8), Barrage de Moiry (v8a/v8b/9a), Grimentz and Zinal (9b).
Vissoie (OR)	**Bus 451:** runs N to Sierre/Siders (where there is a train station). **Bus 453:** runs S to Zinal (9b). **Bus 454:** runs E to St-Luc. From St-Luc, a cable car climbs to Tignousa: from there, it is 0.7km on foot to Cabane Bella Tola (v10b). **Bus 452:** between Moiry Glacier (Stage 8), Barrage de Moiry (v8a/v8b/9a), Grimentz (v9a) and Vissoie.
9b **Sorebois**	**Cable car:** from Sorebois, a gondola runs down to Zinal (9b). You can also travel to Grimentz (v9a).
9b **Zinal**	**Cable car:** from Zinal, a gondola runs up to Sorebois (9b) and Grimentz (v9a). **Bus 453:** runs N to Vissoie. For onward transport from Vissoie, see above. **Bus 455:** between Moiry Glacier (Stage 8), Barrage de Moiry (v8a/v8b/9a), Grimentz (v9a) and Zinal.
10/v10b **Gruben**	**Bus:** in summer, a tourist bus runs between Gruben and Oberems. A cable car operates between Oberems and Turtmann (where there is a train station). See **www.turtmanntal.ch**.
11 **Jungen**	**Cable car:** from Jungen, a cable car runs down to St-Niklaus (11). See **www.jungeralp.ch**.
11 **St-Niklaus**	**Train:** runs S to Herbriggen (12b/v12a), Randa (v12a), Täsch (v13a) and Zermatt (13b/v13a). Also runs N to Visp (which is on the main line between Martigny and Brig). **Bus 551:** between St-Niklaus, Niedergrächen (v12b) and Grächen (v12b). To travel to Gasenried (12a/v12c), change at Niedergrächen onto **Bus 553**. **Bus 552:** between St-Niklaus and Visp. **Bus 554:** between St-Niklaus, Mattsand (v12a) and Herbriggen (12b/v12a). **Cable car:** from St-Niklaus, a cable car runs up to Jungen (Stage 11). See **www.jungeralp.ch**.

Secondary trail-head	Public transport to/from trail-head
v12b Grächen	**Bus 551:** between St-Niklaus (11), Niedergrächen (v12b) and Grächen (v12b). To travel to Gasenried (12a/v12c), change at Niedergrächen onto **Bus 553** **Bus 552:** between Grächen and Visp.
12a/v12c Gasenried	**Bus 553:** runs between Gasenried and Niedergrächen (v12b). Use **Bus 551** to travel between Niedergrächen and St-Niklaus (11) or Grächen (v12b).
v12a Mattsand	**Bus 554:** between St-Niklaus (11), Mattsand and Herbriggen (12b/v12a).
12b/v12a Herbriggen	**Train:** runs S to Randa (v12a), Täsch (v13a) and Zermatt (13b/v13a). Also heads N to St-Niklaus (11) and Visp (which is on the main line between Martigny and Brig). **Bus 554:** between St-Niklaus (11), Mattsand (v12a) and Herbriggen.
v12a Randa	**Train:** runs S to Täsch (v13a) and Zermatt (13b/v13a). Also heads N to Herbriggen (12b/v12a), St-Niklaus (11) and Visp (which is on the main line between Martigny and Brig).
v13a Täsch	**Train:** runs S to Zermatt (13b/v13a). Also heads N to Randa (v12a), Herbriggen (12b/v12a), St-Niklaus (11) and Visp (which is on the main line between Martigny and Brig).
13b Sunnegga	**Cable car:** from Sunnegga, a funicular railway runs down to Zermatt (13b/v13a). See **www.zermatt.ch**.
13b/v13a Zermatt	**Train:** runs N to Täsch (v13a), Randa (v12a), Herbriggen (12b/v12a), St-Niklaus (11) and Visp (which is on the main line between Martigny and Brig).

Further information, timetables and route maps:

Buses and ski-lifts in the Chamonix valley: www.chamonix.net

Mont Blanc Express: www.mont-blanc-express.ch

French Trains: www.sncf-connect.com

Swiss Trains: www.sbb.ch

Swiss buses: www.sbb.ch; www.postauto.ch; www.tmrsa.ch

Meidsee (Stage v10b)

Transport map

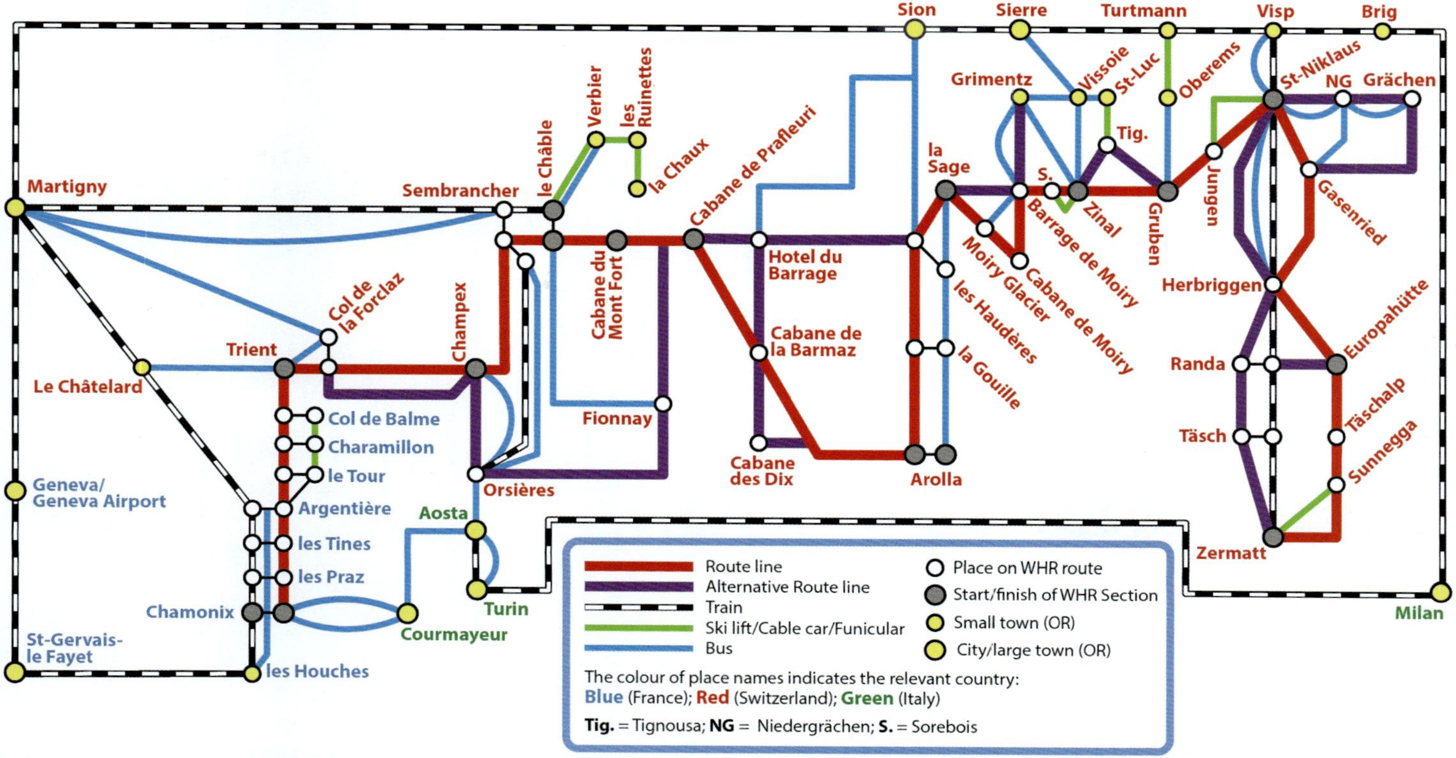

A typical signpost

Costs & budgeting

No permits are required to hike the WHR. However, trekking in Switzerland is slightly more expensive than in other parts of the Alps: food and public transport are particularly costly, however, what you get is normally good quality. In France, both food and public transport are a little cheaper than in Switzerland.

Prices in mountain huts have risen greatly over the last decade but we think that they still offer good value when you consider the high cost of getting supplies to the remote locations. In the huts, the cost of half-board (breakfast, dinner and a dormitory bed) varies widely: in Swiss huts, you will pay CHF68-95; in France, it is around €60-80. Huts which are affiliated to Club Alpin Français or Club Alpin Suisse offer a discount to members of other international alpine clubs: Chalet Alpin du Tour (1b), Cabane du Mont Fort (4), Cabane des Dix (v6b), Cabane de Moiry (8) and Domhütte (Stage 12c; OR).

In hotels along the WHR, double/twin rooms (for 2 people including breakfast) start from around CHF150/€110 in total. Solo travellers will usually pay a single supplement, making hotels relatively expensive for those travelling alone. By camping and/or cooking for yourself, you could save a lot of money.

	Approximate Cost (subject to change) Switzerland/France
Half-board in mountain hut (dormitory bed, breakfast & dinner)	**CHF68-95/€60-80**
Double room in hotel	From **CHF150/€110** upwards (for 2 people sharing a double/twin room)
Campsite	**CHF16-22/€10-20** per person
Main course in restaurant	**CHF20-40/€12-25**
Beer (0.5L)	**CHF6-8/€6-9**

Weather

The Alps have a relatively dry and predictable climate compared, for example, to mountain ranges in the UK: clear and sunny skies are common during the hiking season. However, conditions can still change quickly so be prepared for high winds, rain, low cloud and poor visibility. Furthermore, snow is always possible on cols and summits, even in summer. Sometimes you might experience a mixture of conditions during the day: perhaps some sun and clear skies for a while with cloud and/or rain during other parts of the day. Always remember that mountains can be dangerous so treat them with respect and caution, even if the weather forecast is favourable.

The region has many micro-climates with the weather often differing from valley to valley. It is possible therefore to find blazing sunshine on one side of a ridge and cloud/rain over the other side.

If you can, obtain a weather forecast on your smartphone before setting out each day. MeteoSwiss (the Swiss meteorological office) provides national, regional and local forecasts at **www.meteoswiss.admin.ch**. It also has an excellent smartphone app which provides regularly updated local forecasts. For the French parts of the WHR, Météo-France (the French meteorological office) provides national, regional and local forecasts at **www.meteofrance.com**. It also has an excellent smartphone app which provides regularly updated local forecasts. Many other internet sites and apps also provide forecasts, with a varying degree of reliability. If you are unable to obtain a forecast on your smartphone then it is sensible to speak to the hut wardens: their understanding of local weather conditions can be invaluable and you should follow their advice if they tell you it is not safe to hike. Local forecasts are also displayed at tourist information offices and huts.

Maps

In this book, we have included maps for the entire WHR: each stage has 1:40,000 scale maps produced by Knife Edge Outdoor Guidebooks. Because we were unable to find commercially available maps that suited our purposes, we made our own topographical maps: they are perfect for both planning and navigation while on the trek. However, we also recommend obtaining our sheet map for the WHR: ***Trekking Map: Walker's Haute Route: Chamonix to Zermatt*** (ISBN 9781912933518). It covers the entire trek, clearly shows the WHR route (and its variants) and can be used seamlessly with this book: the scale is 1:40,000 (with larger-scale 1:10,000 insets for sections of the route which are particularly difficult to navigate). With so many variants, the WHR is a complicated trek to plan: being able to view the entire route on a single sheet map will save you a lot of time and effort. A sheet map also makes it easier to navigate in poor conditions and identify peaks along the trail. Our map is available from **www.knifeedgeoutdoor.com**, online retailers and many shops. It is best to buy this map before leaving home, because there are so few book shops along the route.

IGN and Swisstopo (the French and Swiss mapping agencies) also produce maps, however, you need many different sheets to cover the whole trek: this adds a lot of weight to your pack. The French stages are covered on a single 1:25,000 sheet (IGN 3630OT Chamonix-Mont-Blanc). However, for the Swiss stages, you would need about nine Swisstopo 1:25,000 sheets which is not a practical option. Swisstopo also produce 1:50,000 scale maps: although the entire route is covered by two large sheets (5003 Mont Blanc-Grand Combin and 5006 Matterhorn-Mischabel), these maps are often difficult to find. Accordingly, you would probably need to buy the more readily available smaller sheets to cover the whole route: five of these 1:50,000 small sheets are required (282T Martigny, 283T Arolla, 273T Montana, 274T Visp and 284T Mischabel).

Both IGN and Swisstopo also have useful smart-phone apps. Swisstopo's app covers the entire WHR including the French sections (see **www.swisstopo.ch**). IGN's app provides 1:25,000 maps for the French sections (see **www.ign.fr**). Both use GPS to show your location on the map.

Paths and waymarking

Paths and tracks on the WHR are generally well-maintained, straightforward to walk upon and simple to follow but there are rocky, challenging sections too: take care when walking over rocks and boulders. The terrain undulates regularly and some sections are steep and/or exposed: sometimes drops are sheer and occasionally, ropes/chains have been fixed to the rocks for safety. Some paths can be muddy and slippery after rain.

Generally, the route is well marked and navigation is usually straightforward in good conditions: there are often waymarks (painted on trees and rocks) and signs to assist. However, occasionally paths are less easy to follow and navigation is more difficult (particularly in bad conditions): for example, where the trail crosses rocky zones, it can be faint or disappear completely.

In France, waymarks are usually red/white stripes. In Switzerland, there are either red/white stripes or yellow/black diamonds. Waymarks tend to be placed sparingly to avoid sullying the natural environment with man-made marks: often they are found only where absolutely necessary to prevent deviation from the route. A red/white cross on a rock or tree indicates that you are off the route. Yellow signposts often display times and/or distances to specific destinations: the timings are not always reliable. Those who have completed the TMB will be accustomed to following signs and waymarks with the 'TMB' logo on them. However, on the WHR, signs and waymarks do not refer to the WHR itself: rather, they simply direct you to the next place on the route. It is up to you to work out which signpost to follow but this is normally straightforward.

Swiss waymark | Swiss waymark | French waymark | Wrong way

In the route descriptions, we do not highlight every junction because the waymarking is usually good: generally, we only mention junctions if they are particularly significant or if there are no waymarks. As a rule of thumb, remain on the main path unless instructed otherwise by signs/waymarks on the ground or the maps/route descriptions in this book: however, keep your wits about you because there will, of course, be the occasional exception to this rule! Also, bear in mind that waymarking is at the mercy of the environment: for example, signs and waymarks are sometimes destroyed or concealed by rockfall or snow.

On the high points of the WHR, snow can remain into July, covering paths and making progress/route-finding more difficult: follow waymarks carefully because they can be hard to spot against the snow. Normally, early in the season, the trail will become quickly tracked by others ahead of you but always be wary of following someone else's footprints: there is a good chance that they are on the correct path but it is obviously possible that they may have strayed from the route. Also, remember that any fresh snow will obscure footprints.

The following sections of the WHR are particularly difficult:

- **Stage 2b:** challenging boulders on either side of Fenêtre d'Arpette (Knife Edge Outdoor's sheet map shows this area in greater detail, with a 1:10,000 scale inset: see p37).

- **Stage 4:** navigation is fiddly throughout due to the labyrinth of paths/tracks around the ski resort of Verbier (Knife Edge Outdoor's sheet map shows this area in greater detail, with a 1:10,000 scale inset: see p37).
- **Stage 5:** a wild and remote part of the WHR with long sections of rocks and boulders.
- **Stage 6b:** the route is rocky and challenging from Lac des Dix all the way to Col de Riedmatten (Knife Edge Outdoor's sheet map shows this area in greater detail, with a 1:10,000 scale inset: see p37). Navigation is difficult in low visibility.
- **Stages 8 and 9a:** the final climb to, and the descent from, Cabane de Moiry are steep and rocky.
- **Stage 11:** there is a long section of boulders to cross after the Augstbordpass (they are slippery when wet). This area is also prone to rockfall after heavy rain.
- **Sections 12 and 13:** the Europaweg is as tough as it is beautiful. It is not a place to be in bad weather.

Take care if you see mountain biking signs, usually indicated by the letters 'VTT' (Vélo Tout Terrain): mountain bikes are fast and often quiet and a collision between a walker and a mountain bike could be serious.

Water

Drinking water should be one of your primary considerations each day. The sun in the mountains is extremely strong: dehydration and sunstroke are possibilities and you will need more water than usual. Tap water is drinkable and you should fill up your bottles each morning before you depart: it is good practice to start the day with at least 1.5 litres. Along the trail, you can top up at the fountains, bars and shops in villages/towns or from the many streams and rivers: plan carefully so that you know where the next water point is and always check your water levels when you pass a water point.

Remember that the volume of water in streams may vary depending upon the season and the amount of rainfall over previous weeks and months: at the start of the season (June), the rivers are usually in full flow but by the end of the season (September), many of the smaller ones may be dry. Although some do it, we do not recommend drinking water from a river, stream or lake, without first dealing with possible contaminants including visible particulates, bacteria, viruses, protozoa (for example, giardia) and parasites.

It is possible to deal with most contaminants using one or more of the methods described below but you should research thoroughly the specific product you are planning to use to understand its effectiveness and any possible risks:

- **Boiling** is the traditional method. A rolling boil of 1min should kill everything in the water. However, it does not remove visible particulates so the boiled water will remain the same colour as when you found it, which can be off-putting. It also uses up a lot of fuel and takes time so is impractical.
- **Filtering** usually removes visible particulates, working miracles by turning coloured water clear. It also normally removes around 99.9% of bacteria, protozoa and parasites. Filters are often cheap and light. It is the quickest method of treatment so it is useful for long-distance routes. However, most filters cannot remove viruses (although these are unlikely to be an issue on this trek): if you are concerned about viruses then you will need to invest in one of the more expensive filters that remove them or combine filtering with another method (boiling, UV or chemical treatment).
- **Chemical treatment** can remove bacteria, protozoa, viruses and parasites: each product is different so read the labels carefully. However, there are many disadvantages to chemicals: they do not remove visible particulates so the water will remain the same colour as when you found it; water treated with chemicals often has a taste (although you

can usually buy additional chemicals to deal with that); the water usually cannot be drunk immediately as chemicals take time to kill pathogens; and from a health perspective, consuming chemicals may not be good for you.

- **UV treatment** kills bacteria, protozoa, viruses and parasites. However, it does not remove visible particulates so the water will remain the same colour as when you found it: coloured water can be off-putting and the UV treatment is less effective if the water is not completely clear. That said, coloured water is not usually a problem on this trek. The most common products are Steripens which are very light.

	Visible Particulates	Bacteria	Virus	Protozoa	Parasites
Boiling	✗	✓	✓	✓	✓
Filter	✓	✓	Only top of the range filters remove viruses	✓	✓
Chemical Treatment	✗	✓	✓	✓	✓
UV Treatment (such as Steripen)	✗	✓	✓	✓	✓

Perhaps the most practical single method for this trek is filtering: because virus contamination is unlikely, many hikers drink water which has only been filtered with a standard filter, running a small risk of virus contamination. However, if you prefer to be more cautious, you could combine filtration with UV treatment (using a Steripen): this removes or kills practically everything.

The actual effectiveness of individual products varies and is beyond the scope of this book so do your research beforehand. However, it is worth noting that many products claim to be 99.9% effective indicating that drinking water from wild sources can never be said to be 100% risk free. You will have to weigh up the risks and make up your own mind. You drink the water at your own risk!

If, like many, you do decide to drink from natural sources then, as well as treating the water, there are a few rules that you should follow to reduce further any risk:

- Avoid water where there is evidence nearby of animals, especially cows or sheep: carcasses (of dead animals) or faeces can cause contamination.
- Do not collect water downstream from buildings or grazing areas.
- Preferably drink from moving water. The faster the better.
- The bigger the river/stream the better.
- Generally the higher the altitude the better.

Storing bags

Many walkers travel to the WHR carrying only the gear that they will actually take on the trek. However, those who want to spend time elsewhere afterwards will probably have additional baggage which they need to store while trekking. Normally, a hotel that you have stayed at in Geneva or Chamonix will let you store bags until your return: some may charge extra for this so check when booking. At the end of the trek, you can use the train to return from Zermatt to Geneva/Chamonix to pick up your bags (see p31).

You could also use official luggage storage facilities. At Geneva Airport and Geneva Cornavin stations, there are manned baggage counters (near the SBB Travel Centres) where you can leave luggage for CHF12/day. However, you can only deposit/reclaim baggage during the travel centre's opening hours. Zurich Airport also has manned luggage storage. Bounce provides luggage storage facilities in Chamonix: **www.usebounce.com**; €4-6/day.

There are also unmanned luggage lockers at many large Swiss train stations (including Geneva Airport station, Geneva Cornavin and Zurich). However, the maximum storage time is 96 hours which will be insufficient for most trekkers.

Alternatively, there are companies that will transfer your luggage from Geneva/Chamonix to Zermatt and store it while you are hiking the trail: see 'Baggage transfer' below.

Baggage transfer

Businesses offering baggage transfer services can transport your bags to your accommodation so that you only need to carry a small day-pack on the trail. This spares you from the burden of having to carry a heavy backpack and enables you to pack more clean clothes and some luxuries. Although they can facilitate baggage transfer at most towns/villages along the route, they can only service mountain huts which they can access using road vehicles: they cannot reach more remote huts (such as Louvie, Prafleuri, Moiry and the Europahütte).

Most of the companies offering guided and unguided tours will offer baggage transfers as part of the package. In addition, Taxi Follonier offers a baggage transfer service along the WHR: you do not need to book a tour to use this service which makes it useful for independent trekkers. For further information, see **www.taxifollonier.ch**; jm.follonier@taxifollonier.ch; +41 (0)79 427 30 77.

Another option is to have your surplus luggage (that you are not carrying on the trail) transferred from Geneva/Chamonix to Zermatt and stored until your arrival there. This means that you would not need to return to Chamonix to collect your bag after the trek and there would be clean clothes waiting for you when you arrive in Zermatt. Businesses offering this service include Taxi Follonier (from Chamonix to Zermatt; see above) and SBB (the Swiss rail operator; **www.sbb.ch**). SBB's service is a station to station service: you drop off your bags at a Swiss train station (for example, Geneva or Geneva Airport) and collect them at Zermatt's station; you have to buy a train ticket for the route and pay an additional CHF12/bag; there is free storage on the day of arrival of the bag and the following four days; every subsequent day costs CHF 5.

Alternatively, you could mail your bags (as a '*post restante*' consignment) to Zermatt. Swiss Post will store your package at their branch in Zermatt for a month free of charge. For further information, see **www.post.ch**. It is best to mail bags from locations inside Switzerland (for example, Geneva) because customs charges may be payable on packages mailed from outside Switzerland: on arrival in Zermatt, you would not want to find a letter from the Swiss customs authority (requesting payment of customs duties) instead of your bag of clean clothes; remember that Chamonix is in France rather than Switzerland.

For any baggage transfer service, always use a waterproof pack-liner inside the bag to make sure your gear stays dry.

Fuel for camping stoves

Airlines will not permit the transport of fuel so campers will need to source it upon arrival, before setting out on the trek. Standard screw-in gas canisters and Campingaz canisters (pierceable and twist-on) are usually available in Switzerland and France: outdoor shops normally stock them and you may find them in supermarkets, grocery shops and campsites in the region. For outdoor shops, see p42. If you need petrol/diesel for a multi-fuel stove, there are service stations at Chamonix, Orsières, Sembrancher, le Châble, Evolène (OR; near les Haudères), St-Niklaus and Täsch.

Outdoor shops

There are countless outdoor shops in both Chamonix and Zermatt. Mid-route, there are outdoor shops at:

- **Argentière (1a):** Intersport; +33 (0)4 50 54 18 07
- **Orsières (v3a):** Cristal Sport; +41 (0)27 783 2440; info@cristalsport.ch; www.cristalsport.ch.
- **Zinal (9b):** Intersport; +41 (0)27 475 60 58; www.intersportzinal.ch.
- **Grächen (v12b):** Glacier Sport; +41 (0)27 956 12 52; www.glaciersport.ch.

However, those arriving at Geneva Airport may find it more convenient to visit one of the outdoor shops in Geneva city centre: many trains from Geneva Airport to Chamonix stop at Geneva Cornavin which is close to the following stores:

- **Decathlon:** Rue de Lausanne 16-20, 1201 Geneva; +41 (0)22 900 0404; www.decathlon.ch.
- **Univers Sports:** Rue de la Servette 52, 1202 Genève; +41 (0)22 733 3358; www.univers-sports.ch.
- **Ochsner Sport:** Rue du Marché 9/11, 1204 Geneva; +41 (0)22 310 8968; www.ochsnersport.ch.

There are also a few outdoor shops in Martigny:

- **Look Montagne:** Rue du Léman 19, 1920 Martigny; +41 (0)27 722 9155; www.lookmontagne.ch.
- **Sport X:** Av. de Fully 63, 1920 Martigny; +41 (0)27 720 6882; www.sportx.ch.

Ticks

As is often the case in Europe, ticks are present in the Alps. They can carry Lyme disease or tick-borne encephalitis so check yourself regularly. Remove ticks with a tick removal tool (making sure that you get all of it out) and then disinfect the area.

Pastous

The trail enters rural areas and sheep are grazed in the high mountains in summer. Often, the shepherd will live at high altitude in a tiny cabin throughout the grazing season. To protect the sheep from wolves (which are now prevalent again), flocks are often accompanied by dogs. Frequently, the dog is a Pastou (or Patou) which is very large, white and long-haired: it is related to an old Pyrenean breed. They are usually raised with the flock so form a close bond with the sheep. Often they growl or bark if you approach the flock. Although uncommon, occasionally visitors to the Alps are bitten by a Pastou which thought that there was a threat to its sheep. Accordingly, the best advice is to give them a wide berth and assume that there may be a Pastou with any flock you encounter. Remember that from afar, the colour and texture of Pastous' coats makes them hard to spot amongst the sheep.

A Pastou keeping watch over its flock

Equipment

Lac de Moiry (Stage 9a)

The trekker has no influence over challenges like weather and terrain but can control the contents of a pack carried on the trail. Nevertheless, many trekkers set off carrying equipment which is unnecessary or simply too heavy. The more your pack weighs, the harder the trek will be: lugging a heavy pack can lead to exhaustion, injury and/or abandonment. Accordingly, you should give equipment choice careful consideration: it will be crucial to your enjoyment of the trek and the likelihood of success.

Of course, it is easy to understand why a pack should be light, however, it is much more difficult to put this into practice when there are so many things you 'need' in daily life. With experience, it becomes easier to sift between essentials and luxuries but, if you have not been on a multi-day trek before, this can be an unfathomable dilemma. However, if you follow the advice here and limit yourself to the items on our checklist then you should not go far wrong.

A trekker's base weight is the weight of his/her pack, excluding food and water. If you are not carrying camping gear and cooking equipment, it is perfectly possible to get by with a base weight of 5-6kg (13lb) or less. If you intend to carry camping equipment then, by investing in some modern lightweight gear, you could start the trek with a base weight of 8-9kg (17lb) or less. Many people are quick to tell you that the lighter the gear, the greater the price but that is not always the case. While it is true that lightweight gear can be expensive, there are also some excellent lightweight products which are great value. Tents, sleeping bags and backpacks are the three heaviest items that you will carry so they offer the biggest opportunities for weight-saving. But do not ignore the smaller items either as the weight can quickly add up. Accordingly, if you can afford it, it is sensible to invest some money in gear before you leave home. The lighter your gear, the more you will enjoy the trek and the better your chance of success. Be ruthless as every ounce counts.

Recommended basic kit

When undertaking any long-distance route, you should be properly equipped for the worst terrain and the worst weather conditions which you could encounter. In the Alps, this means that you should carry clothing to combat cold, heat, sun, and rain. Becoming cold and wet in the mountains is unpleasant and can be dangerous. Furthermore, if you are lucky and the sun does shine, you will not want to get sunburn (which can put an end to your trek). Also remember that, even in summer, you could experience snow at altitude.

Layering of clothing is the key to managing body temperature. In cool weather, layers can be added: warm air becomes trapped between the layers, acting as insulation. In warmer weather, you simply remove layers and carry them in your pack. Merino wool or man-made materials are preferable: they are lightweight and warm and they wick moisture away from the skin. Do not wear cotton: it is heavy and it does not dry quickly (making you cold). Always carry a spare set of clothes in case you get wet.

Boots/Shoes	Good quality, properly fitting and worn in. Robust soles (such as Vibram) are advisable. Some use trail-running shoes but many prefer boots with ankle support. Shoes/boots with a waterproof membrane (such as Gore-Tex) are good, particularly if there is snow on the ground.	
Socks	2 pairs of good quality, quick-drying walking socks.	
Camp shoes	It is nice to have spare footwear for the evenings. Flip-flops or Crocs are a common choice as they are light. However, if you have comfortable hiking boots/shoes then you might consider not bringing camp shoes to save weight.	
Waterproof jacket and trousers	They should be waterproof and breathable.	
Base layers	2 T-shirts and underpants of man-made fabrics or merino wool, which wick moisture away from your body.	
Fleece	A warm middle layer. Man-made fabrics are best.	
Trousers/shorts	1 pair of lightweight walking trousers and 1 pair of shorts. Alternatively, some prefer 2 pairs of trousers. Convertible trousers are practical as you can remove the legs on warm days.	
Gloves	Lightweight gloves are usually sufficient. However, it is sensible to choose waterproof ones.	
Warm hat & buff	Even in summer it can be cold at altitude, particularly on windy days.	
Down jacket	Even in summer, prepare for low temperatures, especially in the evening and early morning.	
Sunglasses, sun hat, sunscreen and lip salve	The sun is strong: do not set out without these items.	
Sleeping sheet	A thin bag made of silk or cotton. Required to sleep in mountain huts: see p17.	
Head-light with spare batteries	A flashlight is useful (in both huts and tents) if you need to go to the bathroom in the night. Furthermore, it is good practice to carry one for emergencies: it can assist if you get caught out late and enable you to signal to rescuers.	

Backpack	Your backpack is one of the heaviest items that you will carry. The difference in the weights of various packs can be surprisingly large. 35-40 litres should be sufficient if you are not carrying camping gear. 45-60 litres should be adequate for campers. If you need a pack bigger than these then you are probably carrying too much. Look for well-padded shoulder straps and waist band. Much of the weight of the pack should sit on your hips rather than your shoulders.
Waterproof pack-liner	Most backpacks are not very waterproof. An internal liner will keep your gear dry if it rains. Many trekkers use external pack covers but we do not find them to be very useful: they flap in the wind and, in heavy rain, water still leaks into the pack around the straps (so you need an internal liner anyway).
Basic first-aid kit	Including plasters, a bandage, antiseptic wipes and painkillers. Blister plasters, moleskin padding or tape (such as Leukotape) can be useful to prevent or combat blisters. A tick removal tool/card is also recommended.
Map, compass & GPS device	For maps, see p37. A GPS unit or a smart-phone mapping app is a useful addition but they are no substitute for a map and compass: after all, batteries can run out and electronics can fail.
Walking poles	These transfer weight from your legs onto your arms, keeping you fresher. They also save your knees (particularly on descents) and can reduce the likelihood of falling or twisting an ankle. Poles are invaluable in snowy conditions.
Phone and charging cable	A smart-phone is a very useful tool on a trek. It can be used for emergencies. Furthermore, apps for weather, mapping and hotel booking are invaluable. It can also serve as your camera, saving weight.
Ziplock plastic bag	A lightweight way of keeping money and passports dry.
Ear plugs	Useful if staying in huts: you will thank us if someone snores!
Emergency food	Carry some emergency food over and above your planned daily rations. Energy bars, nuts and dried fruit are all good.
Toilet paper and trowel	Bring a backpacking trowel in case nature calls on the trail: bury toilet waste and carry out used toilet paper.
Whistle	For emergencies. Many rucksacks have one incorporated into the sternum strap.
Knife	Such as a Swiss Army knife.
Portable battery pack	Although huts have charging points for electronic devices, they will be in high demand. Accordingly, many people carry their own battery packs: Anker make good ones.
Toiletries	If you wish to take showers at campsites and huts, a small hotel-size bottle of shower gel should be enough to last the trek, saving weight. An almost empty toothpaste tube will also save weight. Leave that make-up behind!
Towel	A lightweight trekking towel is a good idea if you wish to take showers at campsites or huts.

Additional gear for campers

Tent: this is one of the heaviest things that you will carry so it provides a big opportunity for weight saving. Some 2-person tents weigh more than 3kg while others weigh less than 0.6kg. The heaviest ones are normally built for extreme winter conditions and are overkill for the normal Alpine trekking season. Some of the lightest ones, however, are not particularly robust and the thin material can be prone to damage on rocky ground.

Although a few premium brands charge a lot for their products and there are some very expensive tents at the lightest end of the scale, these days there are plenty of mid-weight tents available at reasonable prices. Tents weighing 1 to 1.6kg often strike a good balance between price, longevity and weight. Consider money spent here as an investment in your well-being and enjoyment of one of the world's great trails. Believe us when we say that a few kgs can be the difference between success and failure.

Your tent should be waterproof to ensure that you stay dry during rainy nights. A footprint is a good idea to protect its base: 'footprint' is a trendy, modern word for what used to be known as a groundsheet. Sometimes you can buy footprints specific to your tent model but we prefer to use a sheet of Tyvek which can be cut to size: Tyvek is extremely tough and is cheaper, and normally lighter, than most branded footprints.

Tent pegs: tent weights provided by manufacturers normally exclude the weight of the pegs. The pegs actually provided with tents tend to be quite heavy and many trekkers buy replacement ones which are lighter. Six heavy pegs can weigh as much as 240g while 6 light pegs can weigh as little as 6g. There are many different types available these days and it is important to match the peg with the type of ground they will be used in. You will usually find grassy pitches on this trek, and therefore pegs do not need to be overly strong: titanium ones (which are very light) are a good choice although they can be expensive.

Sleeping bag: every sleeping bag has a 'comfort rating': this is the lowest temperature at which the standard woman should enjoy a comfortable night's sleep. There is also a 'lower comfort limit' which is for men. That may sound simple but it is not. Although all reputable sleeping bag manufacturers use the same independent standard, the bags are not tested in the same place so there is a lack of consistency amongst ratings. Also, the ratings are designed with an average man and woman in mind, however, every person is different: some people get colder than others and need a warmer bag. The ratings should therefore be used as a guide only and it is wise to choose a bag with a comfort rating which is at least 5°C lower than the night temperatures that you are likely to encounter.

Between the start of July and the middle of August, a bag with a comfort rating between -5°C and 5°C (depending on whether you sleep hot or cold) is normally sufficient to cope with the likely night temperatures. Outside of this period, it can be prudent to go with something a little warmer in case the weather throws a cold spell at you: perhaps a bag with a comfort rating between -10°C and 0°C. It is quite a difficult decision because although you want to be warm at night, you do not want to bring a bag that is much too warm as that would add unnecessary weight to your pack.

Unfortunately, with sleeping bags, price tends to be inversely proportional to weight. This is largely because the lightest bags are filled with goose/duck down which is expensive. Synthetic bags are also available but they are much heavier so down is a better choice for trekking. The disadvantage of down bags is that they can lose their warmth if they get wet but that is less likely if you have a good tent and pack liner. Our advice is first to decide what comfort rating you will require. Then choose the lightest bag (with that rating) which you can afford.

Sleeping mat: this makes it comfortable for you to sleep on the hard ground and insulates you from the ground's cold surface. There are three types: air, self-inflating and closed-cell foam. The advantages and disadvantages of each are set out below. All factors considered, we prefer air mats although the very lightest ones may not be sufficiently warm for some trekkers. Thermarest's NeoAir Xlite and NeoAir Xtherm are good choices.

Sleeping mat type	Pros	Cons
Air mats: need to be blown up	Lightest **Very comfortable** Most compact when packed **Thicker: good for side sleepers**	Most expensive **Hard work to inflate** Can be punctured **Less warm than self-inflating**
Self-inflating mats: a combination of air and closed-cell foam. The mat partially inflates itself when the valve is opened	Warmest **Very comfortable** Quite compact **More durable than air mats** Firmness is adjustable by adding air	Heavier **More expensive than closed-cell foam** Can be punctured
Closed-cell foam mats	Light **Least expensive** Most durable **Cannot be punctured**	Not compact: needs to be strapped to the outside of your pack **Least warm** Least comfortable

Pillow: some use rolled-up clothing but we prefer inflatable trekking pillows which only weigh around 50g.

Stove: you should choose a stove that uses a type of fuel which is readily available in the Alps. Airlines do not permit you to carry fuel on planes so, if you are flying, you will need to source fuel on arrival. Although white gas/Coleman fuel is sometimes stocked in outdoor shops, these days gas is more widely available. Most gas stoves are designed to fit generic screw-on canisters which are readily available in Europe. Canisters for Campinggaz stoves (which are popular in France) are widely available too. Multi-fuel stoves that burn petrol and/or diesel are useful but they tend to be heavier, dirtier and more complicated than many gas stoves: the locations of service stations are listed on p41

Hundreds of different stoves are available, some more complicated than others. Often the lightest ones are the most simple and often the most simple ones are relatively inexpensive. If, like most campers, you will eat dried food such as pasta and rice then your stove will need to do little more than boil water. A basic stove which mounts on top of a gas canister will therefore be adequate: such a stove should also be cheap and lightweight (less than 100g).

The superb viewpoint at 104 (Stage 11)

Safety

The incredible scenery on Stage v10b

On a calm summer's day, the Alps are paradise. But a sudden weather shift or an injury can alter your circumstances dramatically so treat the mountains with respect and be conscious of your experience levels and physical capabilities. The following is a non-exhaustive list of recommendations:

- The fitter you are at the start of your trip, the more you will enjoy the hiking.
- Start early to avoid ascending during the hottest part of the day and to allow more surplus time in case something goes wrong.
- Do not stray from the waymarked paths so as to avoid getting lost and to help prevent erosion of the landscape.
- Before you set out each day, study the route and make plans based upon the abilities of the weakest member of your party.
- Obtain a weather forecast (daily if possible) and reassess your plans in light of it. Avoid exposed routes if the weather is uncertain.
- Never be too proud to turn back if you find the going too tough or if the weather deteriorates.
- Bring a map and compass and know how to use them. GPS devices are useful too.
- It can be sensible to call ahead to your accommodation and tell them what time you will arrive. If you do not turn up then they can raise the alarm.
- Carry surplus food and clothing for emergencies.
- Avoid exposed high ground in a thunderstorm. If you get caught out in one then drop your walking poles and stay away from trees, overhanging rocks, metal structures and caves. Generally accepted advice is to squat on your pack and keep as low as possible.
- In snowy conditions, follow waymarks carefully and do not leave the route. Be wary of following someone else's footprints: there is always a chance that they have strayed from the trail.
- In the event of an accident, move an injured person into a safe place and administer any necessary first-aid. Keep the victim warm. If possible, use your cell-phone to call for help: for emergency numbers, see p49. If you have no signal then send someone to the nearest mountain hut or settlement for help.
- Mountain biking is very popular in the Alps so watch out. A collision with a bike would not be pleasant.
- When cooking on a camping stove, place the stove on the ground. Avoid using it on a picnic table. We have witnessed a trekker knocking over his stove and spilling boiling water on his legs: this is a sure-fire way to end your trek.

General Information

Language: French is the first language in both France and the Swiss canton of Valais (which the WHR traverses). However, after crossing the Forcletta/Meidpass on Stages 10/v10b, you enter German speaking Switzerland. In most places, locals will have at least some basic English: along the trail, it seems that English has been adopted as the common language of the WHR these days.

Charging electronic devices: almost all accommodation provides charging facilities. In mountain huts, you sometimes have to queue to use communal power points and therefore many trekkers also bring their own portable battery packs. In France, continental two-pin plugs are used. In Switzerland, these days, most tourist accommodation also provides continental two-pin sockets: older properties may still have the traditional three-pin sockets but these are becoming more rare. Travellers from outside the EU should get by in both countries with a Type-C Europlug adapter.

Money: France uses the Euro (€). Switzerland has the Swiss Franc (CHF) but Euros are normally accepted too (although you may not get a great exchange rate). Hotels and most huts accept credit cards, however, it is a good idea to carry some cash in case credit card machines in remote locations are out of order. Along the route, there are ATMs in Chamonix, Argentière, Champex, Orsières, le Châble, St-Niklaus, Grächen and Zermatt: however, it is wise to carry surplus cash in case an ATM is out of order.

Visas: citizens of the UK, EU, Australia, New Zealand, Canada or the US do not need a visa for short tourist trips to Switzerland or France.

Cell-phones: these days, there is cell network along most of the trail (particularly in towns and villages). However, in some remote valleys, network coverage is poor. When network is available, it is likely to be a 4G/5G service, enabling access to the internet from smart-phones.

International dialling codes: the country codes for France and Switzerland are +33 and +41 respectively. If dialling from overseas, the first 0 in both French and Swiss area codes is omitted.

WiFi: most hotels have WiFi. Some huts have WiFi but some do not.

Emergencies and rescue: the emergency number is 144 in Switzerland and 112 in France. However, in fact, 112 is the universal European emergency number and it also works in Switzerland. Generally, rescue services in France are free of charge. However, rescue services in Switzerland are not always free: in particular, helicopter evacuation could cost you a lot of money. Accordingly, it is wise to take out your own rescue insurance. A good option is membership of the British section of the Austrian Alpine Club (which is open to everyone and not just British trekkers): see **www.alpenverein.at/britannia**. Membership costs around £62 and includes worldwide rescue insurance: it also gives you a discount on the price of a bed at huts which are affiliated to Club Alpin Français or Club Alpin Suisse (see p36).

Medical insurance: depending upon your nationality, any required medical treatment in Switzerland/France may not be provided free of charge so it is wise to purchase travel/medical insurance which covers hiking: this is not the same as rescue insurance.

Tourist information: the following websites are useful:

- **www.chamonix.com:** tourist information for the **Chamonix Valley**.
- **www.chamonix.net:** tourist information for the **Chamonix Valley**.
- **www.myswitzerland.com:** the official tourism website for **Switzerland**.
- **www.sac-cas.ch:** the official website for **Club Alpin Suisse** (the Swiss Alpine Club).
- **www.ffcam.fr:** the official website for **Club Alpin Français** (the French Alpine Club).

Wildlife

Ibex

The extremely varied ecosystems mean that there are plenty of vertebrates in the Alps. Generally, early morning is the best time for sightings: often the first party on the trail spots many chamois or ibex but following groups do not see any.

Bouquetin (ibex): a member of the goat family with long scimitar shaped horns (which have deep ridges). It was saved from extinction by the Savoy kings who banned most hunting in 1821 and created a royal reserve in 1856 (which finally became Italy's Gran Paradiso National Park). After a series of reintroductions in the 20th century, they are now fairly widespread throughout the Alps.

Chamois: another type of mountain goat which is smaller than the ibex and is widespread in the Alps. It has shorter horns which do not have deep ridges. Chamois are frequently spotted in herds. They are much more wary of humans than ibex.

Deer: various species are common below the tree line. Chevreuil (roe deer) are reddish or grey-brown and daim (fallow deer) tend to be brown with white spots. Look out for them when climbing through forests early in the morning.

Marmot

Marmots: everyone loves these fat rodents which are easily spotted in summer when they graze relentlessly to put on layers of fat to last the long winter hibernation. They live in colonies in grassy parts of the mountains, often standing upright on their hind legs like a meerkat. They whistle as you approach to warn their colony of an intruder.

Sanglier (wild boar): a member of the pig family with small tusks. They are common in forests. In the unlikely event that you spot one, keep your distance because they can be dangerous.

Wolves: they were hunted almost to extinction in the Alps in the 20th century. In recent decades, conservation efforts in Italy increased numbers and many have crossed the border into neighbouring countries through the mountains. They are protected but their presence is controversial and particularly unpopular with shepherds who lose sheep to them. They are rarely spotted by hikers.

Other mammals: squirrels, foxes, badgers, weasels and mice are fairly common below the tree line.

Fish: species of trout are found in many rivers, streams and lakes. Some high alpine lakes also contain Arctic char.

Lagopède (or ptarmigan): a grouse-like bird. Its plumage is white in the winter and largely brown in the summer.

Golden eagle: during the hot parts of the day, they can sometimes be seen circling in the thermals to gain altitude as they scan the ground for prey.

Gypaète barbu (bearded vulture): a vulture with a wingspan of up to 3m. In Germany it was given the name 'Lammergeier' (lamb-hawk) because it was believed (probably incorrectly) that it attacked lambs. It is the largest bird in the Alps. Although rare, numbers have increased in recent years.

Golden eagle

The Europaweg (Stage 13b)

Plants & Flowers

A flower-filled alpine meadow in June

The Alps are home to thousands of species of plants including the incredible wild-flowers. June is a fabulous month for flowers, which wait patiently throughout the winter for the snow to clear and then rapidly spring to life. At this time, carpets of different colours cover the slopes and pastures. Although spring is the peak time for flowers, there are still plenty throughout the summer. Watch out for the following:

Alpenrose: a bright pink member of the rhododendron family which coats the slopes at altitude in June/July.

Viola: a small flower in a variety of colours including yellow, white and blue (or a combination of those colours). It is often found in grassy areas.

Edelweiss: it is the most famous alpine plant, perhaps because it has a song named after it. This rare white flower is striking and hard to spot because it only grows at high altitude (1800–3300m). It prefers limestone's calcareous soils. Look out for it on Stage 9a.

Route Descriptions

The wonderful Europaweg (Stage 13a)

1 Chamonix to Trient

The WHR begins with Stage 1a's gentle climb up the l'Arve valley: roads and paths lead you through Chamonix's outlying settlements with the jagged towers of les Drus to keep you company. After les Praz de Chamonix, it is a relief to enter the forest: an undulating path leads through it to the attractive village of Argentière (which has shops, restaurants and places to stay).

On Stage 1b, climb steeply out of Argentière into forest, now on the E side of the Chamonix valley: the scenery becomes more beautiful as you continue up the valley and gaps in the trees offer fabulous views of the Aiguilles Rouges (to the W). A little over an hour from Argentière, reach the lovely hamlet of le Tour.

On Stage 1c, the serious exertions of the WHR begin: the gradient increases and, at last, you climb out of the valley and into the high mountains. Quickly, the views open up with the whole of the Chamonix valley and the MB Massif behind you. For the first time on the trek, the scenery really takes your breath away: it will not be the last time! After a long climb, reach Col de Balme, the WHR's first col: the views are exquisite and it is a great setting for the refuge which was built in 1877 and was occupied by German troops during WW2. In front of the refuge, there is a much-photographed stone marker indicating the Switzerland/France frontier: this is the only border crossing on the WHR.

From the refuge, you have three options: Stage 1d is the main route which is described in this chapter; Stage v1d is a challenging variant which visits Refuge les Grands and Chalet du Glacier on the way to Col de la Forclaz (p62); Stage v1e is a high level route which summits

	Start	Finish	Time	Distance	Ascent	Descent	Max Alt
1a	Chamonix	Argentière	2:45	9.3km 5.8miles	274m 899ft	67m 220ft	1252m 4108ft
1b	Argentière	le Tour	1:30	4.0km 2.5miles	252m 827ft	43m 141ft	1475m 4839ft
1c	le Tour	Col de Balme	2:20	4.3km 2.7miles	738m 2421ft	0m 0ft	2191m 7188ft
1d	Col de Balme	le Peuty	1:40	5.2km 3.2miles	0m 0ft	865m 2838ft	2191m 7188ft
1e	le Peuty	Trient	0:20	1.2km 0.7miles	0m 0ft	26m 85ft	1326m 4350ft

Refuge du Col de Balme (with MB to the right)

the magnificent Croix de Fer before descending steeply to le Peuty (p64). All three routes lead you into Switzerland for the first time.

Stage 1d involves a long (but direct) descent from Col de Balme to the pretty hamlet of le Peuty: it is really nothing more than a few buildings set amongst grassy pastures which are littered with wild-flowers in early summer. The refuge is a fantastic place to stay, especially if you could not secure a place at Trient (Stage 1e) or the busy Hôtel du Col de la Forclaz (Stage 2a).

From le Peuty, you have two options: the main route (Stage 1e) involves a short walk along the valley floor to the village of Trient where there are a few places to stay. Alternatively, you can avoid Trient and head directly from le Peuty to Col de la Forclaz (where there is a hotel and campsite): see p60.

Itinerary options: if hiked all on one day, Section 1 is a tough start to the WHR. Consequently, many people prefer to ease into the trek by splitting this section with an overnight stop at Argentière: because Stage 1a is quite short, those arriving in Chamonix in the afternoon could walk to Argentière that day and spend their first night there. This is a good warm up for the more serious endeavours to come. The following day, you would hike to Trient or Col de la Forclaz. Alternatively, you could skip Stage 1a entirely by taking the train from Chamonix to Argentière.

To save time and effort, you could use the Charamillon and/or Autannes ski-lifts to ascend all, or part of, the way from le Tour to Col de Balme.

Terrain	Paths/tracks are clear and well maintained. The climb from le Tour to Col de Balme is long and tiring with some steep gradients. The descent to le Peuty is long too.
Route-finding	Navigating the paths, tracks and roads out of Chamonix can be a little complicated. The route between le Tour and Col de Balme crosses ski slopes where there is a confusing array of paths/tracks. Otherwise, route-finding is straightforward in good conditions. Stages 1c and 1d are high mountain routes and navigation can be more difficult in bad weather/low visibility.
Transport	**Chamonix/les Praz/les Tines/Argentière:** MBE train; buses up and down the Chamonix valley. **Le Tour:** buses up and down the Chamonix valley; Charamillon/Autannes cable car (to Charamillon and Col de Balme; see p32). **Col de Balme:** Charamillon/Autannes cable car (see p32). **Trient:** Bus 213 to Col de la Forclaz, Martigny and le Châtelard (where you can catch the MBE).

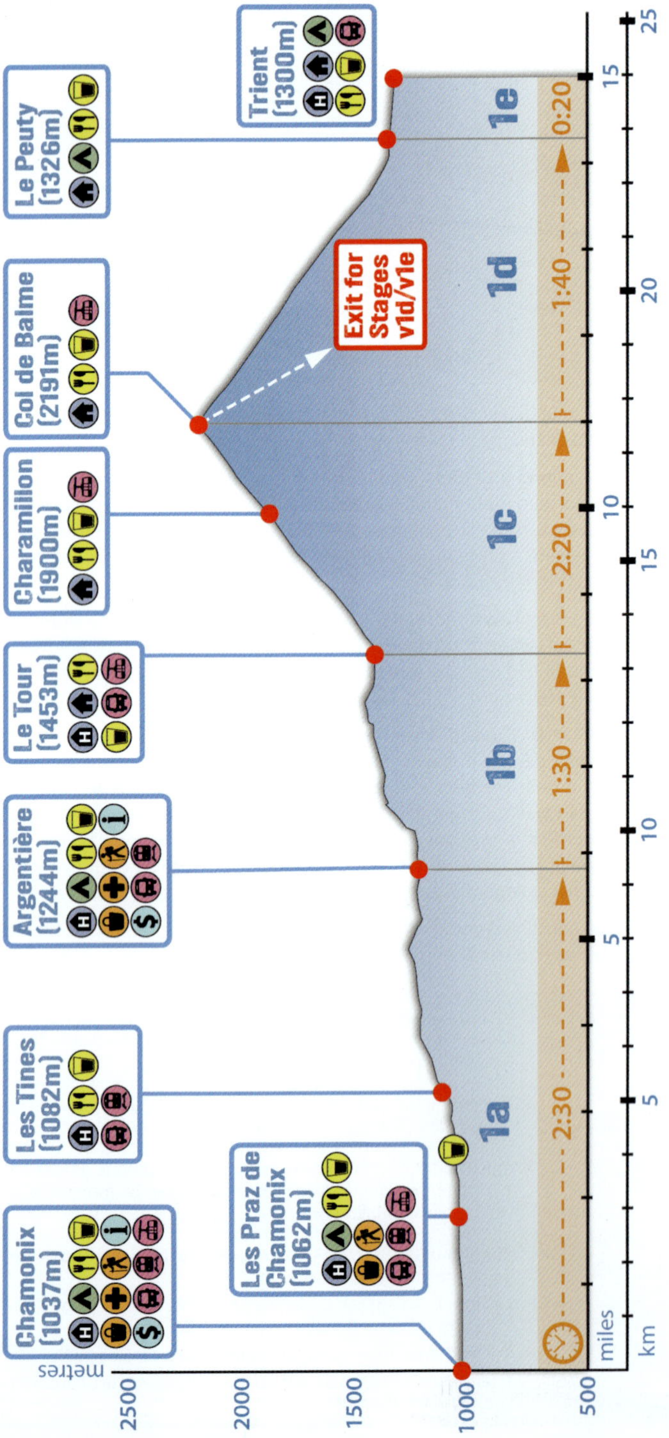

Chamonix (1037m)
Les Praz de Chamonix (1062m)
Les Tines (1082m)
Argentière (1244m)
Le Tour (1453m)
Charamillon (1900m)
Col de Balme (2191m)
Le Peuty (1326m)
Trient (1300m)
Exit for Stages v1d/v1e
1a
1b
1c
1d
1e
2:30
1:30
2:20
1:40
0:20
metres
2500
2000
1500
1000
500
miles
5
10
15
km
5
10
15
20
25

Stage 1a: Chamonix to Argentière

S From the train station, head W, crossing a road. Walk along **Avenue Michel Croz**. TR onto **Rue Whymper**. Shortly afterwards, keep SH at a roundabout ('Argentière').

1 0:15: Immediately after the bus stop at **la Frasse**, TL and cross a footbridge (easy to miss). Just afterwards, TR at a junction. At another junction, take the second right (heading NE). Shortly afterwards, TR at a fork.

2 0:25: Keep SH across a lane, continuing on a path beside a road. After 5min, TL at a fork onto a path. Shortly afterwards, TL onto the road and cross a bridge.

3 0:50: Keep SH across the roundabout in **les Praz de Chamonix** ('Argentière'). Soon, follow the road around to the right. Then take the first lane on the left and walk through the buildings of **Hotel le Labrador**. Keep SH through a car park. Afterwards, keep SH on a track alongside the river. Soon, TL across a footbridge. Then, keep SH, ignoring a path on the right. Shortly afterwards, TR onto a lane. Keep SH at a junction. Keep SH past **Chalet du Paradis** on a track.

4 1:30: Just before **Pont de la Corua**, TL and climb on a path ('Argentière'). At subsequent junctions, follow signs for 'Argentière'. The path climbs for a while and then starts to undulate.

5 2:45: See map on p58. Keep SH on a track to enter **Argentière (1244m)**.

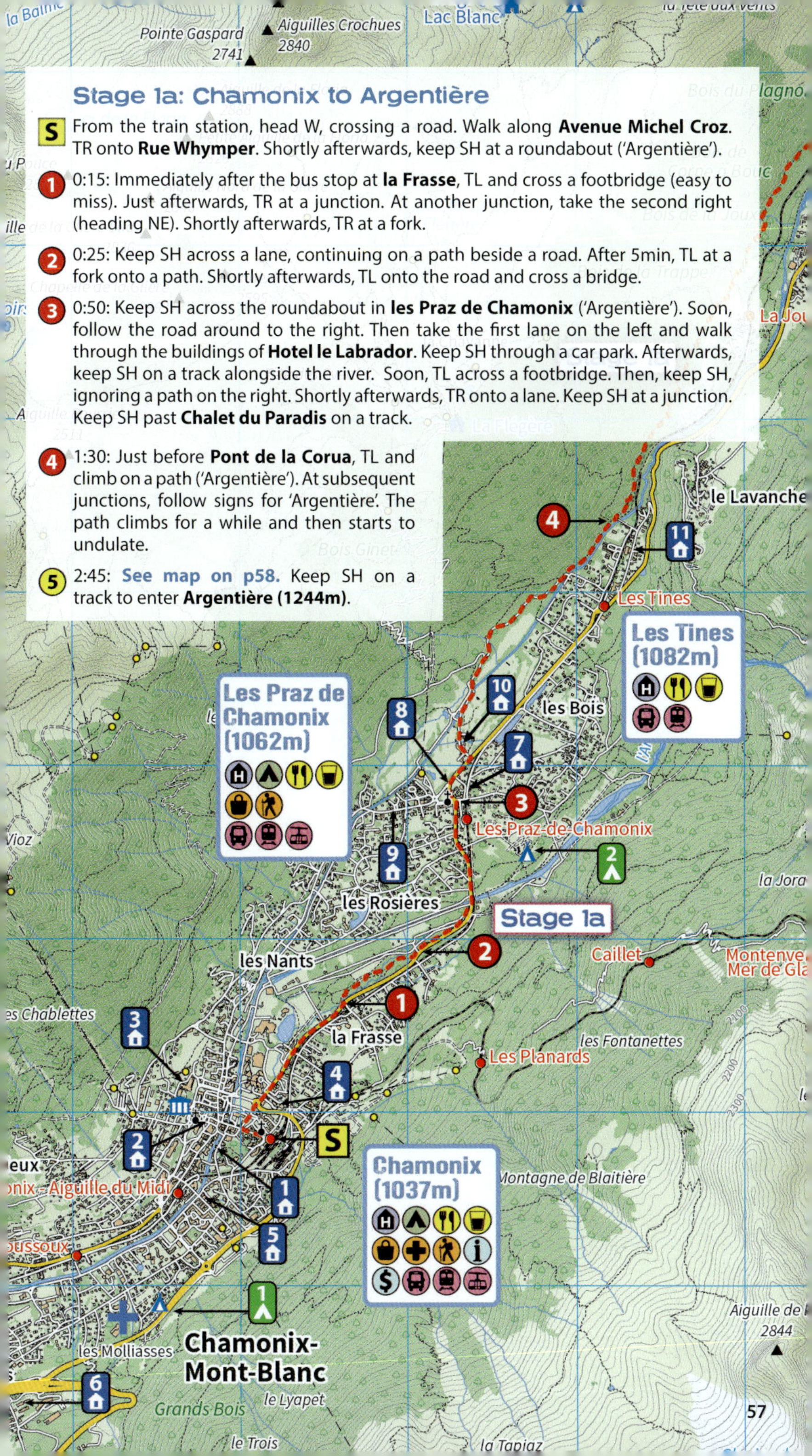

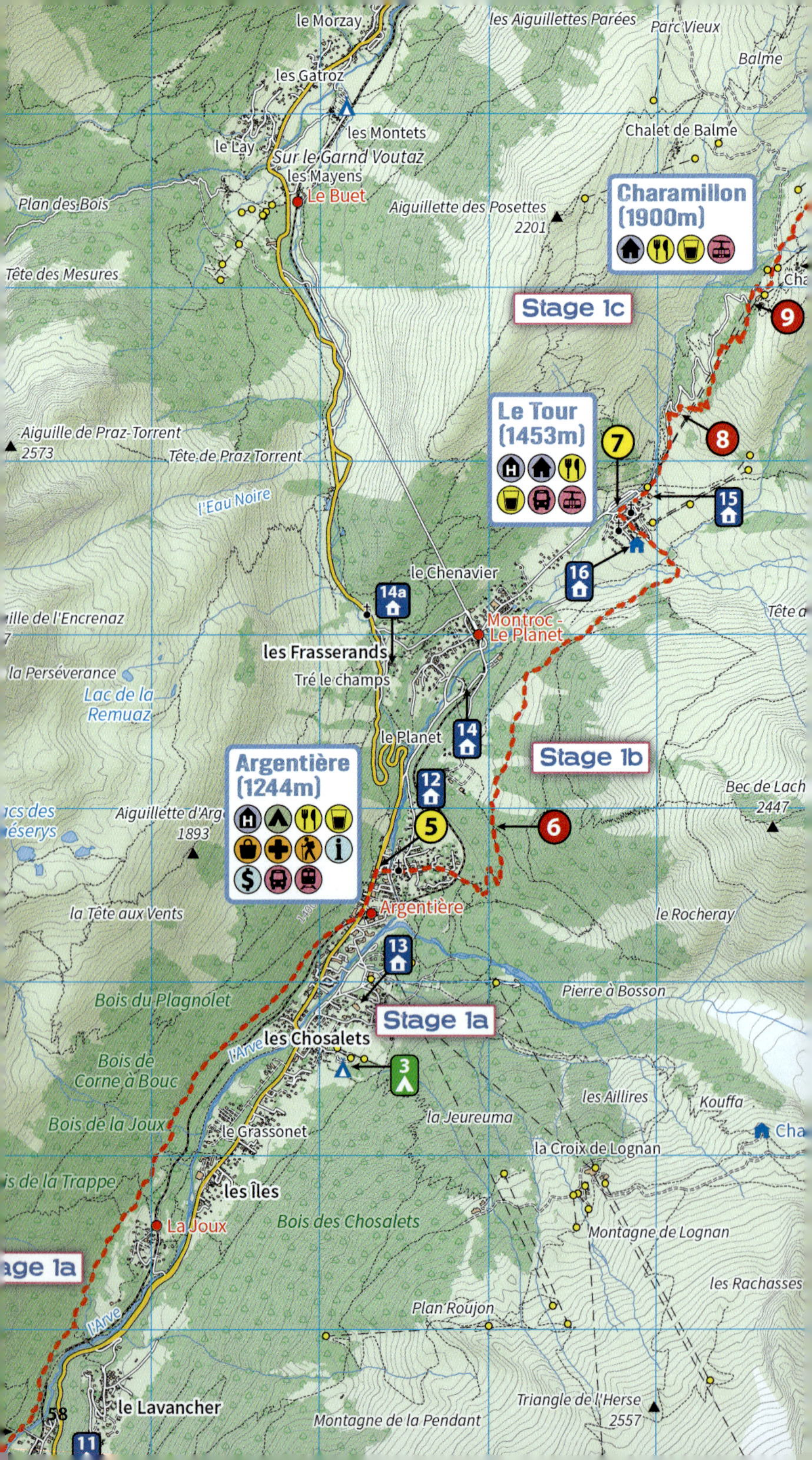

Charamillon (1900m)
Stage 1c
Le Tour (1453m)
Argentière (1244m)
Stage 1b
Stage 1a
le Morzay
les Aiguillettes Parées
Parc Vieux
Balme
les Gatroz
les Montets
Chalet de Balme
le Lay
Sur le Garnd Voutaz
les Mayens
Le Buet
Plan des Bois
Aiguillette des Posettes
2201
Tête des Mesures
Aiguille de Praz-Torrent
2573
Tête de Praz Torrent
l'Eau Noire
le Chenavier
Montroc - Le Planet
les Frasserands
Tré le champs
la Perséverance
Lac de la Remuaz
le Planet
Aiguillette d'Arg
1893
Bec de Lach
2447
la Tête aux Vents
Argentière
le Rocheray
Pierre à Bosson
Bois du Plagnolet
les Chosalets
Bois de Corne à Bouc
Bois de la Joux
le Grassonet
la Jeureuma
les Aillires
Kouffa
la Croix de Lognan
les Îles
La Joux
Bois des Chosalets
Montagne de Lognan
les Rachasses
Plan Roujon
l'Arve
le Lavancher
Triangle de l'Herse
2557
Montagne de la Pendant

Stage 1b: Argentière to le Tour

(5) **See map on p58.** From the centre of **Argentière**, head E on **Route du Village**. Cross the river and, after a few minutes, TR at a junction onto **Chemin de la Moraine**. Soon, pass under a bridge and keep SH on a track. Shortly afterwards, keep SH at a junction ('le Tour'). At the next junction, TL ('Sentier Piétons'). Shortly afterwards, TL at another junction ('le Tour').

(6) 0:35: Keep SH at a junction ('le Tour'). At the next two junctions, keep SH ('le Tour'). Descend gently, cross a bridge and keep SH on a path. Enter **le Tour (1453m)**.

(7) 1:30: Shortly afterwards, arrive at the main road. TR and reach a restaurant and a hotel.

Stage 1c: le Tour to Col de Balme

(7) **See map on p58.** Pass to the right of the **Charamillon cable car station** and climb on a track ('Col de Balme').

(8) 0:20: TR onto a path ('Sentier Piétons').

(9) 1:05: Keep SH at a track. Soon afterwards, TL at a cable car station. Just afterwards, TL at a fork ('Col de Balme'). A few minutes later, TL at a fork. Soon afterwards, TR on a path, climbing quite steeply. At the next junction, TL ('Col de Balme').

(10) 2:15: **See map on p60.** Keep SH at a crossroads.

(11) 2:20: Arrive at **Refuge du Col de Balme (2191m)**.

Stage 1d: Col de Balme to le Peuty

(11) **See map on p60.** Head NE from the refuge, descending the right flank of the **Nant Noir valley**. At any junctions, keep descending generally NE.

(12) 1:30: Ford a river on rocks: take care in early season when there is a lot of water. After a few minutes, keep SH at a junction.

(13) 1:40: Arrive at **le Peuty (1326m)**. For **Trient**, head N on Stage 1e. Alternatively, to head directly to **Col de la Forclaz**, see p60.

Stage 1e: le Peuty to Trient

(13) **See map on p60.** From **le Peuty**, head N: you can either use the road or follow a path/track beside the river (which passes a well-preserved old watermill). After 10min, cross a bridge over the river. Then TR at a fork in the road.

(14) 0:20: Reach the pink chapel in the village of **Trient (1290m)**.

Argentière

Direct route: le Peuty to Col de la Forclaz

(13) **See map on p60.** From **le Peuty** head E on a small road which becomes a track. Cross a road and climb N on a path. 20min from the start, at a junction, there are two paths heading towards the N: take the right-hand one. Cross a modern footbridge over a road and climb steeply on a path.

(15) 0:35: Soon, at a junction, TL to head to Col de la Forclaz: alternatively, TR to start Stage 2b, (avoiding Col de la Forclaz).

(16) 0:45: Arrive at **Col de la Forclaz (1526m)**.

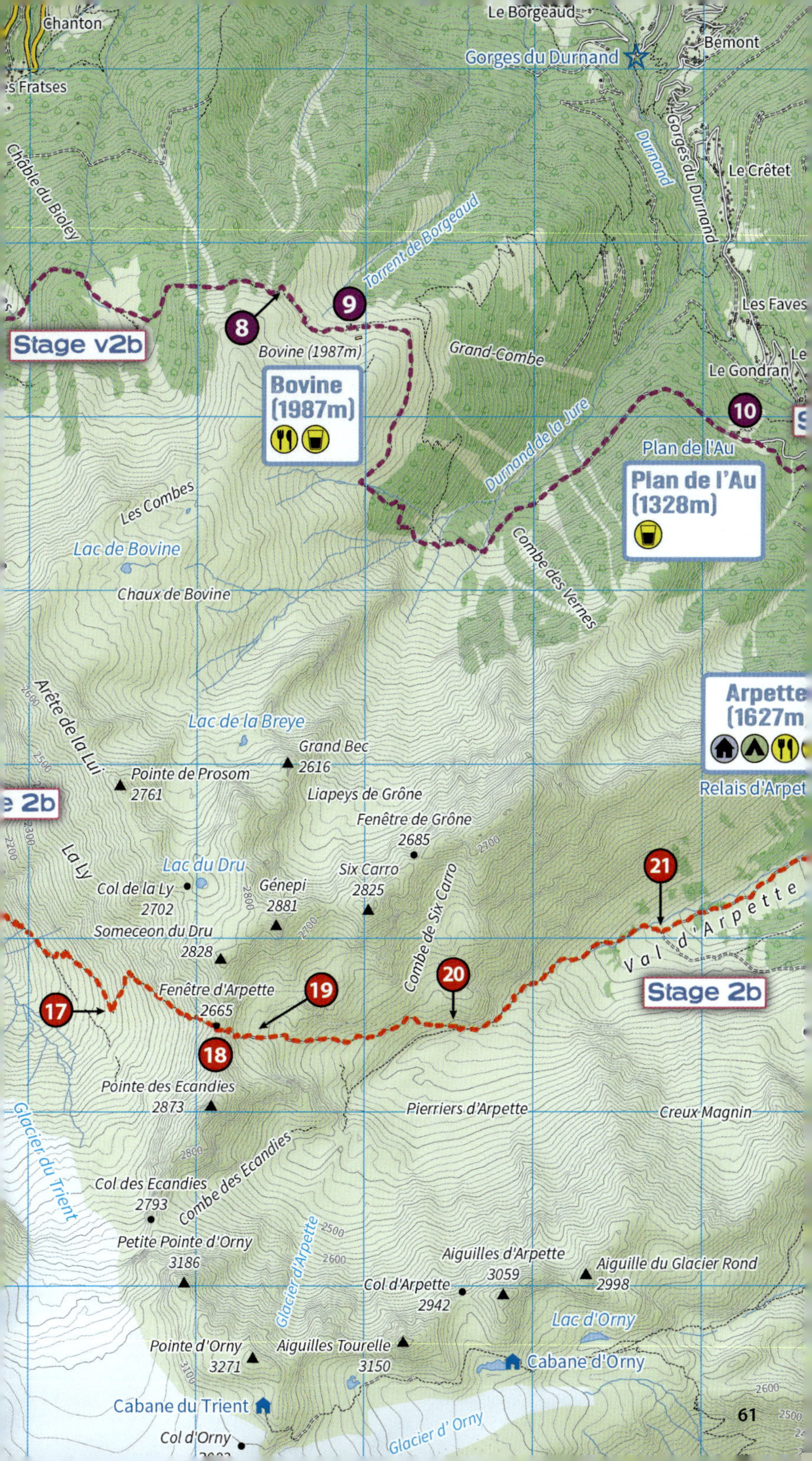

Chanton
Le Borgeaud
Bémont
Gorges du Durnand
es Fratses
Châble du Bioley
Durnand
Gorges du Durnand
Le Crêtet
Torrent de Borgeaud
Les Faves
9
8
Stage v2b
Bovine (1987m)
Grand-Combe
Le Gondran
Bovine (1987m)
10
Durnand de la Jure
Plan de l'Au
Plan de l'Au (1328m)
Les Combes
Lac de Bovine
Combe des Vernes
Chaux de Bovine
Arpette (1627m
Arête de la Lui
Lac de la Breye
Grand Bec 2616
Pointe de Prosom 2761
Liapeys de Grône
Relais d'Arpet
Fenêtre de Grône 2685
La Ly
Lac du Dru
Six Carro 2825
21
Col de la Ly 2702
Génepi 2881
Combe de Six Carro
Val d'Arpette
Someceon du Dru 2828
20
19
Stage 2b
17
Fenêtre d'Arpette 2665
18
Pointe des Ecandies 2873
Pierriers d'Arpette
Creux Magnin
Glacier du Trient
Combe des Ecandies
Col des Ecandies 2793
Petite Pointe d'Orny 3186
Glacier d'Arpette
Aiguilles d'Arpette 3059
Aiguille du Glacier Rond 2998
Col d'Arpette 2942
Lac d'Orny
Pointe d'Orny 3271
Aiguilles Tourelle 3150
Cabane d'Orny
Cabane du Trient
Glacier d' Orny
Col d'Orny

v1d Col de Balme to Chalet du Glacier (via les Grands)

This variant to Col de la Forclaz is scenically superior to the main route (Stages 1d, 1e & 2a). It is also more peaceful because fewer people hike it. In particular, the section between Col de Balme and Refuge les Grands is exquisite, leading you along a magnificent balcony: the views of Glacier du Trient and Glacier des Grands are sublime; the slopes are covered with Alpenrose and Myrtille.

Although Refuge les Grands is superbly situated, it is pretty basic and does not serve meals. As well as the main refuge, there is a winter room in the bergerie next door (although it is not always open). After the refuge, there is a long, steep descent: again, the views of Glacier du Trient are stunning.

Itinerary options: because Refuge les Grands is small, hard to book and does not serve food, most trekkers continue to the hotel at Col de la Forclaz which can be very busy with TMB trekkers. If you cannot get a booking there, then you can avoid Col de la Forclaz altogether by heading E at Chalet du Glacier to proceed directly to Arpette along Stage 2b: however, hiking Stages v1d and 2b on the same day is a challenging undertaking which is suitable only for fit hikers who spent the previous night at Col de Balme.

Terrain	The route between Col de Balme and Refuge les Grands undulates relentlessly and is harder than it appears on the map; paths are often rocky, uneven and tiring; there are sections of boulders to clamber over which are slippery in wet conditions; there are some very steep gradients and narrow/exposed sections with steep drops. Just after the refuge, take care on an exposed section of path cut into the cliffs (protected with a cable). The altitude loss on Stage v1d is significant.
Route-finding	This is a high mountain route which is less frequented than the main route. Do not attempt it in bad weather or low visibility when navigation can be more tricky. There are red/white waymarks.
Transport	**Col de Balme (1c):** Charamillon/Autannes cable car (see p32)

	Start	Finish	Time	Distance	Ascent	Descent	Max Alt
v1d	Col de Balme	Chalet du Glacier	2:55	6.7km 4.2miles	104m 341ft	718m 2356ft	2203m 7228ft

Glacier du Trient

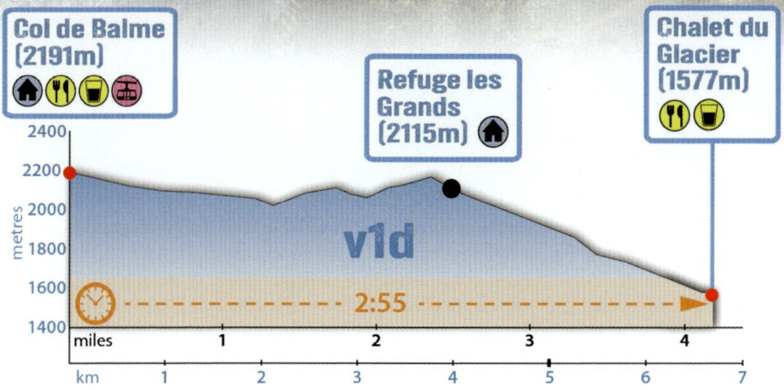

(11) **See map on p60.** From **Refuge du Col de Balme**, cross into **Switzerland** and head E on a path ('les Grands'). The path contours around the hillside with magnificent views of the Swiss Alps to the N. Soon the path becomes rougher and there are short sections of rocks to cross.

1 0:35: Bear right, contouring around the hillside, generally SE. After 30min, incredible views of **Glacier du Trient** suddenly appear.

2 1:10: The path gradually bends right and heads SW. This section is the most challenging.

3 1:30: Descend some steep rocks using a chain. Shortly afterwards, arrive at **Refuge les Grands (2113m)**. Descend SE from the refuge. After a few minutes, descend an exposed and exhilarating section of path cut into the cliffs which has been paved with stone: there is a cable to assist.

4 2:55: TR at a junction. Immediately afterwards, cross a bridge to arrive beside **Chalet du Glacier.** For Col de la Forclaz, TL on a beautiful balcony path, heading down the valley. After 20min, keep SH at a junction ('Col de la Forclaz'). At the next junction, keep SH. 25-30min from Chalet du Glacier, reach **Col de la Forclaz (1526m)**.

Alternatively, TR at **4** for Arpette (Stage 2b).

v1e Col de Balme to le Peuty (via Croix de Fer)

Although this is the least popular of the three routes between Col de Balme and Trient/Col de la Forclaz, we think that it is the most beautiful. The main attraction is Croix de Fer, the summit next to Col de Balme which (as its name would suggest) is topped with an iron cross. Although Croix de Fer is considered to be a minor peak, its position (just N of the MB Massif) ensures that the 360° panorama from the top is sublime: peering directly down the Chamonix valley, the views of MB and the Aiguilles Rouges are completely unimpeded.

In fact, Croix de Fer is a short distance OR: the round-trip to the summit from (5) takes about 45min and leads you along a thrillingly exposed knife-edge ridge with sheer drops on either side. If the weather is fine, the extra distance is well worth the effort but the side-trip is not essential because the views along the rest of the stage are almost as good.

Terrain	Between (5) and the summit of Croix de Fer, the route is narrow and exposed with steep drops and a few sections of rocks to scramble over. Otherwise, paths/tracks are clear and well maintained. The descent to le Peuty is long. Croix de Fer is not a place to be in high winds, foul weather or low visibility: it is very exposed and a fall would be serious.
Route-finding	This is a high mountain route which is less frequented than the main route. Do not attempt it in bad weather or low visibility when navigation can be more tricky.
Transport	**Col de Balme (1c):** Charamillon/Autannes cable car (see p32)

	Start	Finish	Time	Distance	Ascent	Descent	Max Alt
v1e	Col de Balme	le Peuty	2:40	6.6m 4.1miles	190km 623ft	1055m 3461ft	2343m 7687ft

The ridge to Croix de Fer

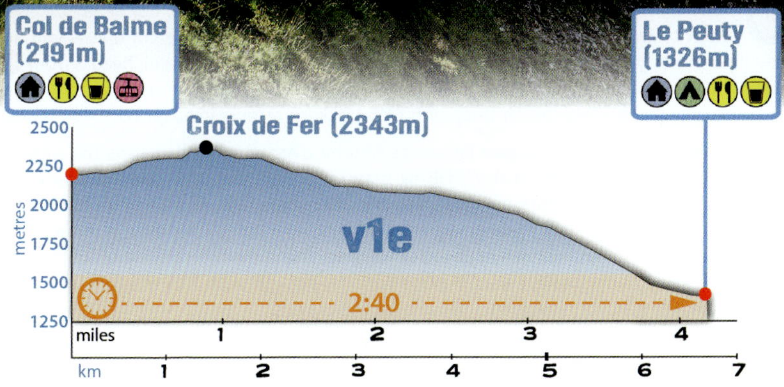

(11) **See map on p60.** From **Refuge du Col de Balme**, head N ('Croix de Fer'). Shortly afterwards, the path bends left and reaches a fork: TR (no signpost).

(5) 0:15: TR at a junction to climb Croix de Fer; alternatively, keep SH to continue to le Peuty (avoiding Croix de Fer). The path to the summit climbs along an exhilarating knife-edge ridge with sheer drops on either side. When the path drifts to the left side of the ridge's crest, there are a few rocks to scramble over.

(6) 0:40: Reach the cross on the summit of **Croix de Fer (2343m)**. After admiring the fabulous views, retrace your steps.

(5) 1:00: At the junction, TR and descend: there are beautiful views of **Lac d'Émosson** and **Mont Buet**. 10min later, TR at a junction ('Trient'). The path contours around the slopes of **Carraye** and soon there are magnificent views of **Glacier du Trient**.

(7) 2:05: Reach a junction. The original route (on the left) has been closed due to rockfall: TR instead, descending steeply through the trees; it is unclear whether this deviation is permanent. Later, TR down a track. Shortly afterwards, TR down a path.

(13) 2:40: TL down a track. Just afterwards, reach **le Peuty (1326m)**.

2 Trient to Champex

On Stage 2a, a short climb through forest leads to 15: from there, Col de la Forclaz is 10min to the N. However, in fact, you do not need to go to the col unless you are staying there or you are planning to hike the v2b variant: to avoid the col, head S from 15 along the route of Stage 2b; this reduces the length of Section 2 by 1.1km. The hotel at the col is the only place to stay and is busy with TMB trekkers: reserve in advance.

Stage 2b crosses a challenging pass known as Fenêtre d'Arpette (which means 'the window of Arpette'). It is a highlight of the WHR so pray for a clear day: the views of Glacier du Trient (to the SW) are exceptional and the path brings you very close to it; a hiker once complained to us that, after posting selfies of himself with the glacier on social media, he was bombarded with accusations of photo tampering! The scenery on both sides of the pass is amazing. Fenêtre d'Arpette is a small place which is popular with TMB trekkers so you are unlikely to have it to yourself: start early to beat the crowds.

Relais d'Arpette, at the end of Stage 2b, is a beautiful place to stay but most people choose to continue to the stunning lakeside town of Champex-Lac, situated at the end of Stage 2c (a short, pretty stage involving a simple descent). As is often the case with place names in French, the correct pronunciation of 'Champex' is not immediately obvious (even to French speakers) and is the subject of much debate amongst trekkers: some French speakers pronounce the 'x' but most locals do not. The busy TMB also passes through Champex so you should book accommodation well in advance. As an alternative, you could descend to Orsières (Stage v3a) and stay there.

	Start	Finish	Time	Distance	Ascent	Descent	Max Alt
2a	Trient	Col de la Forclaz	0:45	1.5km 0.9miles	239m 784ft	13m 43ft	1526m 5007ft
2b	Col de la Forclaz	Arpette	6:00	12.9km 8.0miles	1149m 3770ft	1048m 3438ft	2665m 8743ft
2c	Arpette	Champex	0:40	2.6km 1.6miles	0m 0ft	160m 525ft	1627m 5338ft

Leaving Champex: there are two options:

- **Main route** (to Cabane de Prafleuri) via le Châble and Cabane du Mont Fort (Sections 3/4/5): see p76.
- **High altitude variant** (to Cabane de Prafleuri) via Orsières, Cabane de Mille, Cabane Brunet, Fionnay & Cabane de Louvie (Sections v3/v4/v5c): see p95.

The two routes converge again at 48.

Terrain	On Stages 2a and 2c, paths and tracks are clear and well maintained. However, Stage 2b is one of the hardest parts of the WHR and should not be underestimated. Paths are often rocky, uneven and tiring. Furthermore, at times, there are no paths at all. The rocks are slippery in wet conditions. There are some very steep gradients. The final section of the climb, across rocks, is steep and unstable. The initial descent from the col is also steep and unstable. The subsequent section across boulders is very challenging: often there is no path and some scrambling is required; it would be easy to fall so take it slowly and choose your steps carefully.
Route-finding	Straightforward on Stage 2a. Although Stage 2b is a challenging high mountain route, in good conditions the red/white waymarks are largely straightforward to follow. However, there are a few sections without paths and places where cairns/waymarks are sporadic or hard to spot: do not attempt Stage 2b in bad weather/low visibility when navigation is more tricky. In all conditions, follow waymarks carefully amongst the boulders on the E side of the pass. Sometimes snow can lie near the col until early July: in such conditions, the route is treacherous and difficult to navigate and it is unwise to attempt it. In any difficult conditions, it is preferable to use the Stage v2b variant (p72). The directions for Stage 2c are a little fiddly.
Transport	**Trient:** Bus 213 to Col de la Forclaz, Martigny and le Châtelard (where you can catch the MBE). **Col de la Forclaz:** Bus 213 to Martigny, Trient and le Châtelard (where you can catch the MBE). **Champex:** Bus 271 to Orsières.

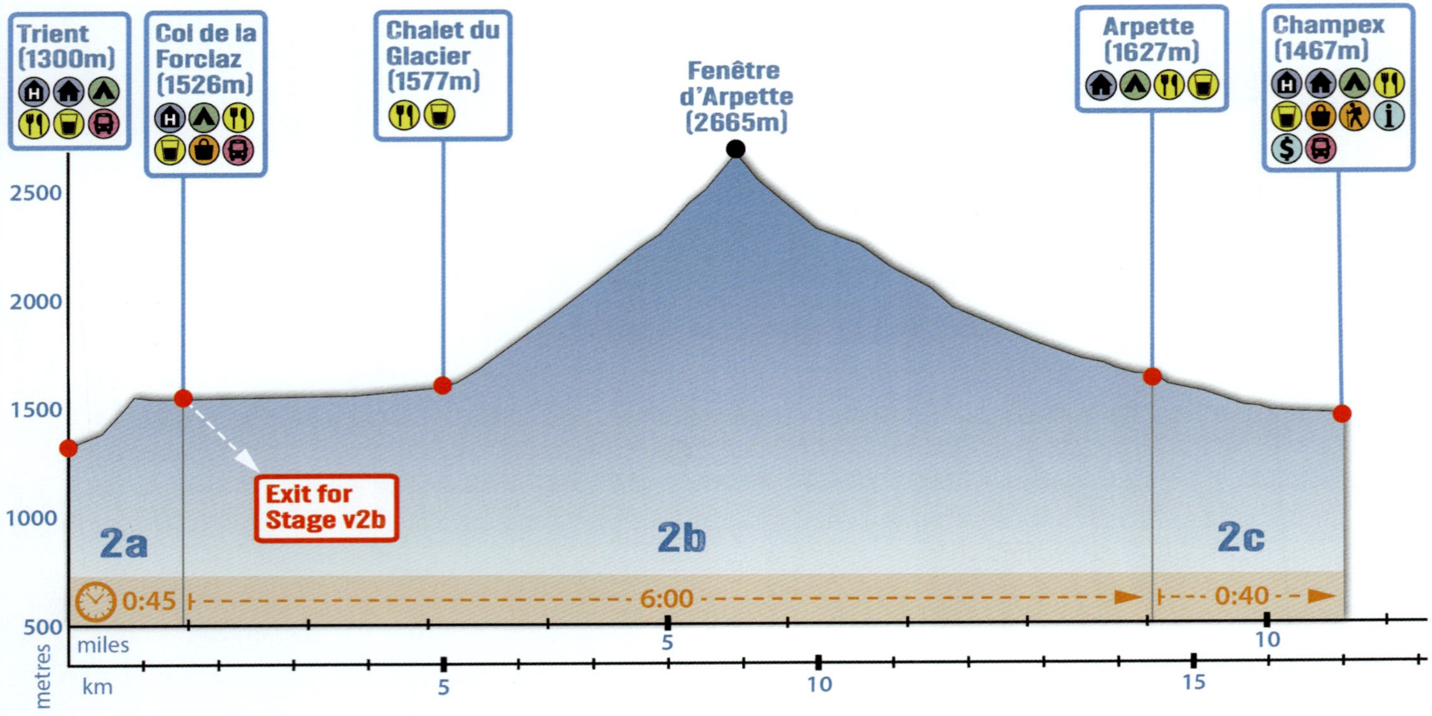
Trient
(1300m)
Col de la
Forclaz
(1526m)
Chalet du
Glacier
(1577m)
Fenêtre
d'Arpette
(2665m)
Arpette
(1627m)
Champex
(1467m)
Exit for
Stage v2b
2a
2b
2c
0:45
6:00
0:40
2500
2000
1500
1000
500
metres
miles
km
5
10
15

Stage 2a: Trient to Col de la Forclaz

14 **See map on p60.** From the centre of **Trient**, head E to reach the road which leads to Col de la Forclaz: TR and head S along it. Shortly afterwards, TL onto a path which climbs S across the slope. At a four-way junction, TL and climb N. Cross a footbridge over a road and climb steeply on a path.

15 0:35: Reach a junction; TL to head to Col de la Forclaz; alternatively, TR to start Stage 2b (avoiding Col de la Forclaz).

16 0:45: Arrive at **Col de la Forclaz (1526m)**.

Stage 2b: Col de la Forclaz to Arpette

16 **See map on p60.** Head S from the hotel, crossing a road to reach a yellow signpost. Keep SH ('Fenêtre d'Arpette') and continue on a path contouring around the hillside (the same path travelled on Stage 2a, between 15 and 16). Keep SH past 15. Soon, walk beside an old irrigation canal. Keep SH at any junctions for now.

4 0:40: TL at a junction to pass **Chalet du Glacier** (where there is a restaurant). Just afterwards, bear left ('Arpette'). After 10min, TL at a junction ('Fenêtre d'Arpette'). As the path climbs, you get closer to the glacier. Take care on a precipitous section of path protected by a rope: a fall would be serious. After a while, pass to the left of an old cabin.

17 2:35: Eventually, bear left and climb a rocky gully, following waymarks: watch your footing. Finally, scramble up a very steep section.

18 3:30: Cross the narrow **Fenêtre d'Arpette (2665m)**. On a fine day, you will want to spend some time here. Descend steeply E on a path that soon splinters into a series of interlinking ones. Watch your footing as the surface is unstable.

19 3:45: In a rocky gully, follow waymarks and cairns across large boulders. This section is challenging and the route is hard to follow: it would be easy to fall from the boulders so take it slowly. After another steep descent, enter a huge mountain bowl: the path descends, more gently now, along the left flank of it.

20 4:50: TL at a junction.

21 5:30: **See map on p70.** TL at a junction ('Champex') and descend on a track.

22 6:00: Pass through a gate at some chalets and descend on a track. Soon afterwards, arrive at **Relais d'Arpette (1627m)**.

Stage 2c: Arpette to Champex

22 **See map on p70.** Descend on the track. Shortly afterwards, TL on a path ('Champex'). After a few minutes, TL across a bridge. Just afterwards, TR on a path heading downhill alongside a torrent. Soon, cross the torrent again on a bridge.

23 0:15: Shortly afterwards, TL at a junction. After a while, TL on another path. Shortly afterwards, TL at a ski-lift. Keep SH under the cables of another ski-lift. Just afterwards, TL onto a road ('Champex').

24 0:30: Shortly afterwards, when you arrive at the main road, turn sharp right and head S on a path. Follow the path around to the left, cross a bridge and then TL on another path. Shortly afterwards, keep SH at a junction. TL at the next junction. Shortly afterwards, TR on a grassy path. Immediately afterwards, TL towards a board-walk. Then TL on a tarmac lane.

25 0:40: Shortly afterwards, TR to walk along the main street of **Champex-Lac (1467m)**.

Surfrête
Chemin-Dessus
Vens (Sembranc
Ravoire
Route du Grand-Saint-Bernard
Le Bougan
Bovernier
Bovernier
Les Valettes (Bovernier)
Forêt du Clou
Bémont
Grand Cheneau
Durnand
Gorges du Durnand
Le Crêtet
Mont Regard
1857
Pouta
Catogne
2598
Comba Névi
Les Faves
Le Cocoro
Le Gondran
La Poya
10
Stage v2b
Plan de l'Au
Plan de l'Au (1328m)
Bonhomme
2436
Champex d'en Haut (1445m)
11
Couloir de Frachay
Champex d'en Haut
Champex (1467m)
Arpette (1627m)
24
28
29
23
24
8
Relais d'Arpette (1627m)
2c
30
22
23
7
25
21
27
25
26
Val d'Arpette
Creux de la Breya
31
32
33
Stage 2b
La Breya
2373
Le Niolet
Prassurny
Col de la Breya

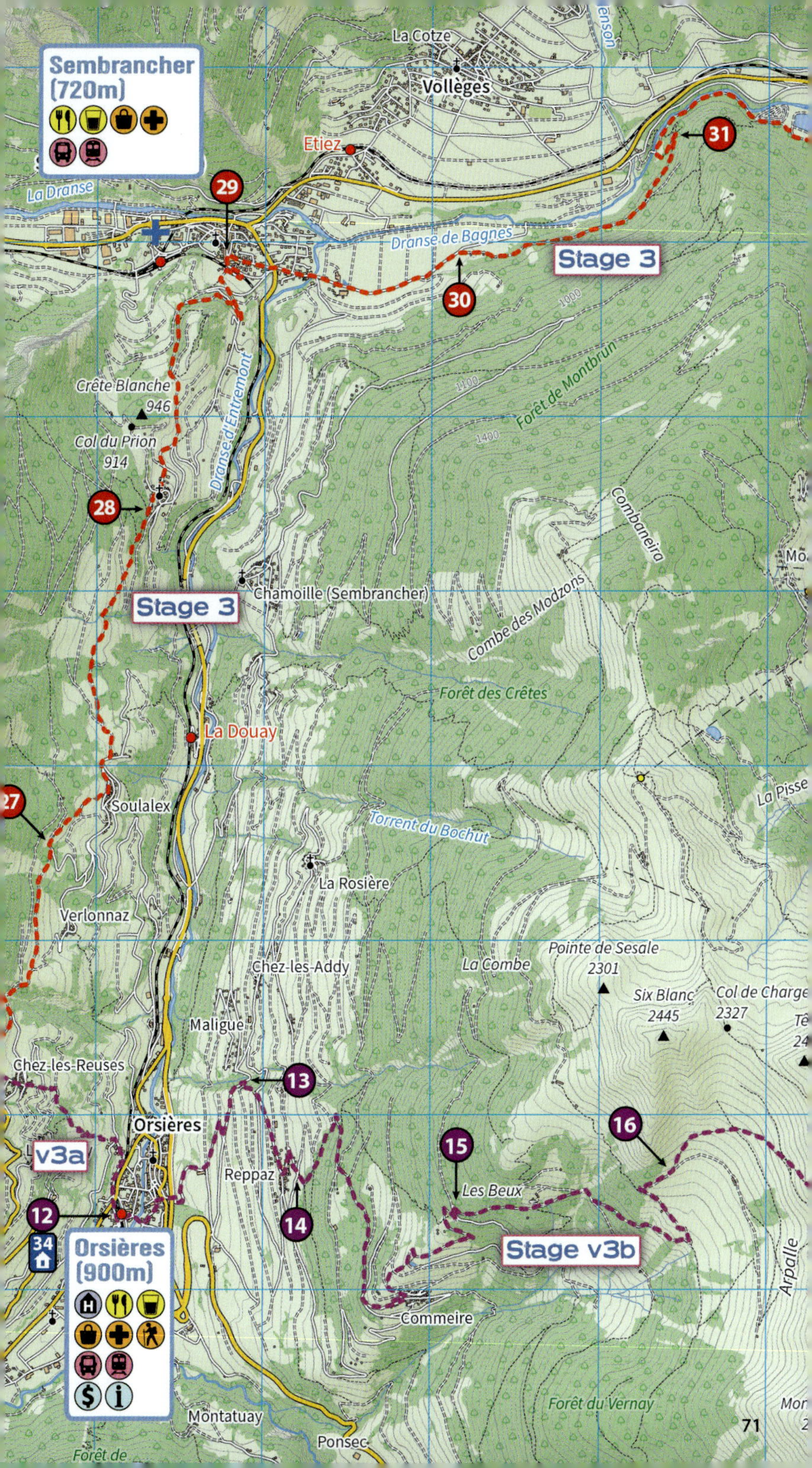
Sembrancher
(720m)
La Cotze
Volléges
Etiez
La Dranse
Dranse de Bagnes
Stage 3
29
30
31
1000
1100
1400
Forêt de Montbrun
Crête Blanche
946
Col du Prion
914
28
Dranse d'Entremont
Combaneira
Chamoille (Sembrancher)
Stage 3
Combe des Modzons
Forêt des Crêtes
La Douay
27
Soulalex
La Pisse
Torrent du Bochut
La Rosière
Verlonnaz
Pointe de Sesale
2301
La Combe
Chez-les-Addy
Six Blanc
2445
Col de Charge
2327
Maligue
Chez-les-Reuses
13
Orsières
16
15
v3a
Reppaz
Les Beux
12
14
34
Stage v3b
Orsières
(900m)
Arpalle
Commeire
Forêt du Vernay
Montatuay
Ponsec
Forêt de

v2b Col de la Forclaz to Champex (via Bovine)

Views of the Rhône valley from the restaurant at Bovine

Climb through aromatic forest with tantalising views of the high peaks between the trees. Emerge from the forest at the stunning pastures around Bovine where there is a restaurant: stop for a drink or food, enjoying sublime views of the Rhône Valley (stretching out towards the E). Afterwards, descend steeply towards Champex: the slopes are covered with Alpenrose which is a vibrant shade of pink in June/July.

Even though the scenery is magnificent, this variant is underrated by WHR trekkers who consider it to be little more than a bad weather alternative to the main route across Fenêtre d'Arpette (Stage 2b). That is a shame because it is a very beautiful route which is, in fact, the main route of the TMB (the most popular trek in the Alps). It also provides an easier alternative for trekkers who have doubts about the challenging boulder crossings on Stage 2b.

Terrain	Paths and tracks are clear and well maintained but they are sometimes steep and rocky. In particular, the descent from Bovine is steep in places (with loose rock).
Route-finding	Straightforward.
Transport	**Col de la Forclaz:** Bus 213 to Martigny, Trient and le Châtelard (where you can catch the MBE). **Champex:** Bus 271 to Orsières.

	Start	Finish	Time	Distance	Ascent	Descent	Max Alt
v2b	Col de la Forclaz	Champex	5:15	14.6km 9.1miles	738m 2421ft	798m 2618ft	2049m 6722ft

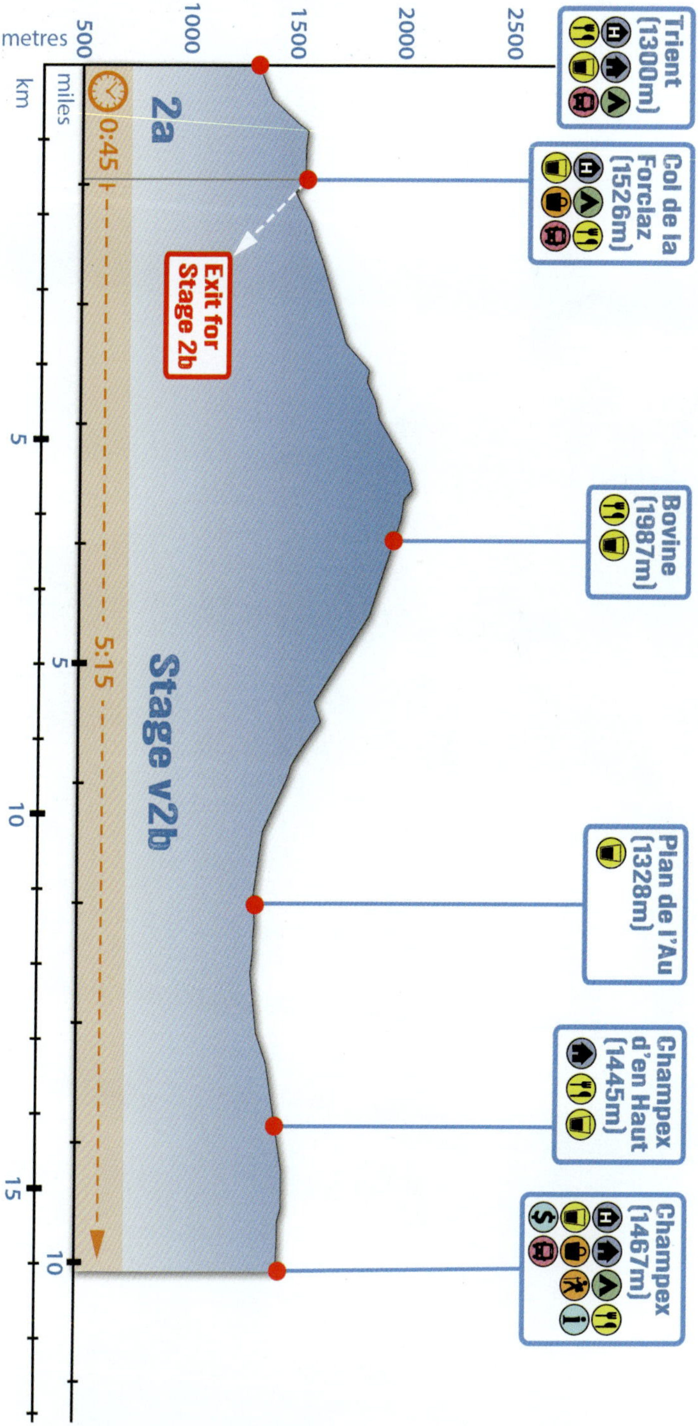

Trient (1300m)
Col de la Forclaz (1526m)
Bovine (1987m)
Plan de l'Au (1328m)
Champex d'en Haut (1445m)
Champex (1467m)
Exit for Stage 2b
2a
Stage v2b
0:45
5:15
metres
500
1000
1500
2000
2500
miles
km
5
10
15

Col de Balme & Croix de Fer viewed from near Col de la Forclaz

Stage v2b: Col de la Forclaz to Champex (via Bovine)

16 **See map on p60.** From the hotel, head E across the road and pick up a path to the left of the shop. Soon, start to climb through forest.

8 1:55: Cross a small col and descend.

9 2:10: Pass the idyllic farm buildings at **Bovine (1987m)** where there is a lovely restaurant. Keep descending as the path contours around the hillside with magnificent views of the **Rhône valley**. After a while, drop below the tree-line and descend more steeply: watch out for loose rocks. Take care crossing a few streams, particularly in early summer when there can be a lot of water.

10 3:45: **See map on p70.** Pass the little buvette at **Plan de l'Au**. Shortly afterwards, TR onto a path. At a junction, keep SH on a track. Keep SH at another junction. Just afterwards, cross a bridge. Immediately afterwards, TR. Pass through **Champex-d'en-Bas**.

11 4:20: Soon TR at a junction and climb: alternatively, keep SH if you wish to stay at **Gîte Bon Abri**. A few minutes later, TL onto a forest track. After 20min, TR onto a main road: take care at blind corners. Pass Champex's **campsite** on the left.

25 5:15: Arrive at **Champex-Lac (1467m)**.

3 Champex to le Châble

This transition stage leads you away from MB towards the Combin Massif. It is a valley hike which is far-removed from the previous high mountain stage and those to come. This part of Switzerland is gentle and green with forests of larch and pine and the bucolic, flower-filled, 'Sound of Music' pastures that one associates with Switzerland. And dotted around the landscape are the neat and tidy chalets found only in Switzerland. A long but easy descent, along the flank of the Val d'Entremont to the town of Sembrancher, is followed by a short, gentle climb to le Châble (along the floor of Val de Bagnes).

Itinerary options: because this is a relatively short stage and there is not much to keep you occupied in le Châble, it can be preferable to spend a leisurely morning in Champex before setting out for le Châble after lunch: you could rent a rowing boat on Champex's lake, or take a stroll around it.

Fit hikers could, in fact, continue beyond le Châble, hiking both Stages 3 and 4 (all the way from Champex to CMF) on the same day. However, this would be too much for most trekkers. A more realistic option would be to hike to le Châble in the morning, have lunch in one of le Châble's restaurants and then use the cable car to ascend to les Ruinettes: from there, it is only 90min on foot to CMF (along Section 4).

	Start	Finish	Time	Distance	Ascent	Descent	Max Alt
3	Champex	Le Châble	4:00	14.1km 8.8miles	192m 630ft	838m 2749ft	1490m 4888ft

The valley scenery that accompanies you all the way down to Sembrancher

Alternatively, from le Châble, you could take the bus to Fionnay and use Stage v4c to climb to Cabane de Louvie to spend the night. The following day, you would rejoin the WHR's main route at 48 (near Col Termin on Stage 5).

Terrain	Good paths and tracks which are simple to follow. Short sections along quiet roads.
Route-finding	The directions for this stage are a little complicated but the route is quite well served with yellow waymarks and signposts.
Transport	You can use public transport to skip Section 3 entirely. Take the bus to Orsières and then the train to le Châble (via Sembrancher). If you stay overnight in le Châble then you are entitled to a free Verbier VIP Pass which gives you free public transport in the Val de Bagnes on your day of arrival and the following day: this includes the cable car to les Ruinettes, buses to Fionnay and trains to Sembrancher. Ask for the pass when checking-in at your hotel: for more information, see **www.verbier.ch**. **Champex:** Bus 271 to Orsières. **Sembrancher:** Train to Martigny/le Châble/Orsières; Bus 211 to Martigny. **le Châble:** Train to Sembrancher/Martigny/Orsières; Bus 253 to Fionnay; Bus 251 to Verbier; Cable car to Verbier, les Ruinettes, la Chaux.

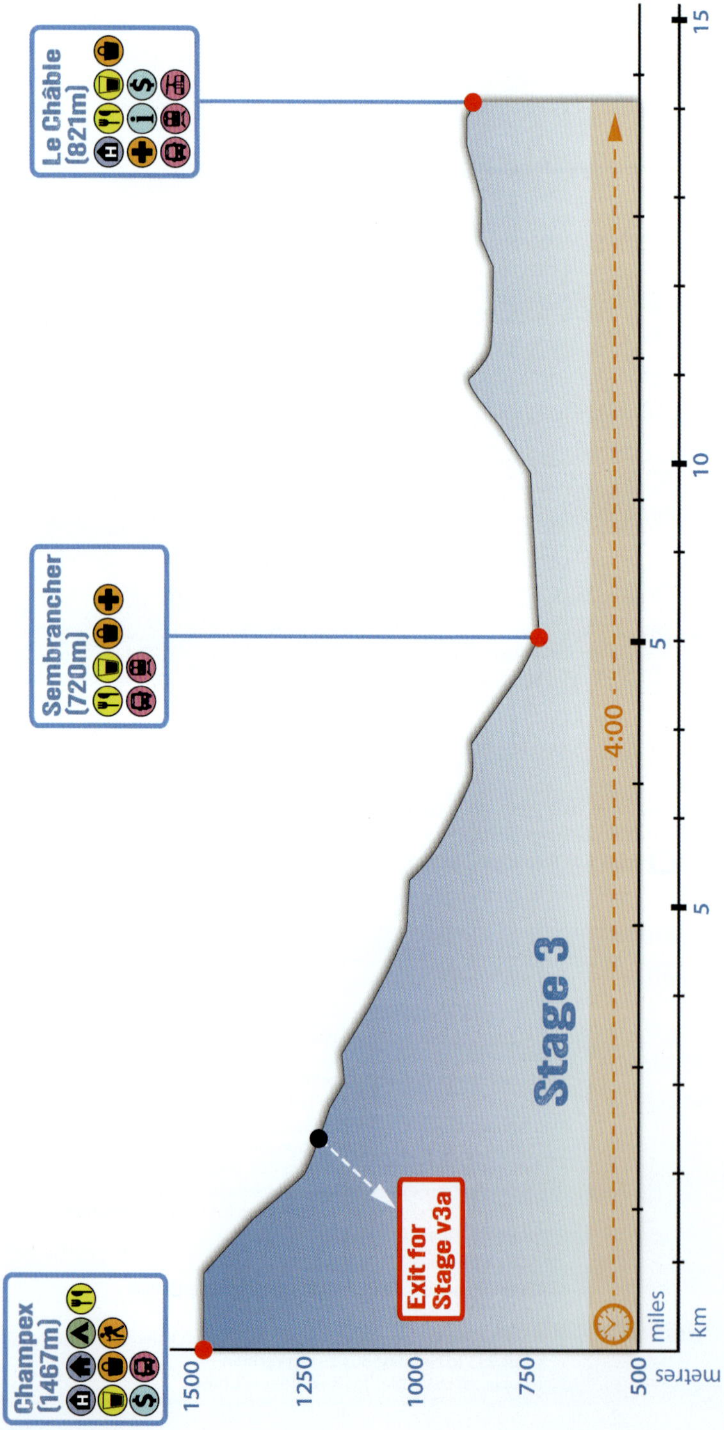

Champex (1467m)
Sembrancher (720m)
Le Châble (821m)
Exit for Stage v3a
Stage 3
4:00
1500
1250
1000
750
500
metres
miles
km
5
10
15
5

Stage 3: Champex to le Châble

25 **See map on p70.** Walk SE alongside the lake on a path. Just after the lake, TL on a road: follow it around to the left past **Hôtel Splendide**. Just after **Hôtel Alpina**, TR and descend on a path ('Sembrancher'): ignore offshoots. Keep SH across a gravel track to descend on a path.

26 0:45: At **Chez-les-Reuses**, keep SH at a junction. A few minutes later, TR at a fork (yellow sign). A few minutes later, TL at a junction ('Sembrancher').

27 1:10: TL on a track. Immediately afterwards, TR downhill on a path ('Sembrancher'). Keep SH onto a track which soon becomes a path. TL just before a trough at the hamlet of **Soulalex** ('Sembrancher'). Soon, TL onto another road. Shortly afterwards, TL at a fork ('Sembrancher'). At a fork beside a park bench, TR (yellow sign). After 15min, cross a track and descend on a path.

28 2:00: Walk through the village of **la Garde (900m)**, following signs for 'Sembrancher'. Leave the village on a road. Keep SH across a junction. Soon the road bends left and becomes a track (yellow sign). Keep on this track, following yellow signs, until it turns sharply right at an electricity pylon: keep SH to pick up a grassy path (yellow waymarks). TR onto a gravel track ('Sembrancher'). Take care crossing a road and continue downhill on a path. Cross the road again and descend on a path. TR at the railway line. Shortly afterwards, TL through a tunnel underneath the railway. Afterwards, TL on a small road and follow yellow signs.

29 2:35: In **Sembrancher (720m)**, TR after a fountain onto **Rue Principale**. After 5min, keep SH at a road junction onto **Route des Moulins**. Just after a fountain, cross a bridge and keep SH ('le Châble'). Follow a tarmac lane through fields.

30 2:55: TR at a fork. Shortly afterwards, keep SH on a track. Soon, start to climb. After a while, descend on a path.

31 3:25: TL on a track. Shortly afterwards, TR before a bridge ('le Châble) and continue on a track alongside the river.

32 3:45: **See map on p80.** TR onto a road: take care as there is no footpath.

33 3:55: TL onto **Ch. De Profray**. Walk past the church and head downhill through le Châble.

34 4:00: Reach the bridge over the river in **le Châble (821m)**.

Champex

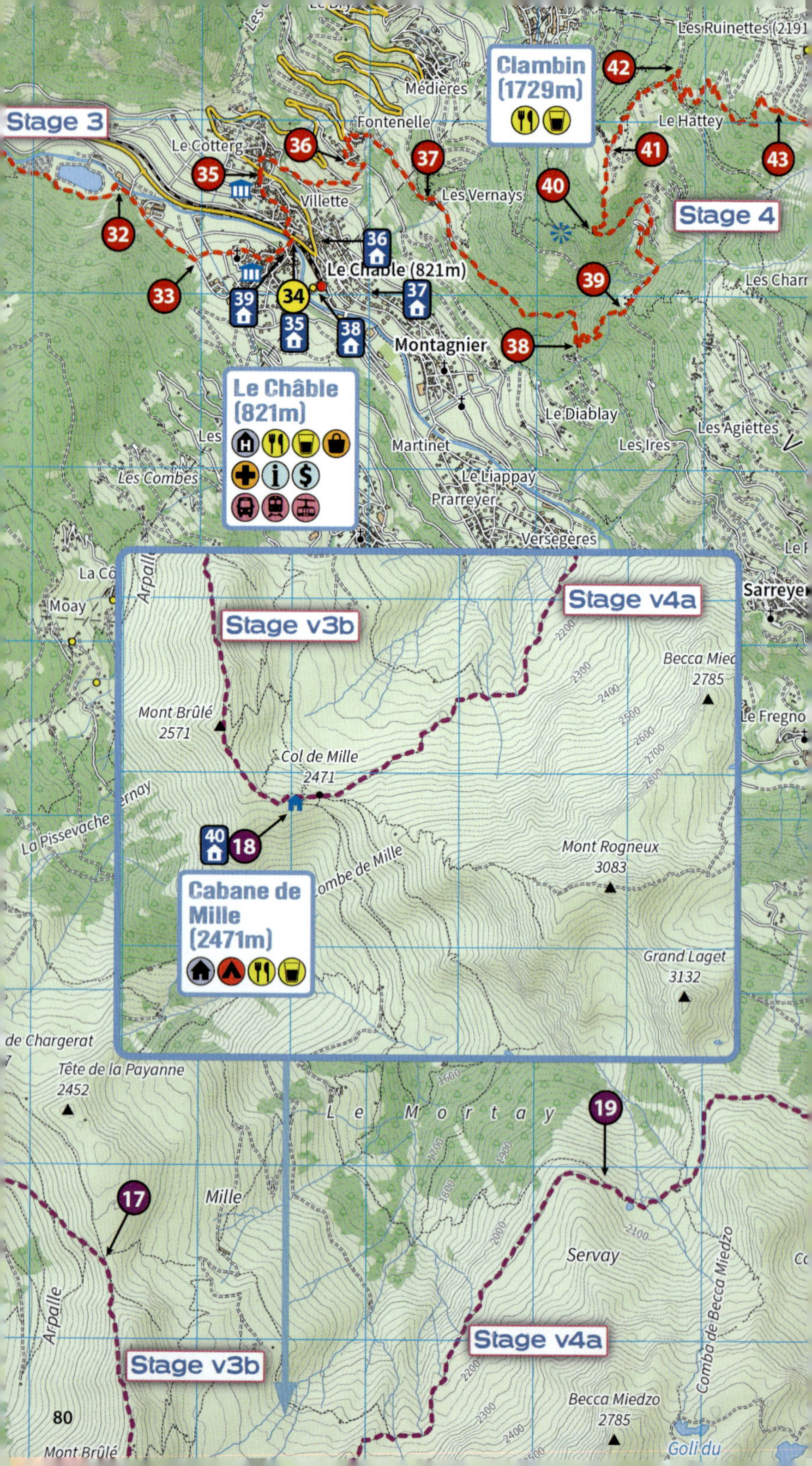
Stage 3
Stage 4
Stage v3b
Stage v4a
Clambin (1729m)
Le Châble (821m)
Cabane de Mille (2471m)
Médières
Fontenelle
Le Cotterg
Villette
Les Vernays
Le Hattey
Les Ruinettes
Montagnier
Le Diablay
Les Agiettes
Les Ires
Martinet
Le Liappay
Prarreyer
Versegères
Sarreyer
Les Combes
La Côt
Moay
Mont Brûlé 2571
Col de Mille 2471
Combe de Mille
Becca Mied 2785
Le Fregno
Mont Rogneux 3083
Grand Laget 3132
La Pissevache
de Chargerat
Tête de la Payanne 2452
Le Mortay
Mille
Arpaille
Servay
Becca Miedzo 2785
Comba de Becca Miedzo
Goli du
Mont Brûlé

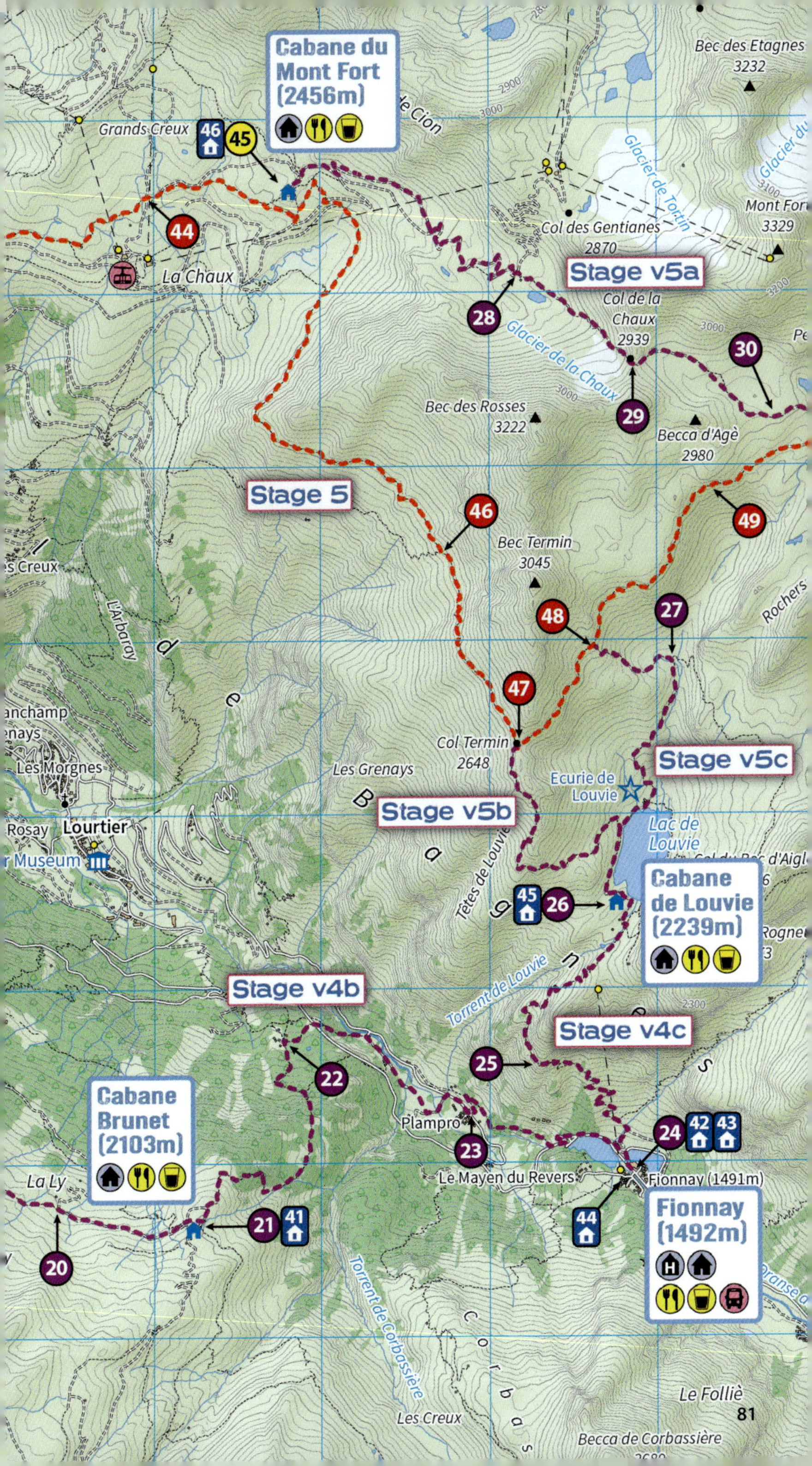
Cabane du Mont Fort (2456m)
Grands Creux
La Chaux
Col des Gentianes 2870
Bec des Etagnes 3232
Glacier de Tortin
Mont Fort 3329
Stage v5a
Col de la Chaux 2939
Glacier de la Chaux
Bec des Rosses 3222
Becca d'Agè 2980
Stage 5
Bec Termin 3045
Les Creux
L'Arbarey
Col Termin 2648
Les Grenays
Stage v5c
Ecurie de Louvie
Stage v5b
Lac de Louvie
Lourtier
Les Morgnes
Rosay
Museum
Têtes de Louvie
Cabane de Louvie (2239m)
Torrent de Louvie
Stage v4b
Stage v4c
Cabane Brunet (2103m)
Plampro
Le Mayen du Revers
Fionnay (1491m)
Fionnay (1492m)
La Ly
Torrent de Corbassière
Les Creux
Le Follié
Becca de Corbassière

4 Le Châble to Cabane du Mont Fort

A long, relentless climb through the forests around the ski resort of Verbier keeps you occupied for much of the day. Fortunately, the excellent views help to take your mind off the significant exertions. When the route finally rises above the trees, you are treated to the spectacular sight of Grand Combin to the SE: this snowy peak will dominate proceedings for the next few days. A superb balcony path now contours around the slopes all the way to Cabane du Mont Fort (CMF) which is a wonderful place for an overnight stop: the MB massif is visible to the SW and sunrise can be spectacular.

Itinerary options: if CMF is full then you could stay at Cabane de Louvie (3hr from CMF; see p93). To get there, use option 3 below. Alternatively, in bad weather, it can be preferable to avoid Col Termin: take the bus from le Châble to Fionnay and then use Stage v4c to climb to Cabane de Louvie (p103).

Moving on from CMF: there are three options:

- **Stage 5:** main WHR route via Col Termin (p86).
- **Stage v5a:** variant via Col de la Chaux (p90).
- **Stage 5/v5b/v5c:** variant via Cabane de Louvie (p93). From CMF, head SE along Stage 5. From Col Termin, follow Stage v5b to Cabane de Louvie. From there, follow Stage v5c to rejoin the main WHR route at 48.

Superb views of Grand Combin on the way to CMF

	Start	Finish	Time	Distance	Ascent	Descent	Max Alt
4	Le Châble	Cabane du Mont Fort	6:45	12.3km 7.6miles	1665m 5463ft	30m 98ft	2456m 8058ft

Terrain	Good paths and tracks which are well maintained. A few short sections on quiet roads/lanes. There is a mammoth 1665m of climbing: start early to beat the midday heat.
Route-finding	There is a complicated labyrinth of paths/tracks around le Châble and Verbier: follow the directions closely and watch for yellow signs/waymarks. Our sheet map shows this area in greater detail, with a 1:10,000 scale inset: see p37.
Transport	You can avoid most of the climb by taking the cable car from le Châble to les Ruinettes (10min on foot from 43): CMF is 3.5km on foot from les Ruinettes. Alternatively, from les Ruinettes, another cable car can take you to la Chaux which is only 2km from CMF. If you stay overnight in le Châble then you are entitled to a free lift pass for the following day: ask for it when you check-in. **le Châble:** train to Sembrancher/Martigny/Orsières; Bus 253 to Fionnay; Bus 251 to Verbier; Cable car to Verbier, les Ruinettes, la Chaux.

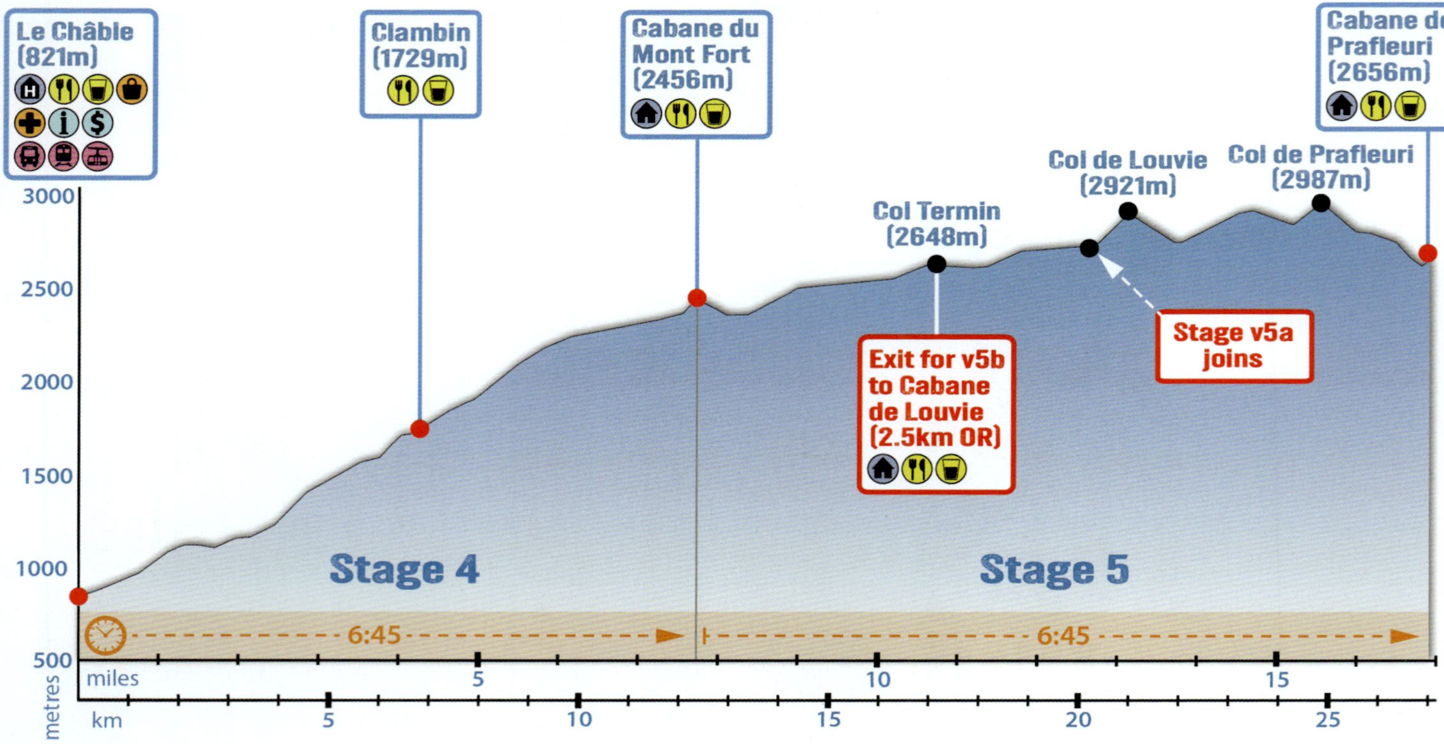
Le Châble (821m)
Clambin (1729m)
Cabane du Mont Fort (2456m)
Col Termin (2648m)
Exit for v5b to Cabane de Louvie (2.5km OR)
Col de Louvie (2921m)
Stage v5a joins
Col de Prafleuri (2987m)
Cabane de Prafleuri (2656m)
Stage 4
Stage 5
6:45
6:45
3000
2500
2000
1500
1000
500
metres
miles
km
5
10
15
20
25

Stage 4: le Châble to Cabane du Mont Fort

34 **See map on p80.** In **le Châble**, cross the bridge over the river and TL. TR onto **Ch. des Etales**. Just afterwards, TL at a junction. Then follow signs for 'Forge Oreiller' up through the hamlet of **Villette**. TR just before the Forge.

35 0:15: Cross a road and climb **Ch. du Reposoir**. Soon, TR ('Chapelle des Verneys') onto **Ch. du Four**: do not go SH uphill following the sign for 'Mont Fort' (this leads to Verbier). After a few minutes, keep SH on a track. Shortly afterwards, TL on a path ('les Verneys').

36 0:35: In the hamlet of **Fontenelle**, at a junction beside a fountain, TR up **Ch. du Grangeret**. At the next junction, TR. Soon afterwards, TR onto a path. Climb steeply and, after a few minutes, TR ('Chapelle des Verneys').

37 1:05: Continue past **Chapelle des Verneys**. After the buildings of **les Verneys**, descend gently. A few minutes later, TL on a path between trees ('Sarreyer').

38 1:50: TL at a junction ('Clambin') and climb steeply.

39 2:35: TL on a broad track. Shortly afterwards, TR at a fork. After a while, TR onto a path (yellow waymark; easy to miss). Follow yellow signs up through trees. TL just after a farm building and contour around the hillside: take care near steep drops.

40 3:20: TR at a junction ('Clambin') and climb. After a steep climb, the path levels and passes some chalets.

41 3:50: A few minutes later, arrive at a junction at **Clambin (1729m)**, near a restaurant: TR ('le Hattey').

42 4:20: At **le Hattey**, TR at a junction ('Mont Fort'). After a few minutes, follow the track around to the left. After 15min, TR on a path ('les Ruinettes') heading through myrtille and raspberry shrubs. Take care crossing some mountain biking tracks. Around **2100m**, emerge from the trees.

43 5:20: At a junction near **les Ruinettes**, TR on a track: the path from the cable car station joins from the left. After a few minutes, the track becomes a path, heading steeply uphill. Shortly afterwards, TR, taking the middle of three paths ('Mont Fort'), and contour around the hillside. A few minutes later, TL on another path ('Mont Fort'). Shortly, cross a track and continue uphill on a path ('Mont Fort') which traverses magnificently around the hillside. Eventually, you should spot CMF up ahead, on a rock outcrop to the E.

44 6:15: Cross a track and continue SH on a path ('Mont Fort'). Soon TR onto a path (yellow waymarks). Pass underneath CMF and then TL at a junction ('Mont Fort').

45 6:45: 10min later, arrive at **Cabane du Mont Fort (2456m)**.

41 Clambin

5 Cabane du Mont Fort to Cabane de Prafleuri

For those who like their hikes wild, this stage will be a highlight of the WHR: much of the route is remote with few signs of human habitation and you will cross three wonderful, and very different, cols. After leaving CMF, climb to Col Termin, enjoying the WHR's last great views of the MB Massif: you are in for a treat if you walk this section as the sun is rising. There are plenty of ibex and chamois too so keep your eyes peeled.

However, the following section between Col Termin and Col de Louvie is the highlight of the stage: it is a remote, beautiful landscape of grassy slopes and snowy peaks which overlooks the shimmering blue Lac de Louvie. The views of Grand Combin are exquisite too. Later, the grass gives way to rock as you climb towards Col de Louvie where both Grand Combin and Mont Blanc are still visible. Afterwards, enter the barren moonscape of the Grand Désert's glacial moraine: the boulders and glacial lakes are a stark contrast to what has come before. It would be easy to lose your way here so navigate carefully. Eventually, climb steeply to the third and final pass, Col de Prafleuri. Then descend equally steeply to Cabane de Prafleuri, set on an outcrop overlooking a barren cirque and surrounded by high peaks.

Itinerary options: Stage v5a is a slightly shorter alternative to Stage 5. After leaving CMF, it crosses Col de la Chaux instead of Col Termin. The two routes converge again at (50). See p90.

	Start	Finish	Time	Distance	Ascent	Descent	Max Alt
5	Cabane du Mont Fort	Cabane de Prafleuri	6:45	14.7km 9.1miles	954m 3130ft	754m 2474ft	2987m 9800ft

The Combins Massif

Terrain	This is one of the hardest stages of the WHR and should not be underestimated. It is very long and the terrain is remote, making it difficult to find help if something were to go wrong. Paths are often rocky, uneven and tiring. Furthermore, sometimes there are no paths at all: on the many sections of rocks/boulders, watch your footing and follow waymarks carefully; the rocks are slippery in wet conditions. There are some steep gradients and often the route is exposed (with steep drops): take care on the narrow, precipitous sections, a few of which are protected with fixed chains.
Route-finding	The route is well marked (blue/white markings in the vicinity of CMF; red/white for the rest of the stage). Nevertheless, this is a high mountain route which should be avoided in bad weather/low visibility when waymarks are harder to follow and navigation can be challenging across the long sections of rock (without paths). In particular, route-finding through the Grand Désert (between Col de Louvie and Col de Prafleuri) requires careful attention. Snow can remain on large parts of the route well into July, making it treacherous and difficult to navigate: in such conditions, it is unwise to attempt it.
Transport	**No transport available.** In bad weather, it is unwise to attempt Section 5. To bypass it, hike from CMF back to les Ruinettes (or la Chaux). Then take the cable car down to le Châble: if the cable car is not operating, you can take the bus from Verbier to le Châble or walk down. From le Châble, take the train to Sion. From Sion, Bus 372 runs to Barrage de la Grande Dixence: you can stay at Hotel du Barrage or hike up to Cabane de Prafleuri (following Stage v6a in reverse from Hotel du Barrage). We had to do exactly that in August 2023.

Stage 5: Cabane du Mont Fort to Cabane de Prafleuri

45 **See map on p81.** Take the path heading E from the rear of CMF and descend ('Col Termin'). TR at a junction. Immediately afterwards, TL at a blue signpost onto a narrow path (blue/white waymarks). After a few minutes, TR and descend on a track. Shortly afterwards, leave the track for a path (blue signpost). Take care crossing a few streams. Soon, traverse SW across the face of the slope, heading directly towards the MB Massif. After a while, the faint, narrow path starts to climb more steeply: take care near steep drops.

46 1:20: Keep SH at a junction ('Col Termin'). A few minutes later, cross a rocky gully (cairns): do not linger here as there are rockfalls. Afterwards, take care on a precipitous section protected by chains.

47 2:00: Cross **Col Termin (2648m)** and descend on a path which quickly bears left to head NE. Almost immediately, **Lac de Louvie** appears to the SE. Soon, there are narrow sections with precipitous drops.

48 2:20: Keep SH at a junction ('Col de Louvie'): climb and then cross a boulder field. Afterwards, the undulating path contours around the hillside.

49 2:50: **See map on p88.** Enter a huge boulder field: watch your footing and follow waymarks. Soon, the path undulates again.

50 3:15: Keep SH at a junction ('Col de Louvie'): the path to the left comes from **Col de la Chaux** (Stage v5a).

51 3:45: Cross **Col de Louvie (2921m)**. Head initially E through a barren, rocky landscape (waymarks). Shortly, start to descend steeply: the path is faint and hard to follow.

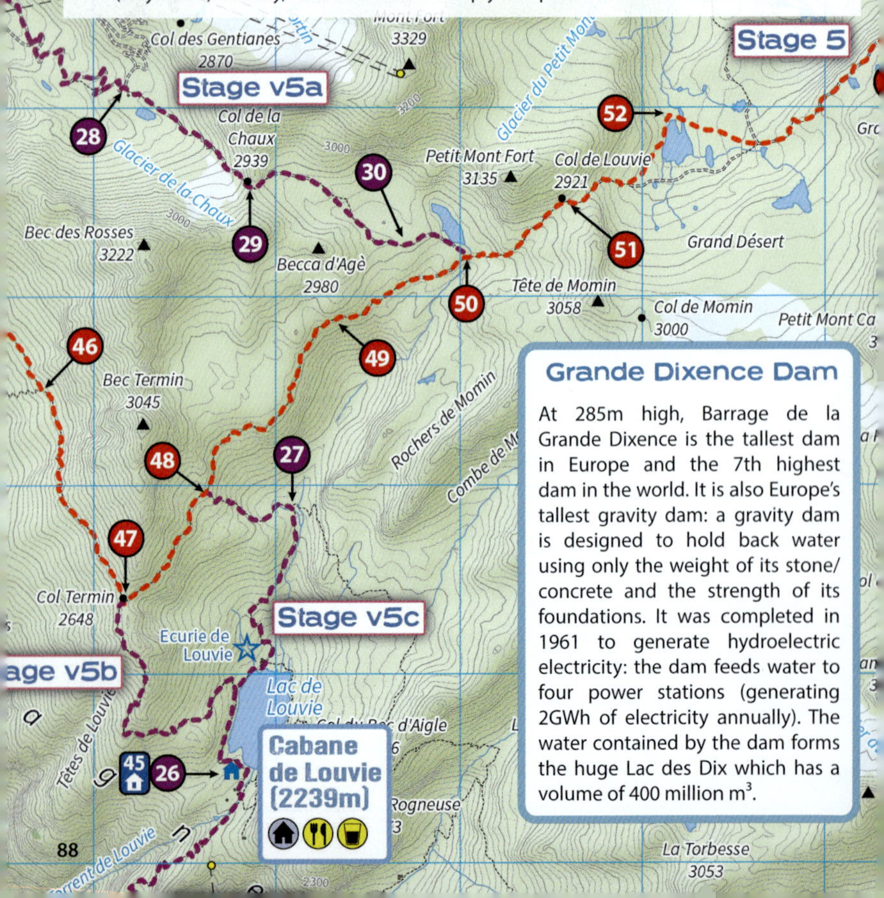

Grande Dixence Dam

At 285m high, Barrage de la Grande Dixence is the tallest dam in Europe and the 7th highest dam in the world. It is also Europe's tallest gravity dam: a gravity dam is designed to hold back water using only the weight of its stone/concrete and the strength of its foundations. It was completed in 1961 to generate hydroelectric electricity: the dam feeds water to four power stations (generating 2GWh of electricity annually). The water contained by the dam forms the huge Lac des Dix which has a volume of 400 million m^3.

52 4:10: Pass along the left side of a lake: at a huge boulder on the N side of it, TR and head SE (waymarks/cairns). Cross the outflow stream of the lake and head E on a faint path. After 20min, bear left at a signpost beside a large boulder and head NE ('Col de Prafleuri'). After climbing, the gradient levels: proceed across a rocky plateau.

53 5:00: Descend towards three turquoise lakes: the path is steep and rocky. There are a few short sections where scrambling is required. Soon, the faint path heads to the left of the lakes. After the lakes, climb steeply through a boulder field. When the path disappears, scramble over boulders (waymarks).

54 5:45: TL at **Col de Prafleuri (2987m)** ('Prafleuri') and soon descend steeply. After 20min, cross a barren plateau. Then, descend through hillocks. TR at a junction onto a track. After a few minutes, TL on a path.

55 6:45: Finally, climb for a few minutes to arrive at **Cabane de Prafleuri (26m)**.

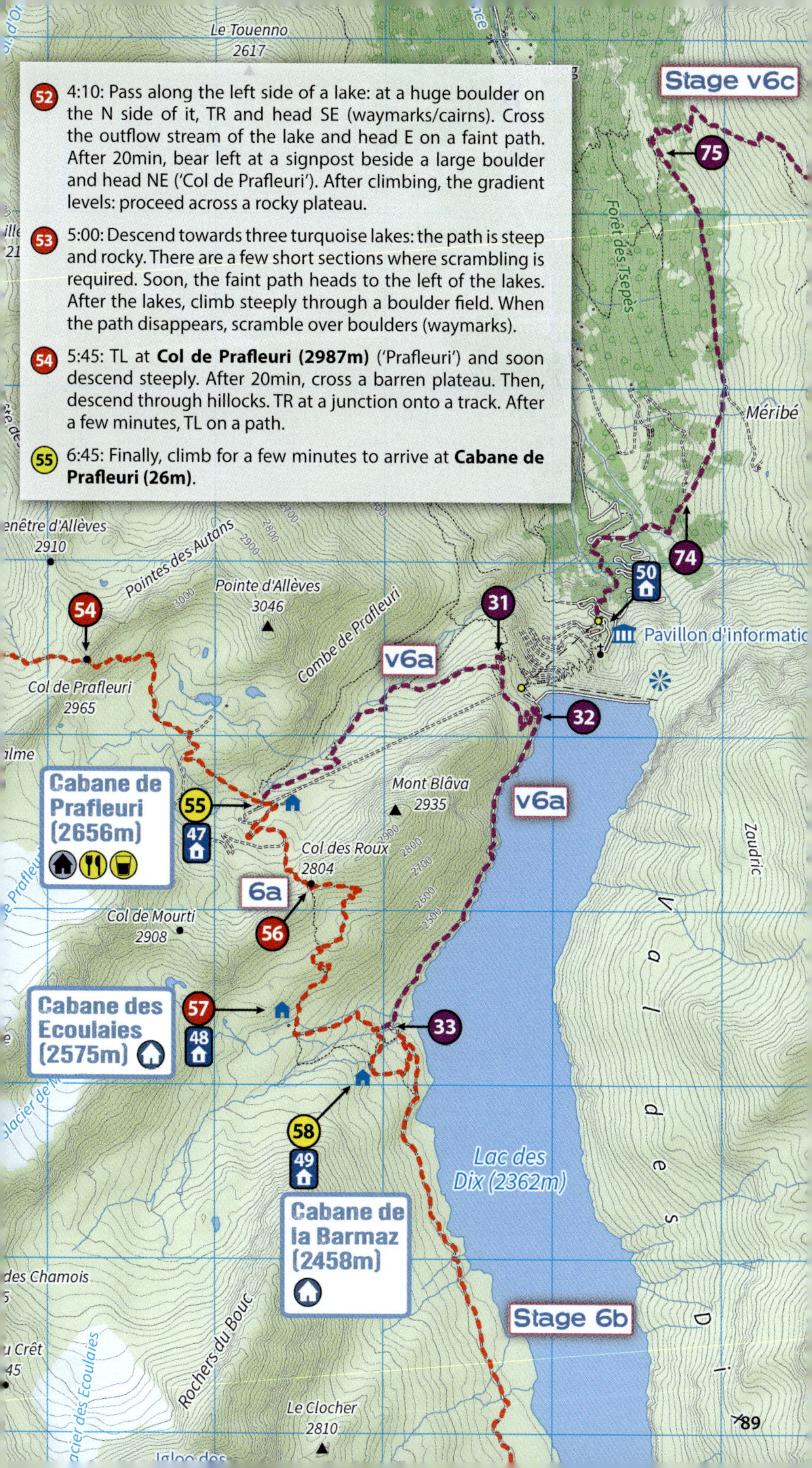

v5a Cabane du Mont Fort to Cabane de Prafleuri (via Col de la Chaux)

The Mont Blanc Massif

This spectacular variant shortens Stage 5 by avoiding Col Termin and taking a more direct route straight over Col de la Chaux. Some suggest that this is a bad weather alternative but we disagree: Col de la Chaux is no place to get caught in low visibility/bad conditions. Furthermore, Stage v5a still requires you to cross the Grand Désert (between Col de Louvie and Col de Prafleuri), a barren place where navigation is tricky. Although, the route over Col de la Chaux is a fabulous hike in its own right, we still prefer Stage 5. It is, however, useful if you are short of time.

Terrain	This stage is long and the terrain is remote, making it difficult to find help if something goes wrong. Paths are often rocky, uneven and tiring. Furthermore, at times there are no paths at all: watch your footing and follow waymarks carefully on the many sections of rocks/boulders; the rocks are slippery in wet conditions. There are some very steep gradients and often the route is exposed (with steep drops): take care on narrow, precipitous sections, some of which are protected with fixed chains.
Route-finding	Although the route is waymarked, this is a high mountain route which should be avoided in bad weather/low visibility when waymarks are harder to follow and navigation can be challenging across the long sections of rock (without paths). In particular, route-finding between Col de Louvie and Col de Prafleuri requires careful attention. Snow can remain on large parts of the route well into July and, in such conditions, it would be unwise to attempt it: paths are treacherous and difficult to navigate
Transport	**No transport available.** See p87.

	Start	Finish	Time	Distance	Ascent	Descent	Max Alt
v5a	Cabane du Mont Fort	Cabane de Prafleuri	6:00	11.6km 7.2miles	987m 3238ft	781m 2562ft	2987m 9800ft

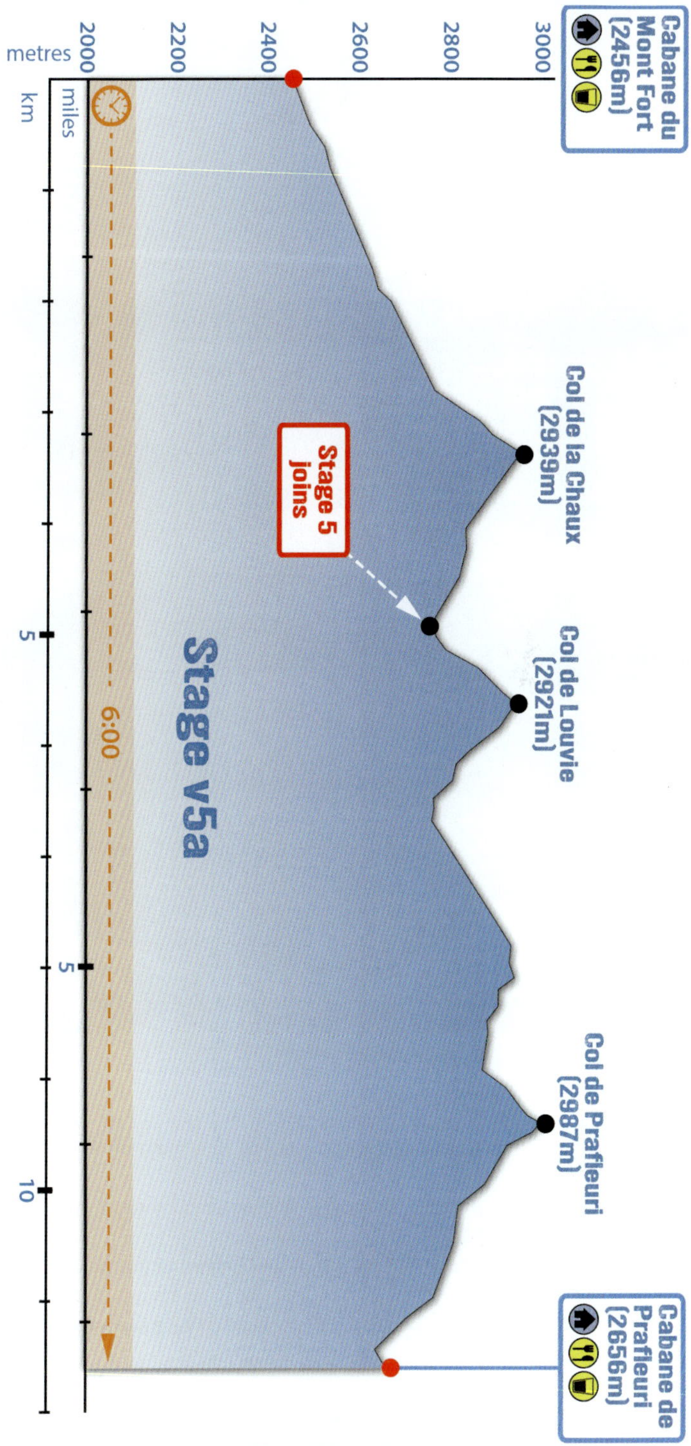

Cabane du Mont Fort (2456m)
Col de la Chaux (2939m)
Stage 5 joins
Col de Louvie (2921m)
Col de Prafleuri (2987m)
Cabane de Prafleuri (2656m)
Stage v5a
6:00
metres
3000
2800
2600
2400
2200
2000
miles
km
5
5
10

Heading towards the Grand Désert

Stage v5a: Cabane du Mont Fort to Cabane de Prafleuri (via Col de la Chaux)

45 **See map on p81.** Take the path heading NE from the rear of CMF. Keep NE at a junction, continuing on a track. At the next junction, turn sharp left. Soon the track bends right to head SE.

28 0:45: TR onto a path **(2704m)**. Follow cairns and waymarks through rocky terrain: sometimes the path disappears.

29 1:45: **See map on p88.** Cross **Col de la Chaux (2939m)** and head into a rocky cirque.

30 2:10: TL at a junction and soon pass to the right of **Lac du Petit Mont Fort (2763m)**.

50 2:30: TL at a junction (where you meet Stage 5). Follow the Stage 5 directions to Cabane de Prafleuri (p88).

55 6:00: Arrive at **Cabane de Prafleuri (2656m)**.

v5b Col Termin to Cabane de Louvie

Col Termin

From Col Termin, a path heads S along the ridge of Bec Termin and then drops into the valley to the E to reach the beautiful Lac de Louvie. From there, Cabane de Louvie is only a short walk away and it is a wonderfully peaceful place to spend the night.

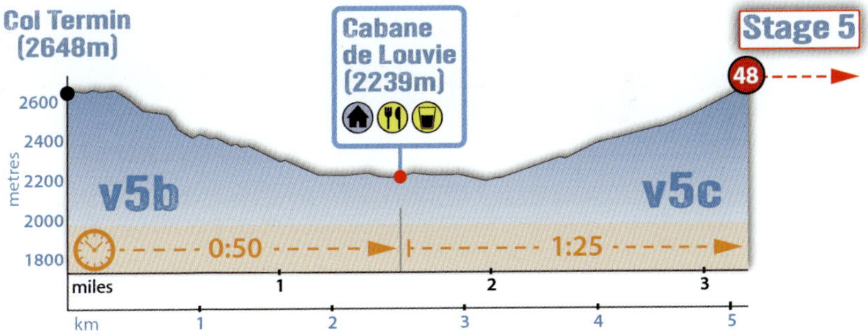

Terrain	This is a high mountain route which should be avoided in bad weather, low visibility or snowy conditions. Paths can be rough, rocky and steep.
Route-finding	Fewer hikers use this route so paths are sometimes rocky and harder to follow than the main WHR. That said, in good conditions, it is not too difficult to follow. Avoid this route if there is snow on the ground (when navigation could be challenging).
Transport	None

	Start	Finish	Time	Distance	Ascent	Descent	Max Alt
v5b	Col Termin	Cabane de Louvie	0:50	2.5km 1.6miles	11m 36ft	420m 1378ft	2648m 8688ft

47 **See map on p88.** From **Col Termin**, head S on a path which initially drops down the W side of the ridge. Follow the ridge S and eventually cross it, descending E towards **Lac de Louvie**. When you reach the lake, TR and head S along the shore.

26 0:50: Reach **Cabane de Louvie (2239m)**.

v5c Louvie Link Route

Lac de Louvie

This short section links Cabane de Louvie with the main route of the WHR (joining Stage 5 at 48, a short distance NE of Col Termin). From there, you follow Stage 5 all the way to Cabane de Prafleuri.

Terrain	This is a high mountain route which should be avoided in bad weather, low visibility or snowy conditions. Paths can be rough, rocky and steep.
Route-finding	Fewer hikers use this route so paths are sometimes rocky and harder to follow than the main WHR. That said, in good conditions, it is not too difficult to follow. Avoid this route if there is snow on the ground (when navigation could be challenging).
Transport	None

	Start	Finish	Time	Distance	Ascent	Descent	Max Alt
v5c	Cabane de Louvie	48	1:25	2.7km 1.7miles	417m 1368ft	30m 98ft	2626m 8615ft

26 **See map on p88.** From **Cabane de Louvie**, follow a beautiful path along the W side of **Lac de Louvie**. At the N end of the lake, pass the buildings known as **les Écuries de Louvie** ('Stables of Louvie'). Shortly afterwards, the path climbs to the N.

27 1:00: TL at a junction at **Plan de la Gole (2429m)**.

48 1:25: Reach a **junction (2626m)**: TR and follow the Stage 5 directions to Cabane de Prafleuri (p88).

Champex to Cabane de Prafleuri (High Altitude Variant)

Although the scenery is beautiful, Sections 3 and 4 are not the finest parts of the WHR: as a lower-level valley walk, Section 3 is less dramatic than many other parts of the route; furthermore, many people do not look forward to Stage 4 and its long climb from le Châble to CMF. Nevertheless, over the years, the routes of Sections 3 and 4 have become generally accepted as the standard route for the WHR. However, there is another route which is used by those 'in the know': it is seldomly documented as part of the WHR but is scenically superior, sending you back up to high altitude soon after leaving Champex.

This alternative route is described here as Sections v3 (p96), v4 (p100) and v5c (p94). It leads you E from Champex, crossing Val d'Entremont at Orsières and then climbing the slopes of the Combins massif. After a spectacular traverse overlooking Val de Bagnes, you will descend into it and reach the village of Fionnay. Then a stiff climb brings you to Cabane de Louvie. Climb again and soon rejoin the main WHR route at 48 in the middle of Stage 5 (shortly above Lac de Louvie).

Because you avoid Sections 3 and 4 of the main WHR route, you will not stay at CMF but overnight stops at Cabane de Mille, Cabane Brunet or Cabane de Louvie should make up for that. The variant is more challenging than the main route (with more climbing) and is therefore better suited to trekkers who are in good shape or have the time to take things slowly.

The Combins massif & Mont Vélan viewed from Cabane de Mille (Stage v3b)

v3 Champex to Col de Mille (via Orsières)

From Champex, an easy descent leads to the village of Orsières at the base of Val d'Entremont: you could skip this stage by taking the bus. From Orsières, however, the route is tougher with a long climb to the hut at Col de Mille. Immediately after leaving Orsières, the path starts upwards and it barely relents until the end: the good news is that although the route heads consistently upwards, rarely is the gradient particularly steep, facilitating a comfortable, steady pace. Furthermore, from the outset until the finish, the scenery is exquisite: classic alpine terrain of jagged peaks, deep green valleys and flower-filled pastures (grazed by herds of the miraculously pristine cows that seem only to exist in Switzerland). Eventually, you reach the top of a ridge, high above the valley, and good paths lead you S along it, across the summit of Mont Brûlé, towards Cabane de Mille.

At the end of Section v3, Cabane de Mille is a modern hut with a spectacular location on Col de Mille: it was rebuilt completely in 2013/2014. It is a comfortable hut with 59 beds in 7 dormitories but can feel crowded in high season. The views from the dining room are stunning. To the S, Combin de Grafeneire (the highest summit in the Combins massif), rises above a dramatic ridge, drawing the eye. However, to its right and slightly further away, the

	Start	Finish	Time	Distance	Ascent	Descent	Max Alt
v3a	Champex	Orsières	1:00	4.0km 2.5miles	19m 62ft	586m 1923ft	1490m 4888ft
v3b	Orsières	Cabane de Mille	6:00	12.5km 7.8miles	1689m 5541ft	118m 387ft	2571m 8435ft

Cabane de Mille

jagged summit of Mont Vélan is even more beautiful. Both summits look particularly fine at sunset when the alpenglow lights up their snowy faces. To the W, the MB massif is only a stone's throw away: the Grandes Jorasses, Mont Dolent and l'Aiguille d'Argentière look magnificent and it hardly matters that you cannot see MB itself from here. If you are arriving at the hut early in the day, bring surplus drinking water because taps are sometimes shut off during the day (due to water shortages): they are switched on again in the evening. Camping is usually permitted beside the cabane.

Mid-section, the only accommodation is at Orsières which is too close to Champex for those who spent the previous night there. However, you could opt for a night in Orsières instead of busier Champex.

Terrain	Paths and tracks are clear, well maintained and straightforward to negotiate. The climb to Col de Mille is long and tiring. Between 17 and Cabane de Mille, the route follows the crest of a ridge which you should avoid in high winds, low visibility or snowy conditions.
Route-finding	Between 13 and 15, there is a complicated labyrinth of paths, tracks and minor roads: follow waymarks and signs carefully. Otherwise, route-finding is largely straightforward in good conditions: most significant junctions have signposts/waymarks.
Transport	**Champex:** Bus 271 to Orsières. **Orsières:** train to Sembrancher/Martigny/le Châble; Bus 271 to Champex; Bus 211 to Aosta in Italy.

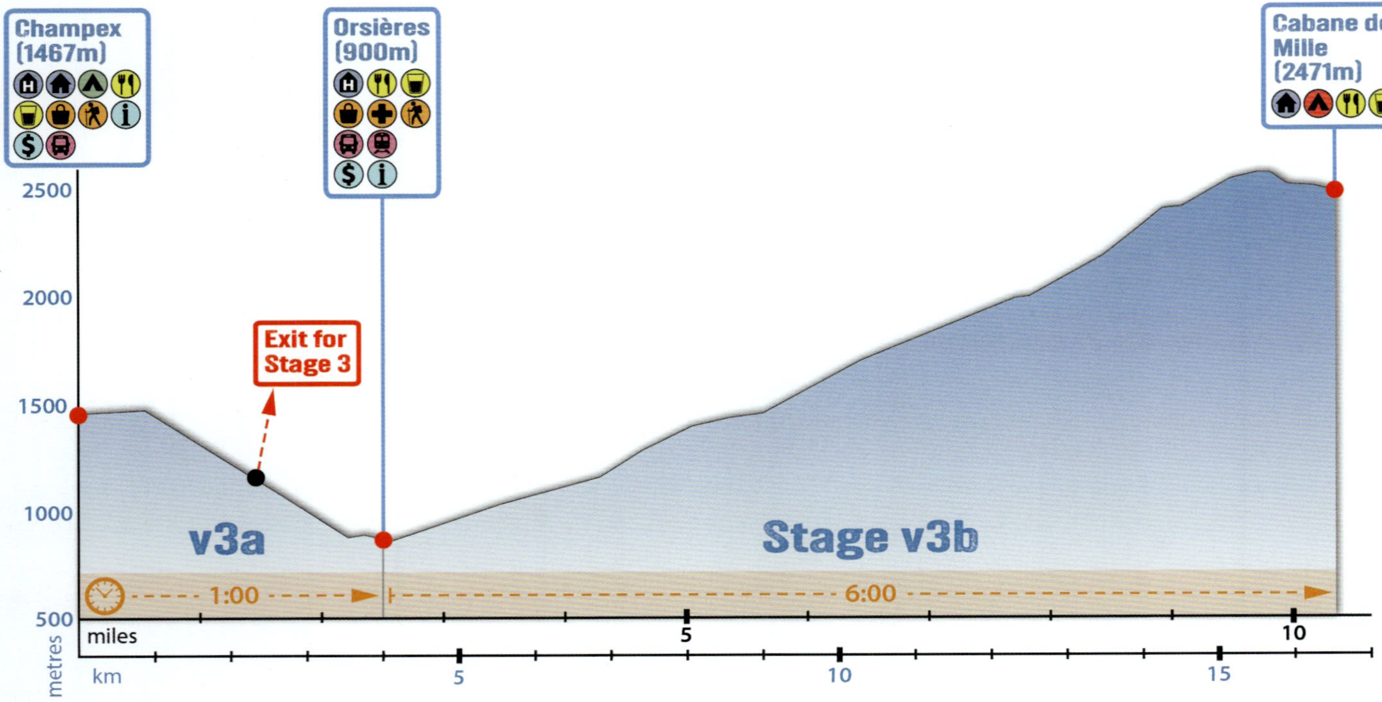
Champex
(1467m)
Orsières
(900m)
Cabane de
Mille
(2471m)
Exit for
Stage 3
v3a
Stage v3b
1:00
6:00
2500
2000
1500
1000
500
metres
miles
5
10
km
5
10
15

Stage v3a: Champex to Orsières

25 **See map on p70.** Walk SE alongside the lake on a path. Just after the lake, TL on a road. Follow the road around to the left past **Hôtel Splendide**. Just after **Hôtel Alpina**, TR and descend on a path ('Sembrancher'): ignore offshoots. Keep SH across a gravel track to descend on a path.

26 0:45: At **Chez-les-Reuses**, TR at a junction and descend on a lane through the hamlet. Then, descend E on a path. At a road junction, head SE towards the railway line. Then follow the road S (parallel to the tracks).

12 1:00: Arrive at the train station in the centre of **Orsières (900m)**.

Stage v3b: Orsières to Cabane de Mille

12 **See map on p71.** From **Orsières station**, head E down **Rue du Châtelard**. Shortly afterwards, descend steps. Then cross a bridge over the river. Shortly afterwards, TL on a road. Soon, TR and climb on a path between houses. Shortly afterwards, keep SH across a road. Now the route climbs using a combination of roads, tracks and paths (yellow/black waymarks).

13 0:30: TR onto a track. Shortly afterwards, TL onto a path (easy to miss). Soon, TR and climb on a road: ignore a smaller track on the right which descends. TL in the hamlet of **Reppaz** and climb between buildings. Shortly afterwards, follow the road around to the right.

14 1:00: Shortly, at a junction, TL onto a path which soon climbs through forest ('Commeire'). At times, the route is unclear and not every junction is waymarked. When you reach a road, follow it up through **Commeire**.

15 2:45: TR at a junction and climb on a track ('les Planards').

16 4:15: TL onto a narrow path (easy to miss; 'Cabane de Mille').

17 5:15: **See map on p80.** Keep SH at a junction. Eventually, the path leads you along the top of the ridge: keep SH across **Mont Brûlé (2571m)**.

18 6:00: Arrive at **Cabane de Mille (2473m)**.

The Mont Blanc Massif viewed from Cabane de Mille

v4 Cabane de Mille to Cabane de Louvie

This spectacular section starts with a fabulous balcony path along the N side of the Combins massif, overlooking the lovely Val de Bagnes: although the route undulates, it never dips below 2000m, ensuring that you retain most of the altitude gained on the previous day and enjoy views of the highest quality. Stage v4a finishes at Cabane Brunet which was built in 1942: it is a lovely place, with views of Petit Combin, but can be quite busy during the day.

	Start	Finish	Time	Distance	Ascent	Descent	Max Alt
v4a	Cabane de Mille	Cabane Brunet	3:00	7.9km 4.9miles	341m 1119ft	709m 2326ft	2473m 8114ft
v4b	Cabane Brunet	Fionnay	1:40	5.5km 3.4miles	165m 541ft	776m 2546ft	2103m 6900ft
v4c	Fionnay	Cabane de Louvie	2:30	3.8km 2.4miles	757m 2484ft	10m 33ft	2239m 7346ft

The route to Cabane Brunet

From Cabane Brunet, Stage v4b descends N into Val de Bagnes to reach Fionnay which has a few places to stay. On Stage v4c, climb out of the valley again to the spectacularly situated Cabane de Louvie: its remote location ensures that this is a tranquil overnight stop; the hut was built in 1997, replacing older buildings which were used by the workers who built the Louvie dam.

Terrain	Paths and tracks are largely clear, well-maintained and straightforward to negotiate. The climb from Fionnay to Cabane de Louvie is steep: you should avoid this area in snowy conditions or after heavy rain (because of avalanches/landslides).
Route-finding	Straightforward in good conditions. Most significant junctions have signposts/waymarks. Sometimes, snow remains on the highest sections of the route into July, making navigation more difficult.
Transport	**Fionnay:** Bus 253 to le Châble.

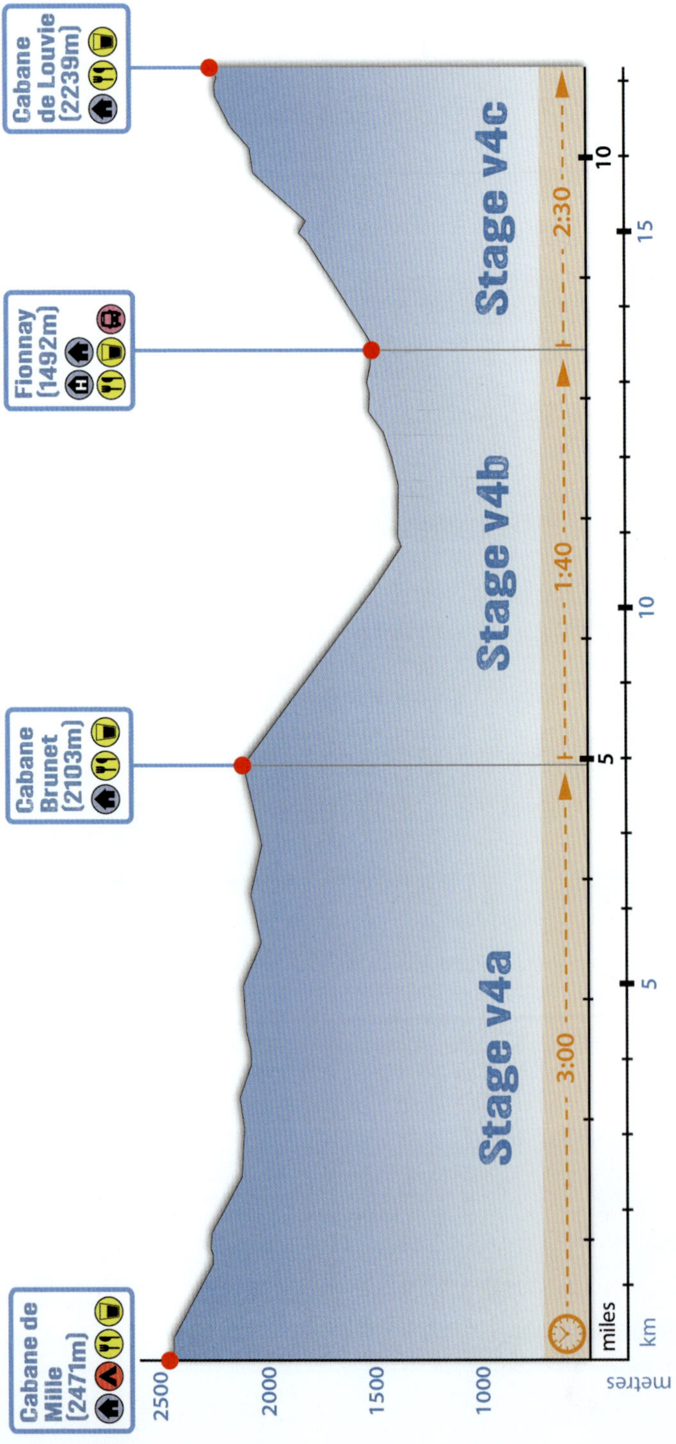

Cabane de Mille (2471m)
Cabane Brunet (2103m)
Fionnay (1492m)
Cabane de Louvie (2239m)
Stage v4a
Stage v4b
Stage v4c
3:00
1:40
2:30
2500
2000
1500
1000
metres
miles
km
5
10
15
5
10

Stage v4a: Cabane de Mille to Cabane Brunet

18 **See map on p80.** From **Cabane de Mille**, head E to nearby **Col de Mille (2471m)**. Cross the col and descend NE on a path which contours around the slopes.

19 1:20: Keep SH at a junction, descending towards a small lake. Continue E past the lake: there are trout in the clear water. Shortly afterwards, keep SH past the farm buildings of **Servay**, ignoring any paths to the left which descend into the valley. An undulating path continues contouring around the slopes.

20 2:40: Keep SH up a track. 15min later, TR and climb on a path.

21 3:00: Arrive at **Cabane Brunet (2103m)**.

Stage v4b: Cabane Brunet to Fionnay

21 **See map on p81.** From **Cabane Brunet**, head NE on a track. A few minutes later, TR on a path and soon descend through trees. At around **1600m**, TL at a junction (descending NW).

22 0:40: At **Barmasse**, TR at a junction. At **la Shleye**, TR on a track. Shortly after crossing a bridge, the path becomes faint: head SE and soon, TL on a grassy track. Shortly afterwards, cross another bridge. Shortly after that, TR on the road.

23 1:15: Shortly afterwards, TL through a parking area: at the end of it, TL and climb NW on a path. Shortly, TR at a junction onto a path which contours around the slopes above **Plampro**. When you reach the road again, TL along it.

24 1:40: Arrive in **Fionnay (1492m)**.

Stage v4c: Fionnay to Cabane de Louvie

24 **See map on p81.** From the bus stop in **Fionnay**, a signposted path runs along the N side of the main road. Soon it bends right (away from the road). Shortly, TL at a junction and zigzag up to the NW: the gradient gradually increases.

25 1:00: Contour around a ridge and then climb N again. Eventually, TL at **Lac de Louvie**.

26 2:30: Shortly afterwards, reach **Cabane de Louvie (2239m)**. **To continue to Cabane de Prafleuri, follow Stage v5c (Louvie Link Route; p94).**

Val de Bagnes

6 Cabane de Prafleuri to Arolla

A short climb out of the barren terrain surrounding Cabane de Prafleuri leads to Col des Roux where you are met by an entirely new, and starkly contrasting, vista: grassy slopes, snowy peaks, glaciers and the incredible Lac des Dix. The colour of the lake is otherworldly and the descent to Refuge de la Barmaz is Alpine walking at its finest. The refuge is usually unmanned, however, it can be one of the most rewarding overnight stops on the WHR. It is clean and fully equipped with blankets and a wood-fired cooker: however, you will need to bring your own food. You can also stay at the unmanned Cabane les Ecoulaies (see p107).

An easy stroll beside the spectacular Lac des Dix leads to probably the most notorious section of the WHR. From the SE tip of the lake, climb a barren but spectacular glacial valley dominated by the peak of Mont Blanc de Cheilon (3870m): watch for Chamois in this area. Then, tackle a very steep and unstable slope on the E flank of the valley which is prone to rockfalls. Soon you will have a decision to make: left for the extremely steep and loose scramble to Col de Riedmatten (a narrow cleft between rocks) or right for the metal ladders of Pas de Chèvres. Both have their pros and cons but whichever you choose, the views are excellent (if you can keep your eyes off the challenging terrain below your feet long enough to enjoy them). A long descent follows all the way to the lovely village of Arolla which is a popular base for mountaineers.

Itinerary options: because the following Section 7 is relatively short, you can restructure Sections 6 and 7 with a stay at Cabane des Dix instead of Arolla. Use the v6b variant (p112) to head to Cabane des Dix, spend the night there and then walk all the way to les Haudères/la Sage the following day.

If you are nervous about the crossing of Col de Riedmatten/Pas de Chèvres, or you are short of time, consider hiking Stage v6c instead (p114). It travels directly between Hotel du Barrage and les Haudères (saving half a day) and avoids Col de Riedmatten/Pas de Chèvres.

	Start	Finish	Time	Distance	Ascent	Descent	Max Alt
6a	Cabane de Prafleuri	Cabane de la Barmaz	1:30	3.2km 2.0miles	195m 640ft	393m 1289ft	2803m 9196ft
6b	Cabane de la Barmaz	Arolla	5:30	15.8km 9.8miles	640m 2100ft	1090m 3576ft	2918m 9573ft

Sunrise at Lac des Dix

Terrain	This is one of the hardest stages of the WHR and should not be underestimated. It is very long and the terrain is remote, making it difficult to find help if something goes wrong. Paths are often rocky, uneven and tiring. Furthermore, at times, there are no paths at all: watch your footing and follow waymarks carefully on the many sections of rocks/boulders; the rocks are slippery in wet conditions. There are some very steep gradients and exposed sections with steep drops: a few of these are protected with fixed chains. In particular, the climb amongst boulders before Col de Riedmatten/Pas de Chèvres is extremely steep, rocky and unstable: rockfalls and landslides frequently damage the path and some scrambling is required. Take great care on this section and do not attempt it in bad weather or low visibility: after rain, dangerous landslides can occur. Furthermore, do not attempt the ladders if you have a fear of heights: they are very exposed and a fall would be serious; however, if you can get your head around the exposure, this route is arguably less challenging than crossing Col de Riedmatten. At the date of press, the ladders at Pas de Chèvres were damaged and closed to hikers: it is not clear if they will re-open.
Route-finding	Although the route is waymarked, it is a high mountain route which should be avoided in bad weather/low visibility when markings are harder to follow and navigation can be challenging across the long sections of rock (without paths). In particular, route-finding between Lac des Dix and Col de Riedmatten/Pas de Chèvres requires careful attention: the path often disappears over rocks and the route below the passes is frequently concealed by rockfalls. Snow can remain on large parts of the route well into July making it treacherous and difficult to navigate: in such conditions, it is unwise to attempt it.
Transport	To bypass Section 6, hike from Cabane de Prafleuri to Hotel du Barrage (using Stage v6a; see p110). Then take Bus 372 down to Sion. From there, Bus 381/382 heads to les Haudères/Arolla (which are both on the main WHR route). **Arolla:** Bus 382 to la Gouille and les Haudères.

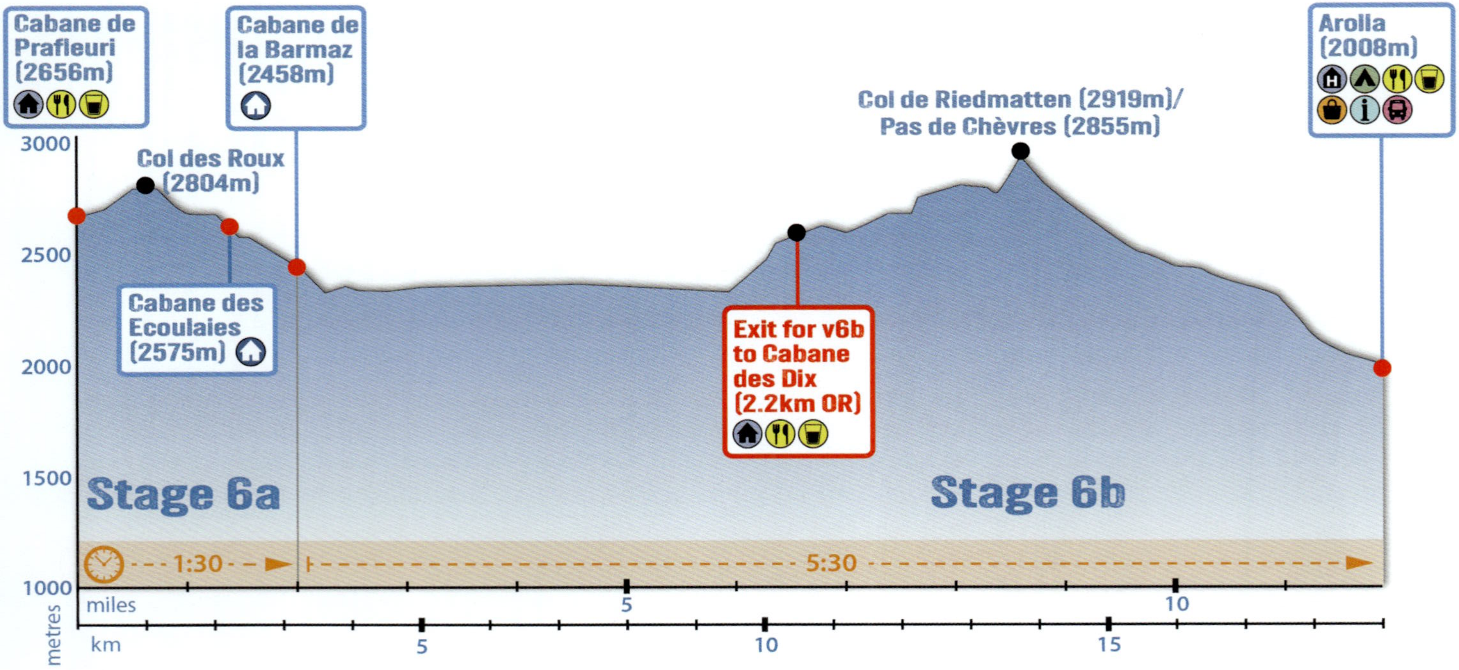

Cabane de Prafleuri (2656m)
Col des Roux (2804m)
Cabane des Ecoulaies (2575m)
Cabane de la Barmaz (2458m)
Exit for v6b to Cabane des Dix (2.2km OR)
Col de Riedmatten (2919m)/ Pas de Chèvres (2855m)
Arolla (2008m)
Stage 6a
Stage 6b
1:30
5:30
3000
2500
2000
1500
1000
metres
miles
km
5
10
15

Stage 6a: Cabane de Prafleuri to Cabane de la Barmaz

55 **See map on p89.** From a signpost in front of **Cabane de Prafleuri**, follow a path heading SE ('Col des Roux'). Follow cairns through a stony plateau and pick up the path on the other side.

56 0:30: Bear left at **Col des Roux (2804m)** and traverse the hillside on a path ('la Barma'). Soon the path starts to descend gently. After 10-15min, cross a short section of boulders, following waymarks.

57 1:10: Pass the unmanned **Cabane des Ecoulaies (2575m)**; there are blankets and a wood-burning cooker but you have to bring your own food; the setting is lovely but it is not as well-kept as Cabane de la Barmaz.

33 1:25: TR at a junction ('Refuge la Barma'). Shortly afterwards, cross a bridge.

58 1:30: 5min later, arrive at **Cabane de la Barmaz (2458m)**.

Stage 6b: Cabane de la Barmaz to Arolla

58 **See map on p108.** Facing the lake, TR onto the path in front of the hut. At a track near the shore of the lake, TR and walk S alongside the lake. At the SW tip of the lake, cross a bridge, bear left and continue following the track along the lake's S side.

59 1:15: TR and climb on a steep path ('Col de Riedmatten'). After 10min, keep SH, heading S amongst rocky crags: ignore a path on the left and instead follow a sign for 'Dix' (painted on a rock). Also ignore a confusing sign for 'Col de Riedmatten' painted on another rock.

60 1:55: Arrive at a fork: TR for Stage v6b to Cabane des Dix (p112); otherwise, TL to continue on Stage 6b ('Col de Riedmatten') and descend into a rocky moraine. Cross a bridge. Immediately afterwards, TR and climb the valley on a path.

61 2:15: Head N and then E around a plateau. After 5min, head NE up a rocky slope. Soon, the path bends right to the SE, sometimes disappearing over rocks. After a while, descend steeply through boulders: the path is unstable and difficult to follow.

62 2:55: The path bears left, heading E straight up an extremely steep and unstable slope: the slope is often damaged by rockfalls and so the directions below may not remain completely accurate. Take great care and do not attempt this section in bad weather or after rain. You will need to use your hands. After 10min, arrive at a faint junction which has directions painted on rocks. TL for Col de Riedmatten or TR for the alternative route over Pas de Chèvres (see box). From the junction, the path to Col de Riedmatten is clearer and can be walked rather than scrambled but it is still steep and unstable. The final approach to the col has chains to assist.

63 3:20: Cross **Col de Riedmatten (2918m)** and descend on a clear path ('Arolla'). Soon, TL at a junction ('Arolla'): the path descending from the right is the alternative route arriving from Pas de Chèvres.

64 4:15: Cross a bridge and continue downhill to the E. After about 25min, keep SH at a junction on a path ('Arolla'). TL after a chalet ('Arolla'). Shortly afterwards, descend on a track. After a few minutes, TR on a path (yellow sign). Soon, TL at a faint junction: from here, there is a confusing array of paths (follow waymarks carefully).

65 5:20: TR and keep downhill on a track past **Grand Hôtel Kurhaus**. Shortly afterwards, TR on a track ('Arolla').

66 5:30: Arrive in **Arolla (2008m)**.

Pas de Chèvres Alternative

TR at the faint junction after 62 and soon arrive at the base of the vertical ladders. Climb these to cross **Pas de Chèvres (2854m)**. Then descend on a path. Soon TR at a junction: the path on the left comes from Col de Riedmatten.

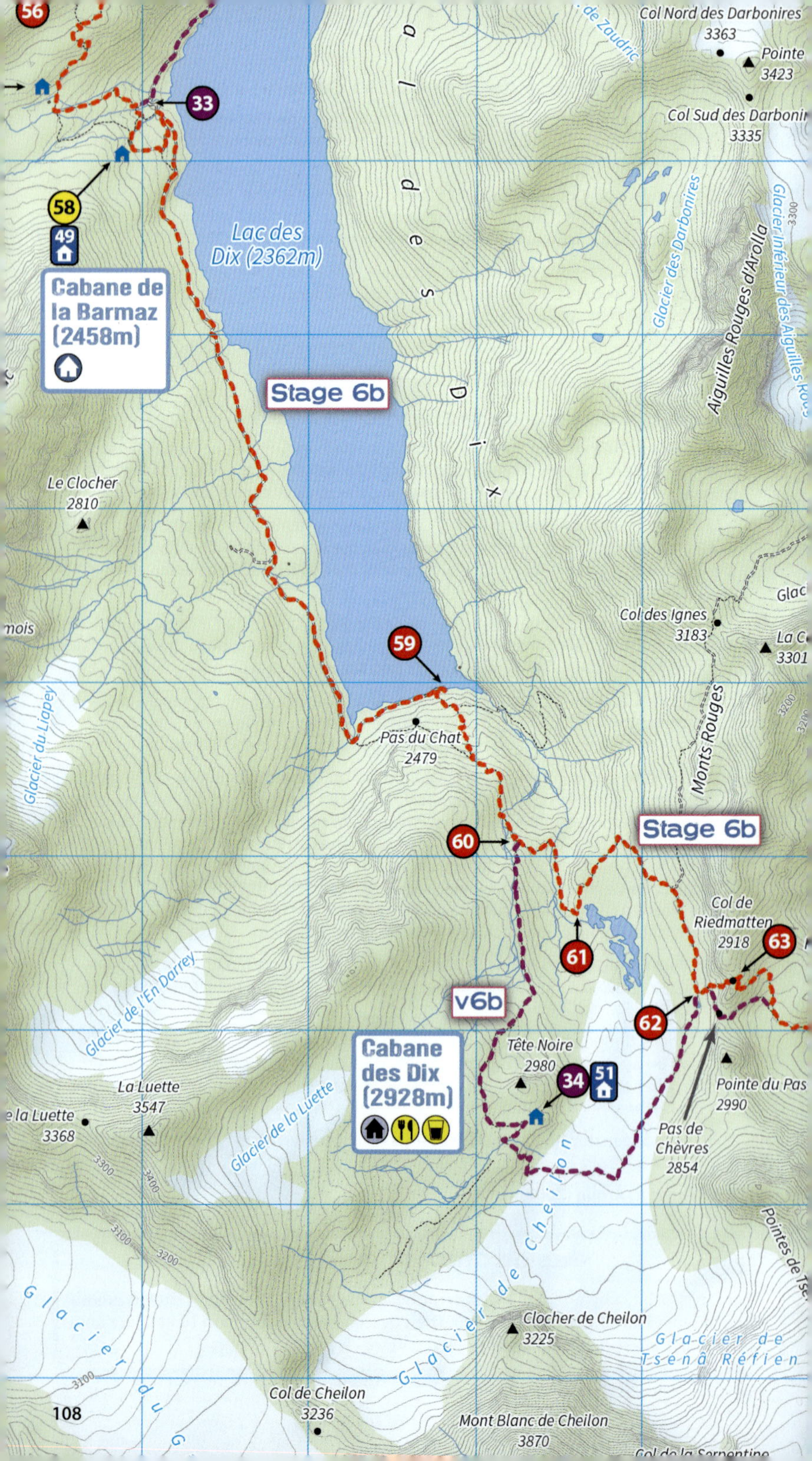
Lac des Dix (2362m)
Stage 6b
Cabane de la Barmaz (2458m)
Cabane des Dix (2928m)
v6b
Le Clocher 2810
Pas du Chat 2479
Col des Ignes 3183
Monts Rouges
Col de Riedmatten 2918
Tête Noire 2980
Pas de Chèvres 2854
Pointe du Pas 2990
La Luette 3547
Glacier de l'En Darrey
Glacier de la Luette
Glacier du Liapey
Glacier de Cheilon
Clocher de Cheilon 3225
Col de Cheilon 3236
Mont Blanc de Cheilon 3870
Glacier de Tsenâ Réfien
Col Nord des Darbonires 3363
Col Sud des Darbonires 3335
Glacier des Darbonires
Aiguilles Rouges d'Arolla
Val des Dix
33
34
56
58
59
60
61
62
63
49
51

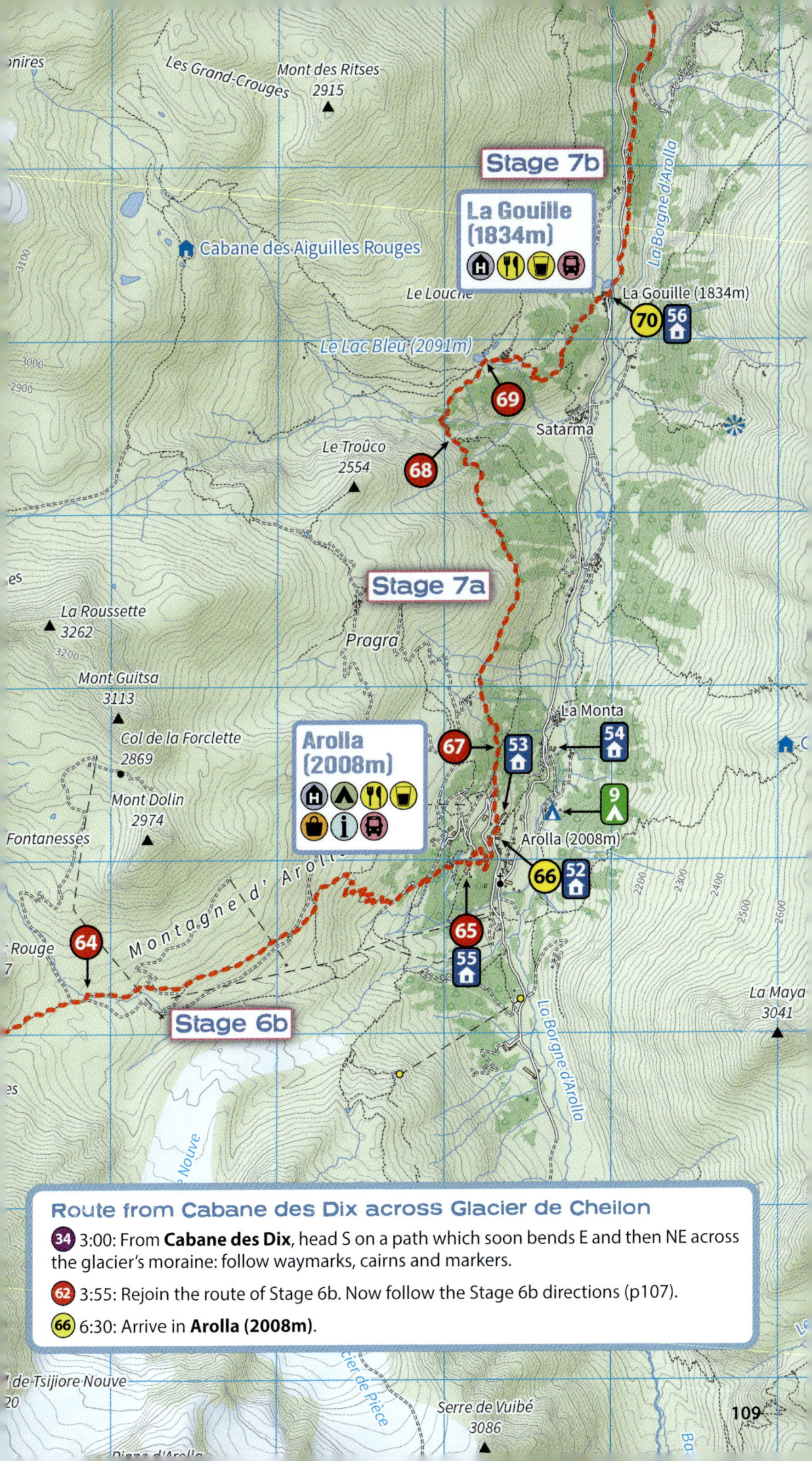

Route from Cabane des Dix across Glacier de Cheilon

(34) 3:00: From **Cabane des Dix**, head S on a path which soon bends E and then NE across the glacier's moraine: follow waymarks, cairns and markers.

(62) 3:55: Rejoin the route of Stage 6b. Now follow the Stage 6b directions (p107).

(66) 6:30: Arrive in **Arolla (2008m)**.

v6a Cabane de Prafleuri to Refuge de la Barmaz (via Barrage de la Dixence)

Although Stage v6a is less dramatic than the main Stage 6a (over Col des Roux), it is still a lovely hike with wonderful views of Lac des Dix. Furthermore, it is a safer option in bad weather/low visibility. The route used is known as 'Sentier des Bouquetins' which is a discovery path, designed to explore the flora, fauna, geology and history of the area: there is a good chance of spotting ibex. From Cabane de Prafleuri, the route descends NE to Barrage de la Grande Dixence (the dam at the N end of Lac des Dix; see p88) and then it follows the shores of the lake S to Refuge de la Barmaz.

Because the route passes close to the top of the dam, you can also use Stage v6a to access Hotel du Barrage at the base of it: the hotel is a short distance OR and is a more comfortable

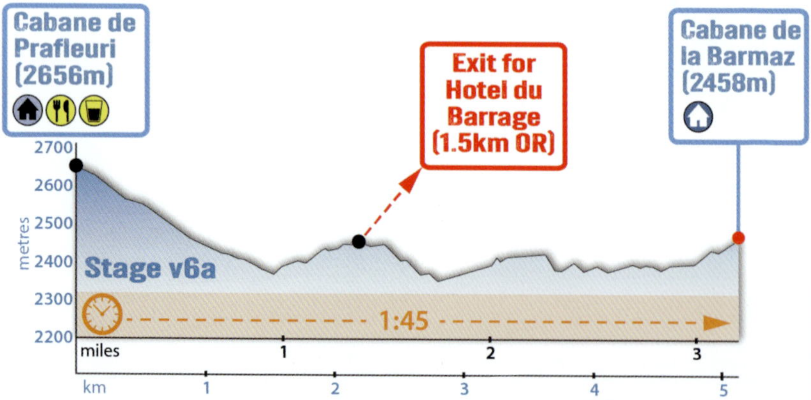

	Start	Finish	Time	Distance	Ascent	Descent	Max Alt
v6a	Cabane de Prafleuri	Cabane de la Barmaz	1:45	5.3km 3.3miles	200m 656ft	398m 1306ft	2656m 8714ft

alternative to busy Cabane de Prafleuri. Hotel du Barrage is also the starting point for the Stage v6c variant (p114) so trekkers proposing to hike that route will first need to follow Stage v6a to reach the hotel. The hotel is an austere structure which was erected in the 1950s to house construction workers building the dam. It has been transformed into a comfortable hotel with an excellent restaurant. A cable car runs between the hotel and the top of the dam wall (200m above): you can use the cable car to save your legs on the descent to the hotel; alternatively, you can walk down using the steep path. After spending a night in the hotel, if you are heading to Cabane de la Barmaz, you will need to hike back up to the top of the dam or use the cable car.

Terrain	Paths and tracks are clear, well maintained and straightforward to negotiate.
Route-finding	Straightforward.
Transport	**Hotel du Barrage:** Bus 372 to Sion; Cable car to/from the top of Barrage de la Grande Dixence (CHF7/10 single/return; 09:00 to 17:50 daily in peak season; **www.visit-grande-dixence.ch**).

(55) **See map on p89.** From **Cabane de Prafleuri**, descend briefly W. TR at a junction and follow **Sentier des Bouquetins** NE along the E bank of **Torrent de Chennaz**. Descending, the path moves away from the torrent. Soon, TL at a junction, descending directly towards the stream again: when you reach it, follow it downhill. 15-20min from the start, TR at a junction and climb to the E.

(31) 0:35: At the top of the slope, reach a junction where you have two options. The path descending steeply E is the most direct route to the dam. However, for the official route of the Sentier des Bouquetins (which is arguably more scenic), TR on a path: shortly afterwards, TR onto a track. Soon, the track zigzags E towards the lake.

(32) 0:50: Reach a junction just S of the dam; TR to continue Stage v6a; alternatively, TL to hike, or get the cable car, to **Hotel du Barrage**. Continuing Stage v6a, the path heads S along the shore of **Lac des Dix**, passing through tunnels.

(33) 1:30: Reach a junction of tracks at **la Barma**. For Refuge de la Barmaz, TR and climb; alternatively, keep SH along the lake shore for Stage 6b.

(58) 1:45: Arrive at **Refuge de la Barmaz (2458m)**.

v6b Refuge de la Barmaz to Arolla (via Cabane des Dix)

Cabane des Dix and Glacier de Cheilon

This fantastic variant enables you to spend an unforgettable night at Cabane des Dix, magnificently situated next to Mont Blanc de Cheilon and the Glacier de Cheilon. The route is the same as Stage 6b all the way to (60): but then, instead of following Stage 6b up the valley floor, head up a fabulous ridge all the way to Cabane des Dix. From there, the original route involved a tough crossing of Glacier de Cheilon to re-join the main Stage 6b route again. However, in the last few seasons, trekkers have been advised not to attempt the glacier crossing and it is now safer to re-trace your steps from Cabane des Dix back to (60) to rejoin the main Stage 6b route. Accordingly, for this edition, we principally describe the safer route (which unfortunately, adds 2.5km to the journey): if you wish to attempt the glacier crossing, then see p109. However, irrespective of whether or not you cross the glacier, you will still have to negotiate Stage 6b's steep and challenging Col de Riedmatten/ Pas de Chèvres to reach Arolla (see p105).

Terrain	Because much of the terrain is shared with Stage 6b, the information on p105 applies equally to Stage v6b. In fact, Stage v6b is a little longer and harder than Stage 6b. And if you do plan to cross Glacier de Cheilon, remember that the route is challenging and prone to change (due to shifting of rock/ice).
Route-finding	The Stage 6 information on p105 applies equally to Stage v6b. Even if the route across Glacier de Cheilon is passable, it can be difficult to navigate, especially in poor conditions.
Transport	**Arolla:** Bus 382 to la Gouille and les Haudères.

	Start	Finish	Time	Distance	Ascent	Descent	Max Alt
v6b	Cabane de la Barmaz	Arolla	7:25	20.0km 12.4miles	956m 3136ft	1405m 4610ft	2928m 9606ft

(58) **See map on p108.** From **Cabane de la Barmaz**, follow Stage 6b to (60): see p107.

(60) Head S up a ridge.

(34) 3:00: Arrive at **Cabane des Dix (2928m)**. Then retrace your steps back towards (60).

(60) 3:50: TR onto the route of Stage 6b. Follow the Stage 6b directions again (p107).

(66) 7:25: Arrive in **Arolla (2008m)**.

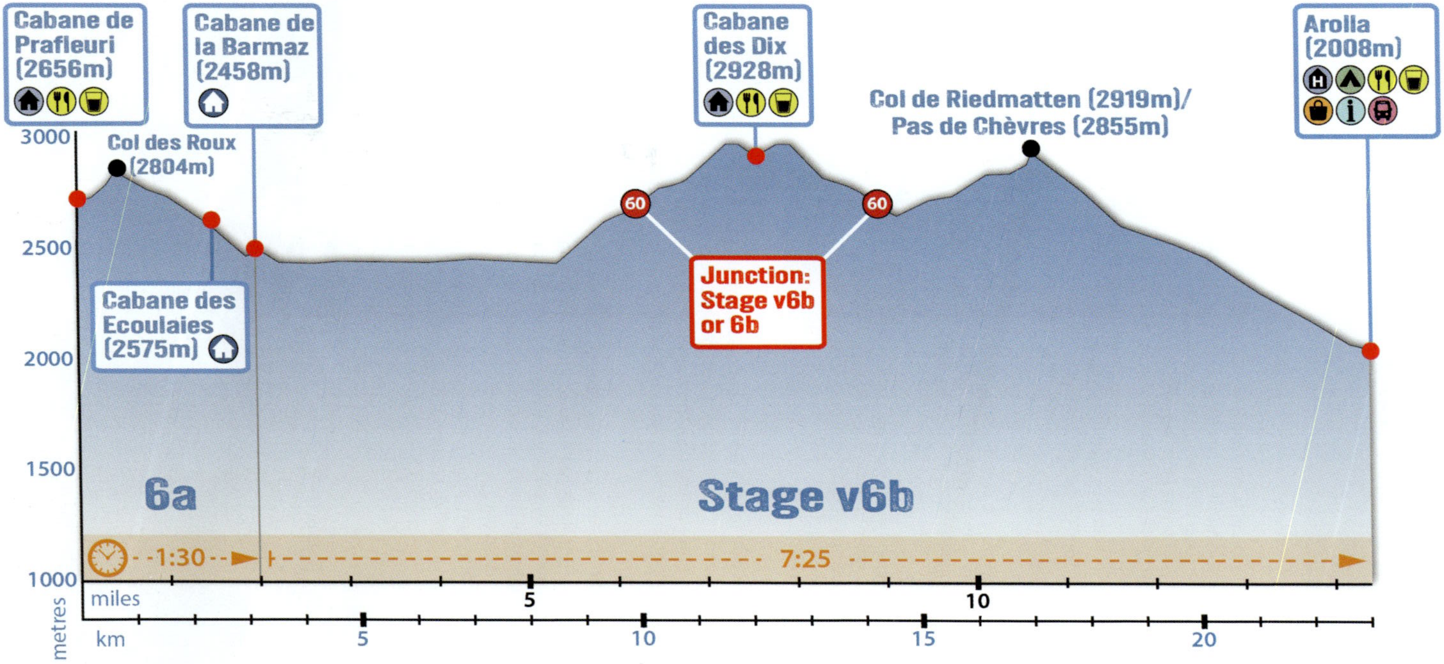
Cabane de Prafleuri (2656m)
Cabane de la Barmaz (2458m)
Cabane des Dix (2928m)
Col de Riedmatten (2919m)/ Pas de Chèvres (2855m)
Arolla (2008m)
Col des Roux (2804m)
Cabane des Ecoulaies (2575m)
60
60
Junction: Stage v6b or 6b
3000
2500
2000
1500
1000
metres
6a
Stage v6b
1:30
7:25
miles
5
10
km
5
10
15
20

v6c Hotel du Barrage to les Haudères

Descending to les Haudères

Stage 6b is a beautiful hike but the unstable terrain on the approach to Col de Riedmatten/Pas de Chèvres is hardly the safest part of the WHR, particularly in bad weather or after rain (when the loose rock is unstable and prone to landslides). Understandably therefore, some trekkers are not keen to attempt that tricky section and instead hike down from Cabane de Prafleuri to Hotel du Barrage and then use public transport to travel around to les Haudères/Arolla: see below. However, there is an alternative which few trekkers know about: Stage v6c is a completely separate route which travels more directly between Hotel du Barrage and les Haudères (using the spectacular Col de la Meina). The views are fabulous and you will see fewer trekkers.

However, although the terrain is safer than Stage 6b's sketchy crossing of Col de Riedmatten/Pas de Chèvres, this is still a high mountain route and you should exercise caution in low visibility/bad weather. It is also long and tiring: the balcony path above the valley on the approach to les Haudères is wonderful but it seems to go on forever and you will definitely be ready to stop at the end of it.

Terrain	Generally, paths/tracks are clear and straightforward to negotiate. However, the paths in the forests between Hotel du Barrage and Novèlé are narrow, steep and slippery when wet. On both sides of Col de la Meina, there are sections of rocks to cross: watch your footing and follow waymarks carefully.
Route-finding	Navigation near the col can be tricky in poor conditions and, because fewer people hike this route, it can feel quite isolated. Sometimes, snow can remain on the highest sections of the route into July, making navigation difficult.
Transport	**Hotel du Barrage:** Bus 372 to Sion; Cable car to/from the top of Barrage de la Grande Dixence (CHF7/10 single/return; 09:00 to 17:50 daily in peak season; **www.visit-grande-dixence.ch**). **Chemeuille** (2.2km OR)**:** to save your legs, you could descend using the Chemeuille-Lanna cable car. The upper station is 2.2km NE of 78 (30min). From the lower station at Lanna, it is a relatively flat walk to les Haudères along the E bank of the river (5.4km; 80-90min). **Les Haudères:** Bus 382 to La Gouille/Arolla; Bus 383 to la Sage; Bus 381 to Sion.

	Start	Finish	Time	Distance	Ascent	Descent	Max Alt
v6c	Hotel du Barrage	les Haudères	7:30	21.6km 13.4miles	959m 3146ft	1647m 5404ft	2702m 8865ft

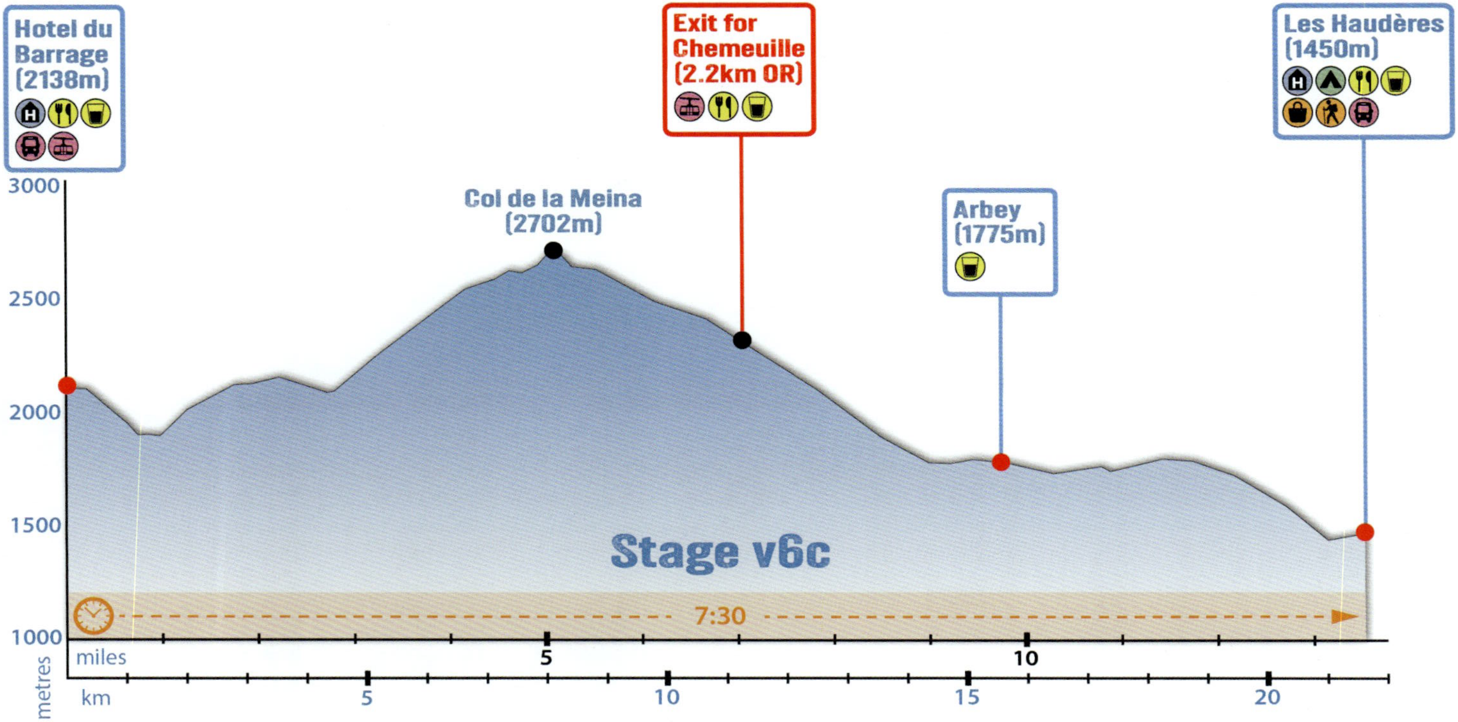
Hotel du Barrage (2138m)
Col de la Meina (2702m)
Exit for Chemeuille (2.2km OR)
Arbey (1775m)
Les Haudères (1450m)
Stage v6c
7:30
metres
3000
2500
2000
1500
1000
miles
5
10
km
5
10
15
20

Stage v6c: Hotel du Barrage to les Haudères

50 See map on p89. From **Hotel du Barrage**, head N down the valley on a steep path through forest (black/yellow waymarks). After 20min, TR and climb gently along the road. A few minutes later, TL onto a path (yellow sign). Cross two streams and then climb through trees.

74 0:50: TR at a junction, climbing on a path. 10min later, at a bend in the track, keep SH on a narrow path that contours along the slope (black/yellow waymarks).

75 1:30: See map on p116. Keep SH at a junction. Just afterwards, pass the buildings of **Novèlé**. Then zigzag steeply upwards to the E. When you emerge from the trees, the path heads SE up the slopes, becoming rockier (occasionally hard to follow). At about **2650m**, the path bends left to make the final approach to the col: climb NE.

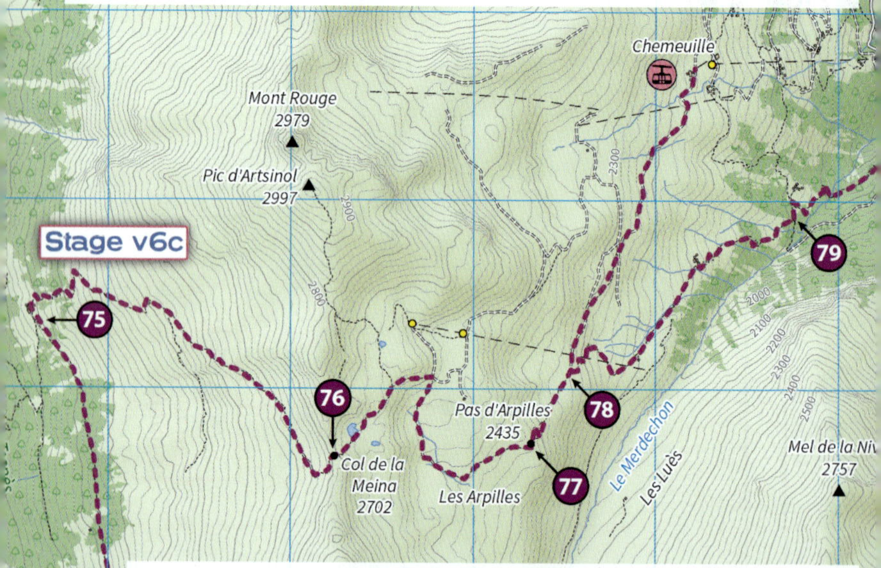

76 3:50: Cross **Col de la Meina/Col de Méribé (2702m)**. The path now zigzags steeply down to the NE, passing between two small lakes. 5min later, TR at a junction and descend towards another signpost (visible below): TR at the signpost, descending S along a valley.

77 4:30: At **Pas d'Arpilles (2435m)**, go through a gate and head downhill on a track.

78 4:50: TR at a junction; alternatively, keep SH for the chairlift at **Chemeuille** (see p114). 25-30min later, enter forest and zigzag down through the trees (red/white waymarks).

79 5:30: TL at a junction. Shortly afterwards, TR at another junction and descend steeply. 15min later, TR at a junction.

80 6:05: Just after the lake at **Arbey**, TR and climb on a track. Just afterwards, TL at a junction, heading SE on the track. 5min later, TR onto a path: head SE across the slopes with superb views of the valley.

81 7:00: Keep SH on a lane past the old chalets at **l'Ata Gieute**. 5-10min later, TL down a road. 5-10min after that, keep SH across a road and descend steeply on a path. Cross a bridge over the **Borgne river** and climb gently.

72 7:30: Arrive in the historic village of **les Haudères (1450m)**.

Sasseneire
3254
Basset
Col de
29
Le Cotter
Stage v8
Lanna
Les Flantses
Evolène
Mayens du Cotter (2058m)
Musée d'Evolène
Hérens
La Borgne
Le Pétérey
Le Pre
La Fauchère
Villa
Stage v6c
Zau Derri
Le Borza
La Sage
(1667m)
Le Tsa
(2167
La Tour VS
La Niva
L'Ata Gieute
Le Gavil
Stage 8
Molignon
7c
La Forclaz VS
Les Haudères
(1450m)
La Bornette
Les Chlistes
Pralovin
La Coutaz
Sepéc
La Vèntura
La Coûta
Stage 7b

7 Arolla to la Sage

La Sage

This underrated section of the WHR is shorter and less challenging than the longer, tougher stages of the previous days. That said, it is more tiring than it looks on paper: Stage 7a's climb, from Arolla to the stunning clear blue waters of Lac Bleu, undulates continuously; however, the paths stay high for the most part and views are consistently excellent. After the lake, pass le Louché, a lovely hamlet with a little restaurant. Then descend to the hotel at la Gouille which is located in the base of the valley next to the road.

From la Gouille, Stage 7b remains close to the valley floor all the way to les Haudères: although the scenery is less dramatic, it is still beautiful. The village of les Haudères is lovely, with many immaculately preserved Valaisian buildings: they are perched on stilts, topped with large stone slabs to prevent rodents from entering. From there, Stage 7c climbs to the hamlet of la Sage, a great place to stop for the night before the exertions of Stage 8: there is only a hotel and a gîte so it is wise to book ahead.

Itinerary options: Stages 7a, 7b and 7c together make for a relatively short day so you could instead tag Stage 7a onto Stage 6b, overnight at la Gouille and then complete Stages 7b, 7c and 8 the following day.

	Start	Finish	Time	Distance	Ascent	Descent	Max Alt
7a	Arolla	La Gouille	1:50	4.8km 3.0miles	252m 827ft	426m 1398ft	2130m 6988ft
7b	La Gouille	les Haudères	1:10	4.0km 2.5miles	20m 66ft	404m 1325ft	1834m 6017ft
7c	les Haudères	la Sage	0:50	2.9km 1.8miles	230m 755ft	13m 43ft	1667m 5469ft

Terrain	The paths are generally clear and easy to follow. However, gradients are occasionally steep and the route's undulations are quite tiring. Before Lac Bleu, take care on some exposed sections protected with cables.
Route-finding	Between Arolla and Lac Bleu, there are quite a few junctions and paths to choose from: follow the directions closely. Otherwise, route-finding is straightforward.
Transport	**Arolla/la Gouille:** Bus 382 to les Haudères. **Les Haudères:** Bus 382 to la Gouille/Arolla; Bus 383 to la Sage; Bus 381 to Sion. **La Sage:** Bus 383 to les Haudères.

Stage 7a: Arolla to la Gouille

66 **See map on p109.** From the **tourist office**, head NE down a road. Shortly afterwards, TL and climb on a path ('Lac Bleu'). Soon, pass to the right of a building. Shortly afterwards, keep SH on a path heading N: ignore offshoots.

67 0:15: TL at a junction ('Lac Bleu'). The path undulates. Take care on exposed sections protected with cables.

68 1:00: Keep SH at a junction ('Lac Bleu').

69 1:30: Cross the bridge to the right of **Lac Bleu (2091m)**. Then TR, descending on a path. Shortly afterwards, TR at the beautiful hamlet of **le Louché (2079m)**. Afterwards, continue descending, ignoring offshoots.

70 1:50: Arrive at the hotel at **la Gouille (1834m)**.

Stage 7b: la Gouille to les Haudères

70 **See map on p109.** Cross the main road and TL to walk on a path alongside it. After a few minutes, TR on a path. At any junctions, follow yellow/black waymarks.

71 1:00: **See map on p117.** Approaching the hamlet of **Pralovin**, TL on a lane. A few minutes later, TR on a road. Then, cross a bridge. Immediately afterwards, TL on a track. When you meet the road again, keep SH.

72 1:10. Cross the bridge at the entrance to **les Haudères (1450m)**. TR onto **Route de la Sage**. After a few minutes, TL on **Route du Vieux Village** and walk past the lovely old barns and houses.

Stage 7c: les Haudères to la Sage

72 **See map on p117.** Head N at a fork ('la Sage'). Keep SH, climbing on a track.

73 0:15: At a right-hand hairpin, keep SH on a path. 5min later, TR at a fork (no waymarks).

74 0:30: Keep SH up a road. Shortly afterwards, TL on another road ('la Sage').

75 0:50: Follow the road up to the village of **la Sage (1667m)**.

Les Haudères:
traditional building on stilts

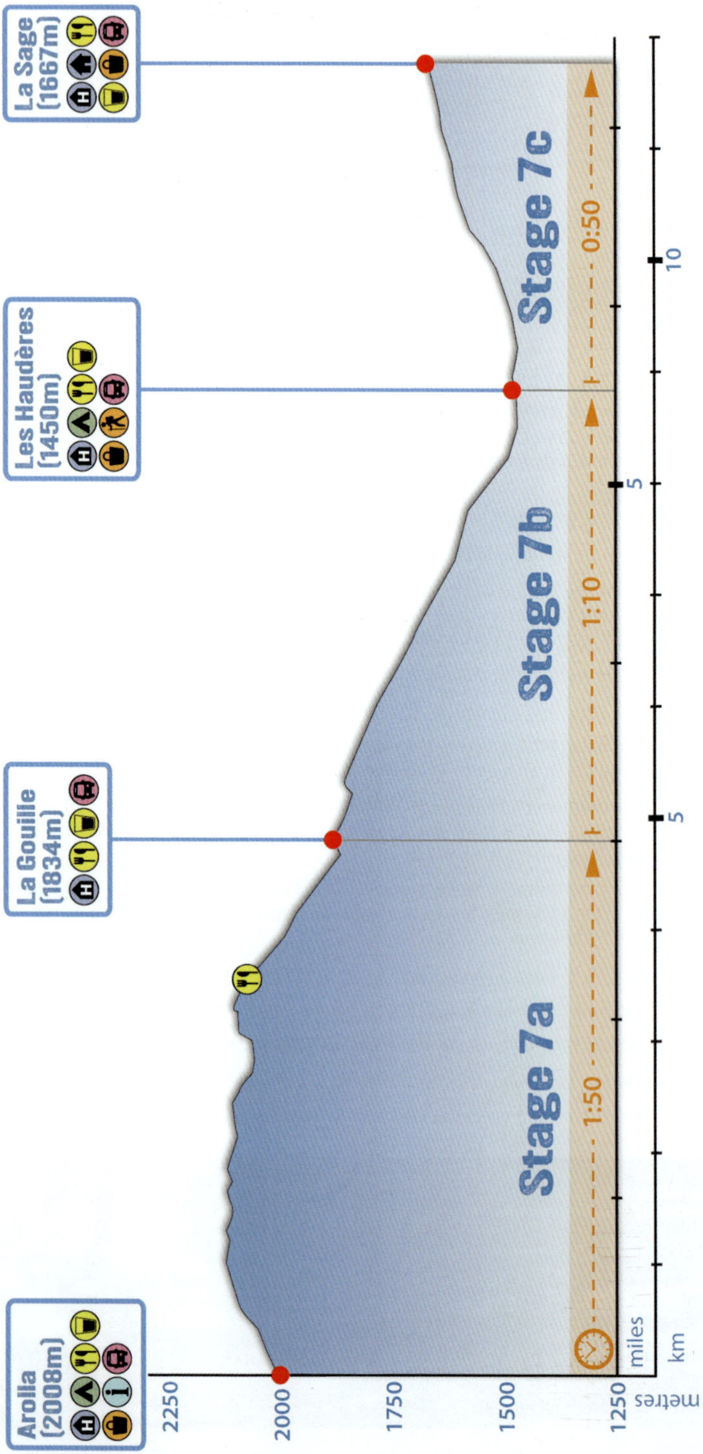
Arolla (2008m)
La Gouille (1834m)
Les Haudères (1450m)
La Sage (1667m)
Stage 7a
Stage 7b
Stage 7c
1:50
1:10
0:50
2250
2000
1750
1500
1250
metres
miles
km
5
5
10

One of the magnificent chalets in the hamlet of la Sage

8 La Sage to Cabane de Moiry

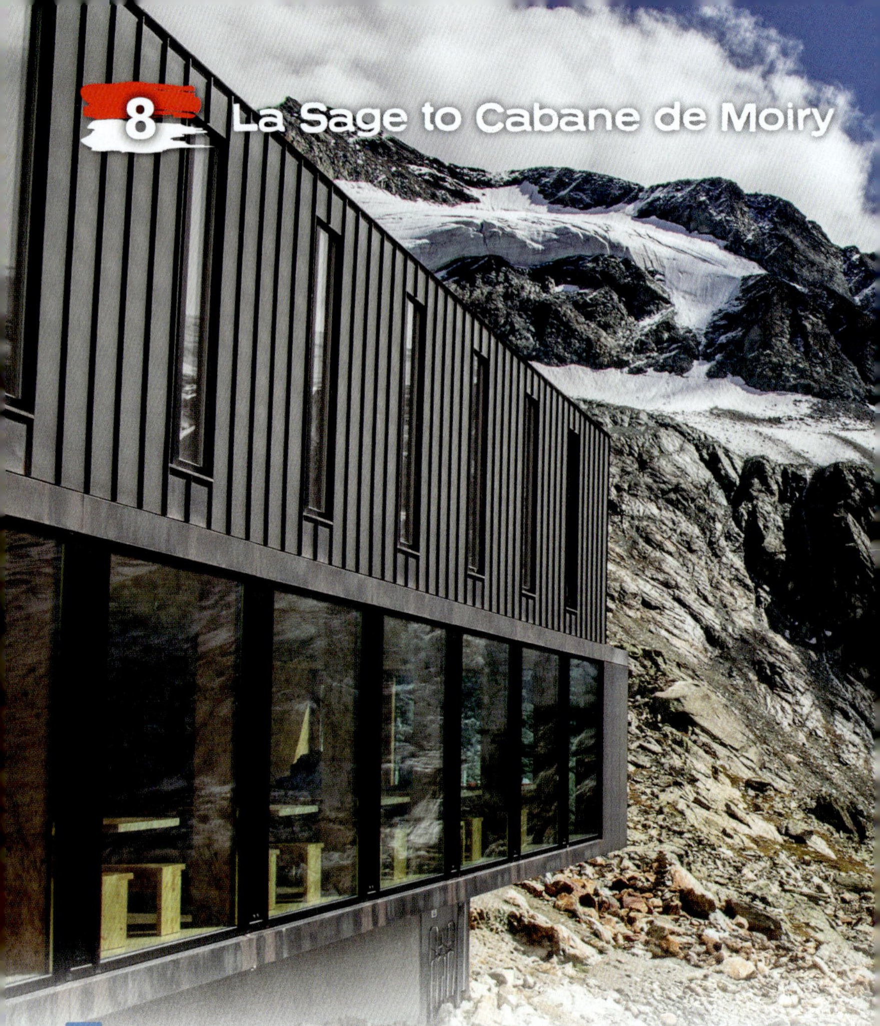

The day begins with one of the WHR's longest climbs: a hefty 1200m of ascent to Col du Tsaté. Fortunately, there are more of the spectacular views to which you will by now be accustomed and Col du Tsaté is a stunning place: to the W, look back over the route of previous days and to the E, Val de Moiry shows itself; Glacier de Moiry also appears in all its glory and, later in the day, you will find yourself very close to it indeed.

The second climb of the day leads to the fabulous Cabane de Moiry, set right beside the glacier: we can think of no better place for a beer! The cabane itself is an old refuge which was extended more recently. The architecture is superb, perfectly marrying the old stone building with a modern structure which blends into the hillside. The wall-to-wall windows in the dining area ensure that you never lose sight of the glacier: book this hut well in advance. Look out for ibex and chamois on the final climb.

	Start	Finish	Time	Distance	Ascent	Descent	Max Alt
8	La Sage	Cabane de Moiry	5:55	11.8km 7.3miles	1676m 5499ft	518m 1699ft	2868m 9409ft

Terrain	The climb to Col du Tsaté is long and tiring and the descent from it is steep and unstable. The final climb to Cabane de Moiry is steep, rocky and exposed: in places, you will need to use your hands and there are some fixed cables. Otherwise, paths are generally clear and easy to follow but gradients can be steep.
Route-finding	Generally straightforward. The route is quite well covered with signs/ waymarks (yellow or red/white). Sometimes, snow can remain on the highest sections of the route into July, making navigation difficult.
Transport	If you stay overnight at Cabane de Moiry, you are entitled to a free Val d'Anniviers pass. This entitles you to free buses and a discount on the price of the cable car from Sorebois to Zinal for the following day (see p135). Request the pass when you check-in. **La Sage:** Bus 383 to les Haudères. **Moiry Glacier (Lac de Châteaupré; 82):** Bus 452 to Barrage de Moiry, Grimentz and Vissoie; Bus 455 to Barrage de Moiry, Grimentz and Zinal.

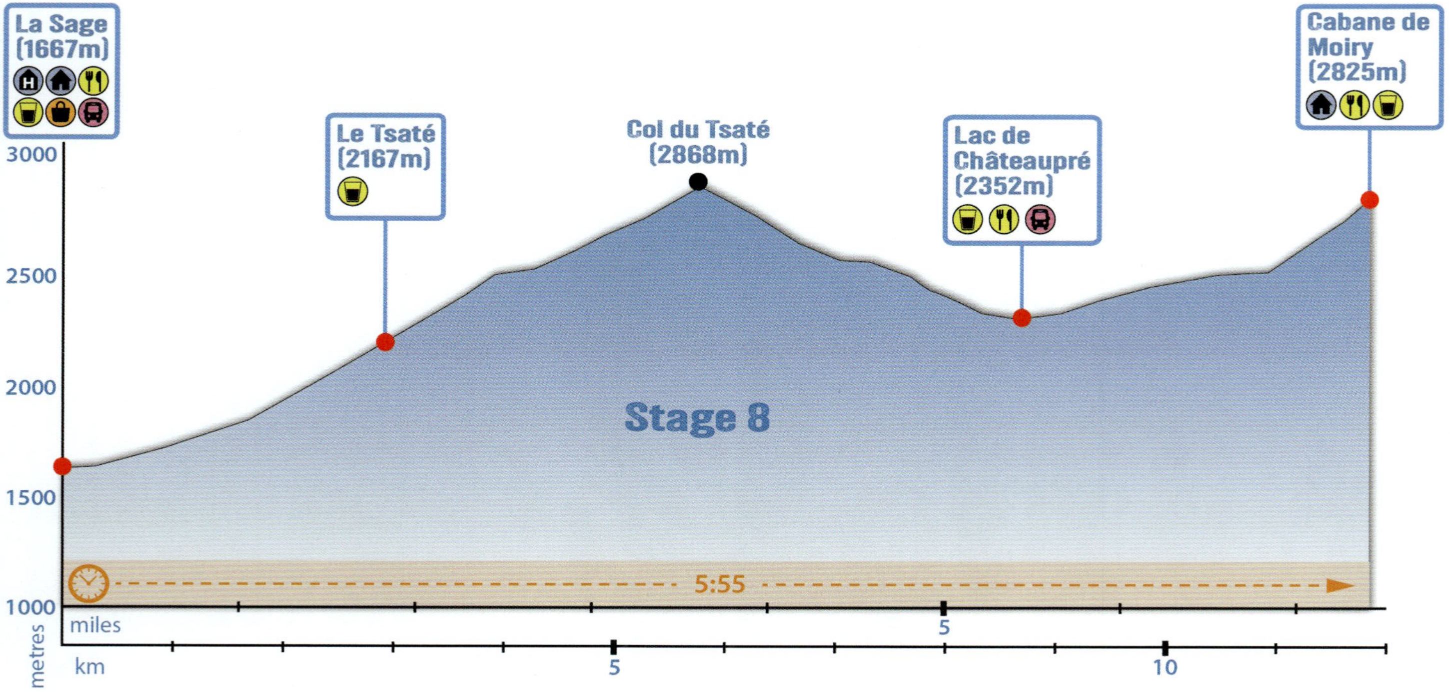
La Sage
(1667m)
Le Tsaté
(2167m)
Col du Tsaté
(2868m)
Lac de
Châteaupré
(2352m)
Cabane de
Moiry
(2825m)
Stage 8
5:55
3000
2500
2000
1500
1000
metres
miles
5
km
5
10

Stage 8: la Sage to Cabane de Moiry

75 **See map on p117.** From **la Sage**, descend S on a road ('Col du Tsaté'). Shortly afterwards, TL on a lane and climb. Soon, keep SH on a track through forest.

76 0:20: TL at a junction ('Col du Tsaté'). A few minutes later, TR (yellow sign). After 10min, at another junction, take the left-hand path (yellow signs). Shortly afterwards, TR on another path (yellow waymarks).

77 0:45: The path passes to the left of the buildings of the spectacular hamlet of **Motô (1925m)**. Keep SH at a junction.

78 1:15: **See map on p130.** Pass the hamlet of **le Tsaté (2167m)**. Afterwards, cross a track and climb steeply NE on a path which heads through beautiful pastures filled with wild-flowers. After 25min, keep SH across a track and continue on a path.

79 2:00: After the farm buildings at **Remointse du Tsaté (2480m)**, TR on a track. Shortly afterwards, TL on a path ('Col du Tsaté'): the path splinters and is tricky to follow. Soon, cross a grassy bowl with a lake beside it. Afterwards, climb NE.

80 3:15: Cross **Col du Tsaté (2868m)** and descend on a path ('Lac Bayenna') which is steep and unstable.

81 3:40: Pass to the left of **Lac de la Bayenna (2548m)**. Then, bear right briefly along the E side of it. Just afterwards, TL on a faint path heading N: this junction is not waymarked. After 20min, keep SH at a junction. Soon the path becomes rough and faint. After 5min, TL at a junction and follow a rough path.

82 4:10: TR at a car park near **Lac de Châteaupré (2352m)** and climb E on a path ('Cabane de Moiry'). After a while, the path heads along the top of a little ridge: the views are incredible. Then, the path bears left, dropping off the ridge. Afterwards, climb on a path, contouring upwards across the hillside. Soon, the gradient increases as the path climbs amongst rocks.

83 5:55: Finally, cross some boulders to arrive at **Cabane de Moiry (2825m)**.

Climbing to Cabane de Moiry

v8 La Sage to Barrage de Moiry

August snow near Col de Torrent

This is a spectacular alternative to Stage 8/9a: the vista from Col de Torrent is arguably superior to that at Col du Tsaté with the startlingly turquoise Lac de Moiry just below to the E. It is also shorter than the main route, heading more directly to Barrage de Moiry and saving you about half a day's walking. However, you will miss out on a night at Cabane de Moiry and Stage 9a's wonderful traverse along the E side of Lac de Moiry.

The climb, through beautiful pastures, is another big one with slightly more altitude gain than Stage 8's climb to Col du Tsaté. The views are fabulous all the way up, however, the highlight is the sublime descent to Barrage de Moiry: this is one of our favourite parts of the entire trek. The only accommodation is the peaceful Gîte de Moiry which is a short climb above the dam: you will have to descend back to the restaurant at the dam for your evening meal.

Itinerary options: because Gîte de Moiry is the only place to stay, it books up quickly. If you are strong, you could push on to Zinal along Stage 9b: this makes for a long day but you could use the cable car from Sorebois to Zinal to avoid much of the steep descent into Zinal (see p135). However, after crossing Col de Torrent, most trekkers will not have the surplus energy even to contemplate another climb: for this reason, many trekkers use Stage v9a to hike down to Grimentz where there are hotels and restaurants (see p129). Alternatively, buses run from Barrage de Moiry to Grimentz (see below).

Terrain	Paths/tracks are generally clear and easy to follow. However, gradients are occasionally steep. Both the climb and descent are long and tiring.
Route-finding	Generally straightforward. The route is generally well covered with signs and waymarks. Sometimes, snow remains on the highest sections into July, making navigation difficult.
Transport	**La Sage:** Bus 383 to les Haudères. **Barrage de Moiry:** Bus 452 to Moiry Glacier, Grimentz and Vissoie; Bus 455 to Moiry Glacier, Grimentz and Zinal.

	Start	Finish	Time	Distance	Ascent	Descent	Max Alt
v8a	La Sage	Barrage de Moiry	5:40	13.0km 8.1miles	1251m 4104ft	688m 2257ft	2916m 9567ft
v8b	Barrage de Moiry	Barrage de Moiry Junction	0:30	1.5km 0.9miles	124m 407ft	0m 0ft	2374m 7789ft

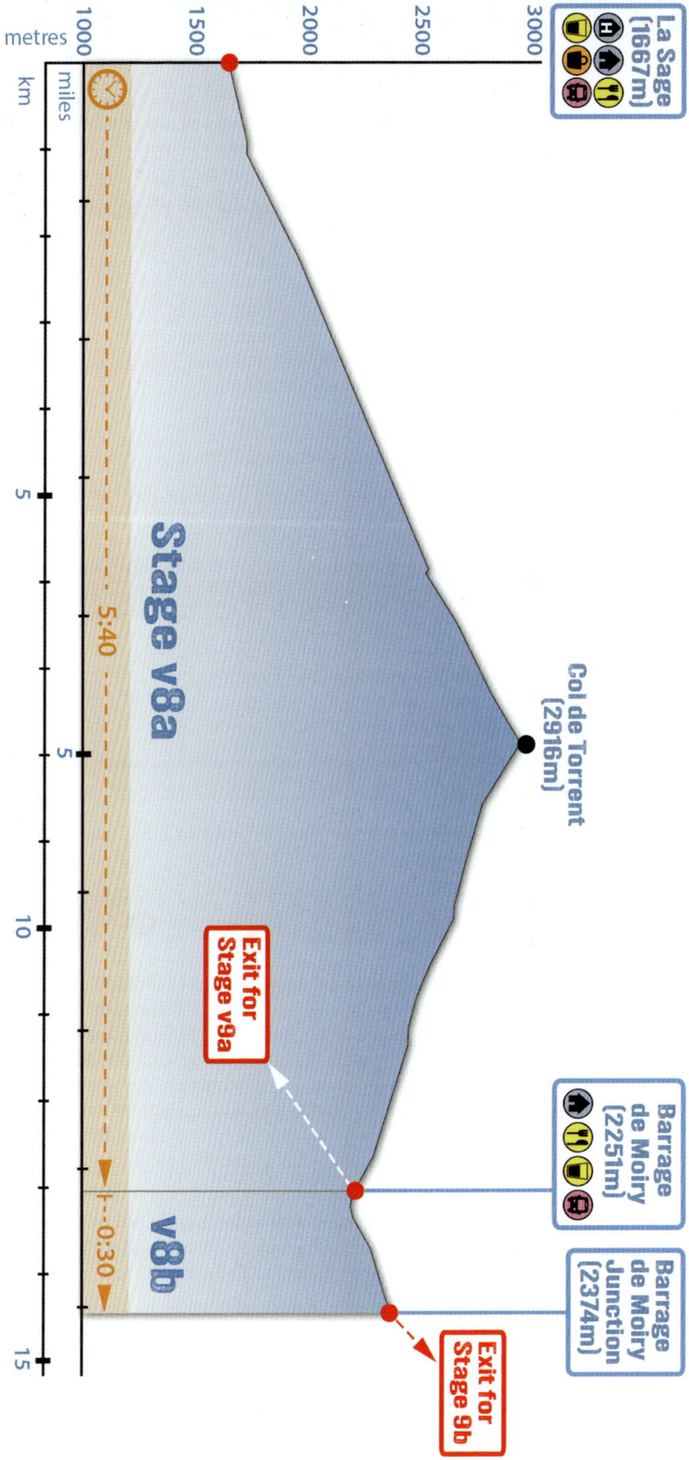
La Sage
(1667m)
Col de Torrent
(2916m)
Barrage
de Moiry
(2251m)
Barrage
de Moiry
Junction
(2374m)
Exit for
Stage v9a
Exit for
Stage 9b
Stage v8a
v8b
5:40
0:30
metres
1000
1500
2000
2500
3000
miles
km
5
5
10
15

Stage v8a: la Sage to Barrage de Moiry (via Col de Torrent)

75 See map on p117. From the road junction near **Gîte l'Ecureuil**, climb N on the road. At the chapel in **Villa (Evolène)**, TR ('Col de Torrent'). Shortly afterwards, TR at a junction: follow waymarks up through houses. Keep SH on a track: ignore offshoots.

35 0:45: Keep SH at a fork. Shortly, keep SH onto a path which soon crosses a stream. Climb generally N.

36 1:20: At **Mayens du Cotter (2058m)**, TL onto a track. Shortly afterwards, TR at a junction and climb on a path.

37 2:40: Pass a little **tarn (2535m)** and keep climbing.

38 4:10: See map on p130. Cross **Col de Torrent (2916m)** and descend NE. After 20min, pass the magnificent **Lac des Autannes (2685m)**.

39 5:10: From **Alpage de Torrent (2479m)**, head SE on a track.

40 5:40: Reach the dam at the N side of **Lac de Moiry (2250m)**.

Stage v8b: Barrage de Moiry to Moiry Junction (2373m)

40 See map on p130. Head E across the top of the dam.

41 0:10: Reach the restaurant at the E side of the dam. Head initially E on a path and climb. After a few minutes, TL on a track. Shortly afterwards, TL on a path if you wish to stay at **Gîte de Moiry**: it is 5min away, just N of the dam. Otherwise, keep climbing on the track: you can cut across some of the hairpins.

85 0:30: Arrive at **junction (2373m)** where Stage 9b begins.

Moving on from Grimentz: possible options

- **Head back up to Barrage de Moiry and hike Stage 9b to Zinal:** hike Stage v9a in reverse to reach Barrage de Moiry or catch bus 452/455.
- **Hike to Cabane de Moiry:** buses 452/455 run from Grimentz to Moiry Glacier (via Barrage de Moiry). From Moiry Glacier (Lac de Châteaupré; 82), Stage 8 leads to Cabane de Moiry.
- **Head to Zinal to hike Stage 10/v10 to Gruben:** in high season, bus 455 runs from Grimentz to Zinal. Out of high season, take bus 452 to Vissoie: then change onto bus 453 to Zinal (the buses are timed to connect). You can also travel by cable car between Grimentz and Zinal (changing at Espace Weisshorn and Sorebois): see **www.valdanniviers.ch**. If you stay overnight in Grimentz, you are entitled to a free Val d'Anniviers pass, giving you free buses and a discount on the price of the cable car to Zinal for the following day. Alternatively, a clear path runs SE from Grimentz to Zinal (through the forest on the W side of the valley): follow signposts from Grimentz; 8.1km; 2.5hr.
- **Head to Cabane Bella Tola to hike Stage v10b to Gruben:** take bus 452 to Vissoie and then change onto bus 454 to St-Luc. A funicular railway runs daily from St-Luc to Tignousa: from there, it is 20min on foot (uphill) to Cabane Bella Tola.
- **Hike to Hotel Weisshorn** (4.25hr; 9.2km; ⬆1066; ⬇312): from Grimentz, a signed path descends NE into the valley and then up to Mission (Mèssion). From there, it is a long steep climb to the hotel. You could also walk from Tignousa to Hotel Weisshorn (1hr): see above.

v9a Barrage de Moiry to Grimentz

Lac de Moiry

Most trekkers who reach Barrage de Moiry using the challenging Stage v8 over Col de Torrent, will not have the energy to hike to Zinal that same day (over Col de Sorebois). However, the only accommodation at Barrage de Moiry is Gîte de Moiry which books up very quickly. For this reason, many trekkers descend to Grimentz where there are comfortable hotels and good restaurants. **For itinerary options from Grimentz, see p128.**

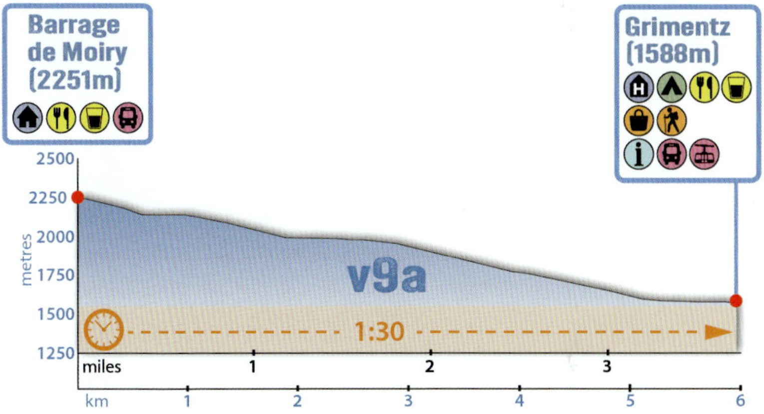

Terrain	Good paths and tracks which are simple to follow.
Route-finding	Straightforward.
Transport	**Barrage de Moiry:** Bus 452 to Moiry Glacier, Grimentz and Vissoie; Bus 455 to Moiry Glacier, Grimentz and Zinal. **Grimentz:** Bus 452 to Barrage de Moiry, Moiry Glacier and Vissoie; Bus 455 to Barrage de Moiry, Moiry Glacier and Zinal; Cable car between Grimentz and Zinal (see p128).

	Start	Finish	Time	Distance	Ascent	Descent	Max Alt
v9a	Barrage de Moiry	Grimentz	1:30	5.9km 3.7miles	14m 46ft	676m 2218ft	2250m 7382ft

Stage v9a
Stage v8a
Stage v8b
Stage 8
Barrage de Moiry (2251m)
Le Tsaté (2167m)
Sotier
Torrent de Lona
Lac de Lona
Ché de Mareinda 2903
Basset de Lona 2791
Diablon 3053
Sasseneire 3254
Basset de Levron 2898
La Madeleine 2776
Lac des Autannes
Col de Torrent 2916
Moiry
Le Cotter
Combe Duran
Pointe du Prélèt 2999
Pointe du Tsaté 3078
Le Prélèt
Pointe du Bandon 3073
La Bayenna
Lac du Tsaté
Col du Tsaté 2868
Lac de la Bayenna
Le Tsaté
Col de Bréonna 2916
Cherra Neire
La Gougra
Corne de
Pointe d
Fache
Les
Col de la Cou

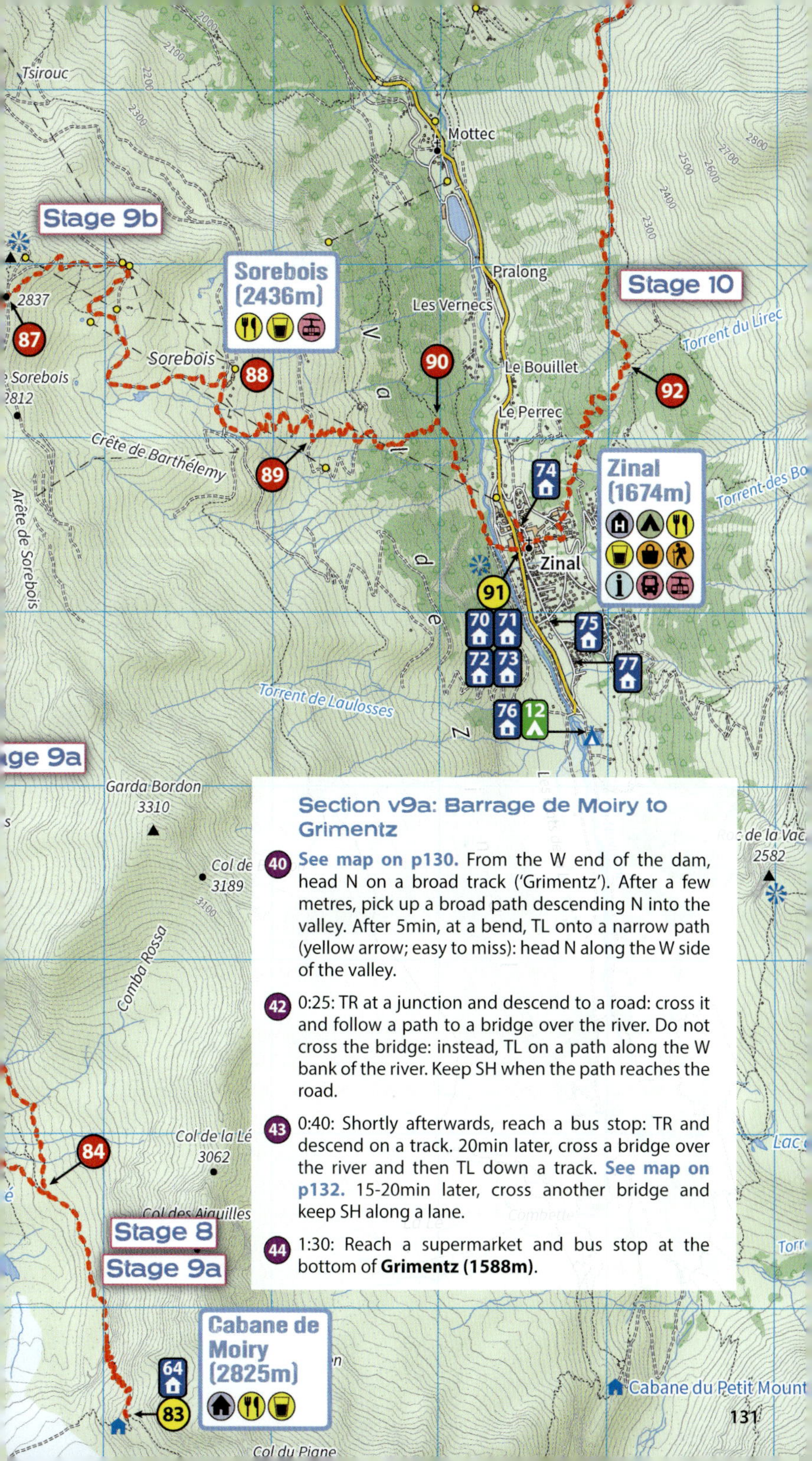

Section v9a: Barrage de Moiry to Grimentz

40 See map on p130. From the W end of the dam, head N on a broad track ('Grimentz'). After a few metres, pick up a broad path descending N into the valley. After 5min, at a bend, TL onto a narrow path (yellow arrow; easy to miss): head N along the W side of the valley.

42 0:25: TR at a junction and descend to a road: cross it and follow a path to a bridge over the river. Do not cross the bridge: instead, TL on a path along the W bank of the river. Keep SH when the path reaches the road.

43 0:40: Shortly afterwards, reach a bus stop: TR and descend on a track. 20min later, cross a bridge over the river and then TL down a track. See map on p132. 15-20min later, cross another bridge and keep SH along a lane.

44 1:30: Reach a supermarket and bus stop at the bottom of **Grimentz (1588m)**.

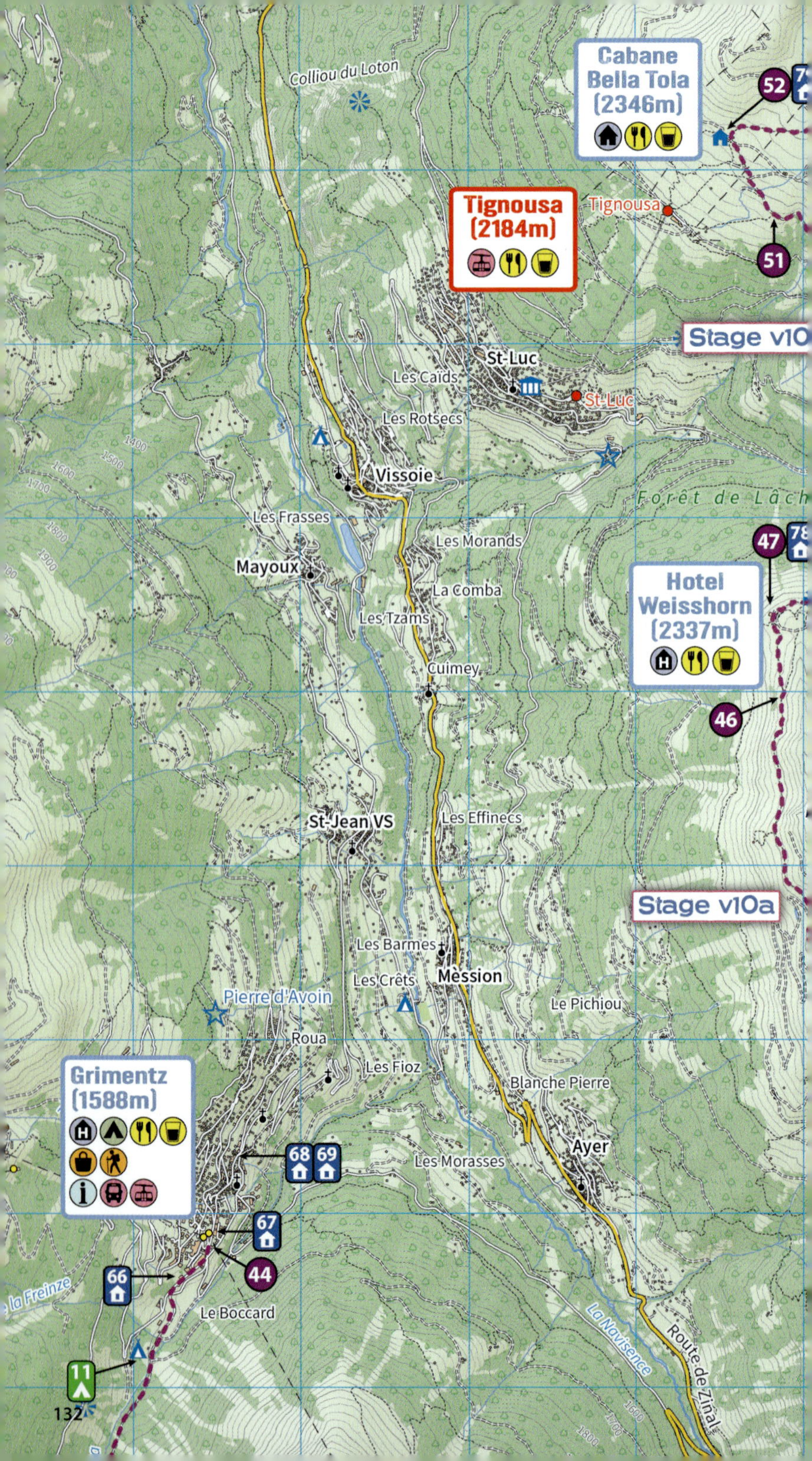

Cabane Bella Tola (2346m)
Colliou du Loton
52
Tignousa (2184m)
Tignousa
51
Stage v10
St-Luc
Les Caïds
St-Luc
Les Rotsecs
Vissoie
Forêt de Lâch
Les Frasses
Mayoux
Les Morands
47
78
La Comba
Hotel Weisshorn (2337m)
Les Tzams
Cuimey
46
St-Jean VS
Les Effinecs
Stage v10a
Les Barmes
Mèssion
Les Crêts
Le Pichiou
Pierre d'Avoin
Roua
Les Fioz
Grimentz (1588m)
Blanche Pierre
68
69
Ayer
Les Morasses
67
44
66
la Freinze
Le Boccard
La Navisence
Route de Zinal
11

Combe du Guerni
53
54
Runds Horli
2959
Pas de Boeuf
2816
Bortertälli
Tällispitze
2862
Simmig
Lac de la
Bella Tola
Stage v10b
Borterpass
2840
Rotighorn
2959
2800
2500
Aiguilles du Meiden | Meidspitz
2934
Rotigtälli
Piolousa
Lac de
l'Armina
55
56
Meidsee
Rotiggrat
alet Blanc
50
Meidpass
2789
Meidu
Chlei
Seewji
49
Meidtälli
Meidpass
Short-cut
Meidzänd
Läng
Seewji
Lac de
Combavert
Gämschwart
2790
Äugsttolu
Meidbach
48
Le Toûno
3018
Gälus Häupt
2917
Meidhoru
2876
2900
Pointe de Tourtemagne | Turtmannspitze
3082
3000
Lac du Toûno
Äugsttälli
Tsa du Toûno
Col de Vijivi
2916
Wyssgrat
Burgihorn | Le Boudri
3071
96
Blüomatt
Pointes de Nava
Bella Vouarda
2621
Chalte Berg
45
2700
Hirsihorn | Pointe de la Forcletta
3077
Stage 10
Sänntumbach
95
Blüomatttälli
Tsahèlett
Col de la Forcletta | Furggilti
2875
Nava
94
2600
Minugrat
Col de l'Omen Roso
3000
Turtmaschafalpu
Crête de Barneuza
Col de Barneuza | Frilijoch
3010
Frilitälli
Frilihorn
3145
3100
Turtmann
93
Barneuza
Wängerjoch

9 Cabane de Moiry to Zinal

Although you descend from Cabane de Moiry initially using the same path travelled on the previous stage, this is no imposition: you can enjoy a different perspective of Glacier de Moiry as it basks in the low light of sunrise; and if you are lucky, you may see some ibex or chamois (which are easier to spot at first light). Anyway, you will soon leave this path, heading N on a superb balcony, high above the unforgettable, turquoise coloured, Lac de Moiry: it leads you all the way to a junction above Barrage de Moiry (at the N end of the lake) and, on a fine day, this is a highlight of the WHR. Keep your eyes peeled for Edelweiss.

From the Barrage de Moiry junction, a steep climb leads to a saddle near Col de Sorebois: there are fantastic views of Lac de Moiry all the way up. At the saddle, you are greeted by the incredible vista to the E which is dominated by the Weisshorn (4506m). Descend steeply through ski infrastructure to the small ski station of Sorebois with its lovely restaurant. Afterwards, leave the ski-fields behind as you descend steeply through beautiful pastures and forest to Zinal (on the valley floor).

	Start	Finish	Time	Distance	Ascent	Descent	Max Alt
9a	Cabane de Moiry	Barrage de Moiry Junction	2:15	7.2km 4.5miles	96m 315ft	548m 1798ft	2825m 9268ft
9b	Barrage de Moiry Junction	Zinal	3:30	9.4km 5.8miles	478m 1568ft	1177m 3862ft	2837m 9308ft

Lac de Moiry

Itinerary options: you could avoid much of the long, steep descent by taking the cable car from Sorebois to Zinal. Alternatively, if you wish to leave the WHR after your stay at Cabane de Moiry, you can descend to the bus stops at Moiry Glacier (Lac de Châteaupré) or Barrage de Moiry (see below).

Terrain	Take care on the descent from Cabane de Moiry as the path is steep, rocky and unstable. Stage 9a's balcony path undulates continuously and is tiring. The descent from Col de Sorebois to Zinal is a 'knee-jerker'.
Route-finding	Generally straightforward: signs and waymarks.
Transport	If you stay overnight at Cabane de Moiry, you are entitled to a free Val d'Anniviers pass. This entitles you to free buses and a discount on the price of the cable car from Sorebois to Zinal for the following day. Request the pass when you check-in. See p128. **Moiry Glacier** (Lac de Châteaupré 82; 1km OR from 84)**:** Bus 452 to Barrage de Moiry, Grimentz and Vissoie; Bus 455 to Barrage de Moiry, Grimentz and Zinal. **Barrage de Moiry** (41; 0.9km from 85)**:** Bus 452 to Moiry Glacier, Grimentz and Vissoie; Bus 455 to Moiry Glacier, Grimentz and Zinal. **Sorebois 88:** cable car to Zinal/Grimentz (see p128). **Zinal:** Bus 453 to Vissoie (for onward transport from Vissoie, see p33); Bus 455 to Grimentz, Barrage de Moiry and Moiry Glacier; Cable car to Sorebois/Grimentz (see p128).

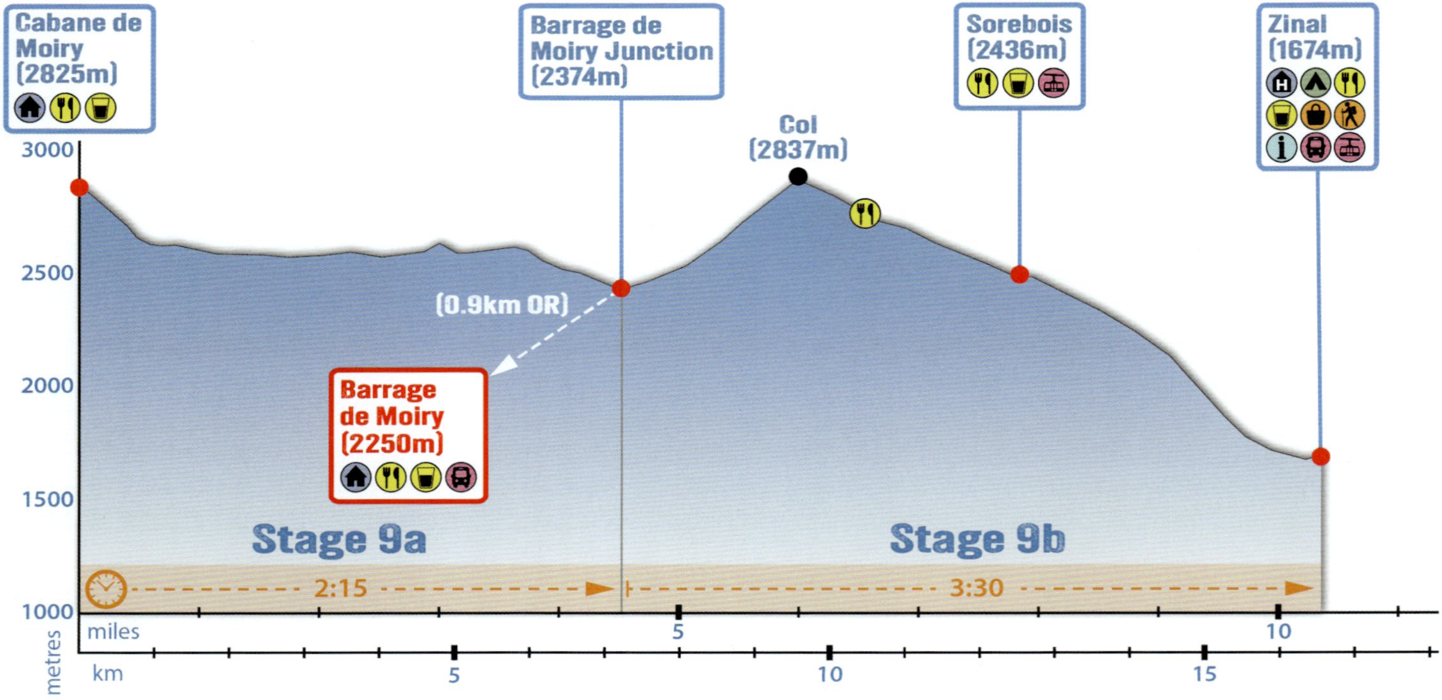
Cabane de Moiry (2825m)
Barrage de Moiry Junction (2374m)
Col (2837m)
Sorebois (2436m)
Zinal (1674m)
(0.9km OR)
Barrage de Moiry (2250m)
Stage 9a
Stage 9b
2:15
3:30
3000
2500
2000
1500
1000
metres
miles
km
5
10
15

Stage 9a: Cabane de Moiry to Barrage de Moiry Junction

83 **See map on p131.** Retrace your steps from the cabane and descend steeply.

84 0:50: TR at a junction ('Moiry Barrage') onto a lovely path traversing the hillside. After 20min, keep SH at a junction ('Moiry Barrage'). Soon, get your first glimpse of **Lac de Moiry**. The path undulates with some quite big height gains/losses. Take care crossing rocky stream beds and gullies, which can be quite slippery.

85 2:15: Arrive at **junction (2373m)**, above **Barrage de Moiry**. This is where Section v8 rejoins the main WHR. Descend on the track if you wish to stay at **Gîte de Moiry** (which is just below, about 50m above the dam).

Stage 9b: Barrage de Moiry Junction to Zinal

85 **See map on p130.** From the junction, climb on the grassy track ('Zinal').

86 0:20: TL on a path heading up to the NE: this junction is easy to miss (rock with a faint waymark).

87 1:30: Arrive at a **saddle (2837m)**, just below **Corne de Sorebois**: this saddle is slightly N of **Col de Sorebois** (as indicated on the map). TL if you wish to climb a few more metres to the summit of Corne de Sorebois. Otherwise, head NE across the saddle and pick up a path. Soon, TR onto a track and follow it downhill, ignoring offshoots. Eventually, the track bears right into a hanging valley, amongst ski infrastructure: keep on the track down through the valley.

88 2:00: TR at the ski station of **Sorebois (2436m)** ('Zinal'). There is a restaurant with a terrace overlooking the Weisshorn: a good place for a break. 5min later, TL on a path: just afterwards, there is an alternative track on the left which also goes to Zinal: it is less steep but longer.

89 2:35: TL onto a path (yellow sign). 10min later, TR at a junction ('Zinal'). Eventually, the path heads into trees and becomes very steep: take care.

90 3:10: TR at a junction ('Zinal'). After 5-10min, keep SH at a junction. TL and cross a bridge. Shortly afterwards, keep SH up a small road.

91 3:30: Shortly afterwards, enter **Zinal (1674m)**.

Cattle on the descent to Zinal

10 Zinal to Gruben

Val d'Anniviers: the chisel-shaped peak is the Matterhorn

Another incredible day out. A long ascent out of Val d'Anniviers to Col de la Forcletta is followed by a long descent into the Turtmanntal Valley. On the climb, the Matterhorn appears: it is wedge-shaped from this angle and looks very different to the familiar crooked form that it takes when viewed from Zermatt. The views from the col are fantastic: the ridge on which the col is situated is the dividing line between the French and German speaking parts of the Valais ('Wallis' in German). The Turtmanntal is one of the most remote valleys in Switzerland and is completely cut off by winter snow.

Hotel Schwarzhorn (which has dormitories and private rooms) is the only place to stay in Gruben itself: book in advance, especially at weekends. Alternatively, Grindjisand Mountain Inn is 2.3km OR (down the valley from Gruben).

Terrain	Paths/tracks are generally clear and easy to follow. However, gradients are occasionally steep. Both the climb and descent are long and tiring.
Route-finding	Generally straightforward. The route is generally well covered with signs and waymarks. Sometimes, snow can remain on the highest sections of the route into July, making navigation difficult.
Transport	**Zinal:** Bus 453 to Vissoie (for onward transport from Vissoie, see p33); Bus 455 to Grimentz, Barrage de Moiry and Moiry Glacier; Cable car to Sorebois/Grimentz (see p128). **Gruben:** in summer, a tourist bus runs between Gruben and Oberems. A cable car operates between Oberems and Turtmann (where there is a train station). See **www.turtmanntal.ch**.

	Start	Finish	Time	Distance	Ascent	Descent	Max Alt
10	Zinal	Gruben	6:40	17.7km 11.0miles	1270m 4167ft	1126m 3694ft	2875m 9432ft

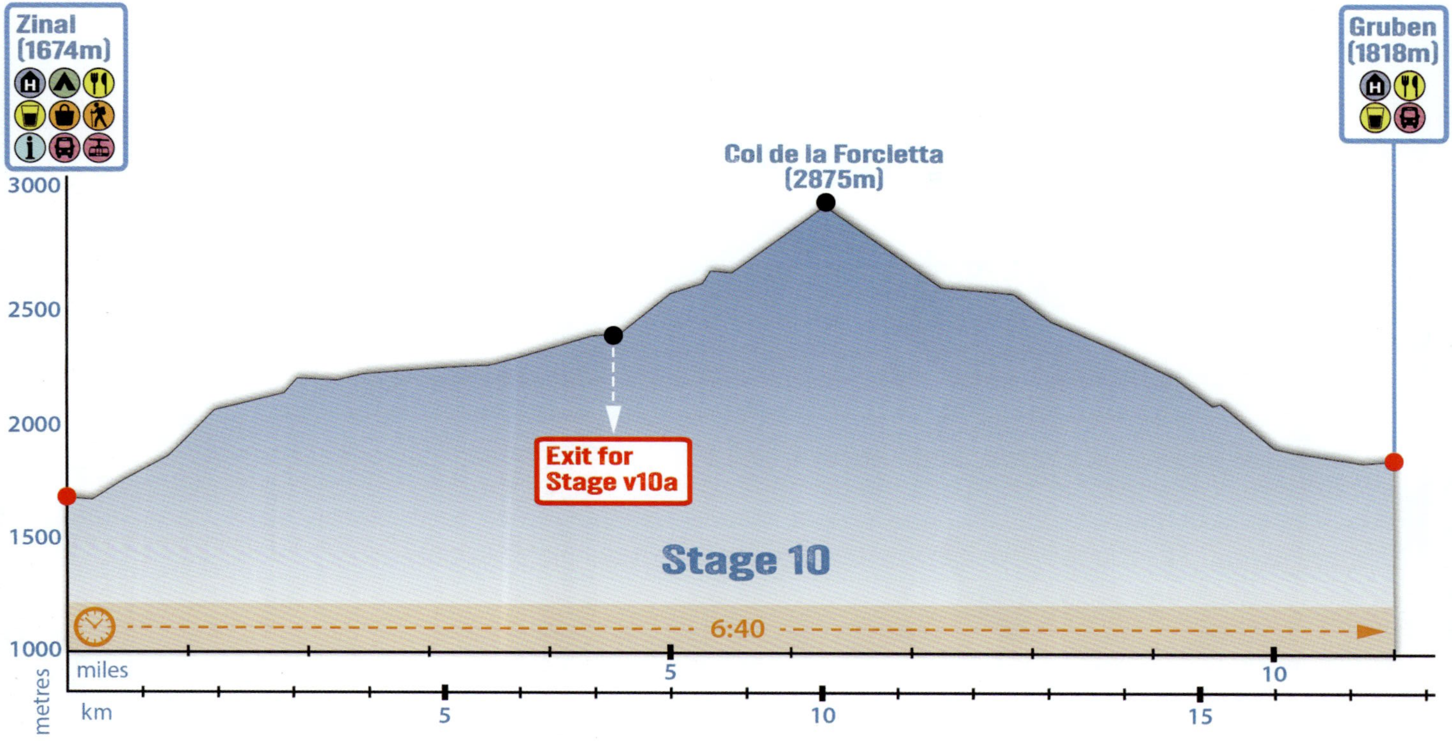
Zinal
(1674m)
Col de la Forcletta
(2875m)
Gruben
(1818m)
Exit for
Stage v10a
Stage 10
6:40
3000
2500
2000
1500
1000
metres
miles
km
5
10
15

Stage 10: Zinal to Gruben

91 **See map on p131.** From the tourist office, head briefly N down the road. Then TR on another road ('Hôtel Weisshorn'). Shortly afterwards, keep SH at a junction. TL before **Hôtel le Besso**. Soon, TL on a track. Then keep SH across a road ('Hôtel Weisshorn').

92 1:00: TL at a junction (2027m) and climb ('Hôtel Weisshorn'). After a while, the gradient eases and the path undulates. After 20min, climb a steep ramp to a junction: keep SH ('Hôtel Weisshorn'). Afterwards, the gradient eases again and you proceed along a superb balcony, high above the valley.

93 2:00: **See map on p133.** Pass farm buildings at **Barneuza Alpage (2210m)**. Immediately afterwards, keep SH on a path ('Hôtel Weisshorn'), ignoring the path descending to the left. After 5min, cross boulders following waymarks.

94 2:45: TR at a junction (2340m), climbing on a path which is faint in places (waymarks). After 20min, pass the wooden cross at **Tsahèlett (2524m)**. The path now heads E across pastures and then zig-zags up a rocky slope.

95 4:15: Cross **Col de la Forcletta (2875m)**. Head NE down a shale slope into a rocky valley. Keep following a path down the valley beside a stream. After a while, the path bears left, leaving the stream.

96 5:15: Pass between the buildings of **Chalte Berg (2495m)**. Then head E on a path down a grassy slope (waymarks). TL onto a track. Shortly afterwards, bear right on a path running parallel to the track. **See map on p146.** At **Massstafel (2239m)**, TR down a path. Soon, TR onto a track. Just after a right-hand hairpin, TL on a path which soon enters forest. Zig-zag down to the E.

97 6:25: Pass to the right of some farm buildings and head N on the road. After a few minutes, TL onto a path along the river.

98 6:40: Cross the river on a bridge. Immediately afterwards, TL and enter **Gruben (1818m)**.

The Turtmanntal Valley

Descending towards Gruben

v10 Zinal to Gruben (via Meidpass)

Stage v10a from Zinal to Hôtel Weisshorn is one of the most stunning parts of the WHR. After a climb out of Zinal (initially, on the same path as Stage 10), follow an amazing balcony all the way to the historic Hôtel Weisshorn. Looking backwards, there are fabulous views of the Matterhorn: from this angle, it is wedge-shaped. The slopes are carpeted with myrtille and alpenrose (which is a vibrant pink in early summer). Hôtel Weisshorn was first opened in 1883 but was destroyed in a fire in 1889. It was re-opened (in its current form) in 1891. The materials for its construction were carried up by mule: apparently, the piano was carried on the backs of six men. It is a fabulous place to spend the night.

Stage v10b from Hôtel Weisshorn to Gruben is one of our favourite parts of the WHR. The scenery leading to Cabane Bella Tola is sublime and it is no surprise that the paths are also popular with day walkers: there are wide views of the valley and the high peaks to the S, including the Weisshorn (4506m), the Zinalrothorn (4221m), Dent Blanche (4357m) and the Matterhorn (4478m). The vista from Cabane Bella Tola is particularly good and it is a more relaxed and informal place to spend the night than Hôtel Weisshorn.

	Start	Finish	Time	Distance	Ascent	Descent	Max Alt
v10a	Zinal	Hôtel Weisshorn	4:15	11.5km 7.1miles	819m 2687ft	156m 512ft	2423m 7949ft
v10b	Hôtel Weisshorn	Gruben	5:30	16.3km 10.1miles	715m 2346ft	1234m 4049ft	2789m 9150ft

The author at the Meidpass

If you can believe it, the scenery is even better after Cabane Bella Tola. After climbing through ski-fields for about an hour, leave civilization behind and enter more remote terrain: you will see few other hikers here. After passing the wonderful Lac de l'Armina (spectacularly set in a beautiful grassy bowl, surrounded by peaks), climb to the awesome Meidpass where you enter German-speaking territory. From the pass, you will see that the best has been saved for last: descend through a wilderness of tarns and grassy slopes (overlooked by snowy summits). Pass Meidsee (a magnificent lake) and then descend into the lovely Turtmanntal valley. We cannot recommend this variant more highly.

Terrain	The route between Zinal and Cabane Bella Tola uses good paths/tracks although gradients are sometimes steep. Between Cabane Bella Tola and the Meidpass, paths are rockier and more challenging. The descent from the Meidpass is long and tiring.
Route-finding	The route between Hôtel Weisshorn and Cabane Bella Tola is a little fiddly to follow. After Lac de la Bella Tola, the terrain is remote so navigate carefully: avoid this section in low visibility/bad weather (when it would be easy to lose your way). Sometimes, snow remains on the highest sections of the route into July, making navigation difficult. Otherwise, route-finding is straightforward: there are plenty of red/white waymarks.
Transport	**Zinal:** see p138. **Tignousa** (0.7km OR from Cabane Bella Tola 52)**:** funicular railway to St-Luc, where you can catch a bus to Vissoie (see p33). **Gruben:** see p138

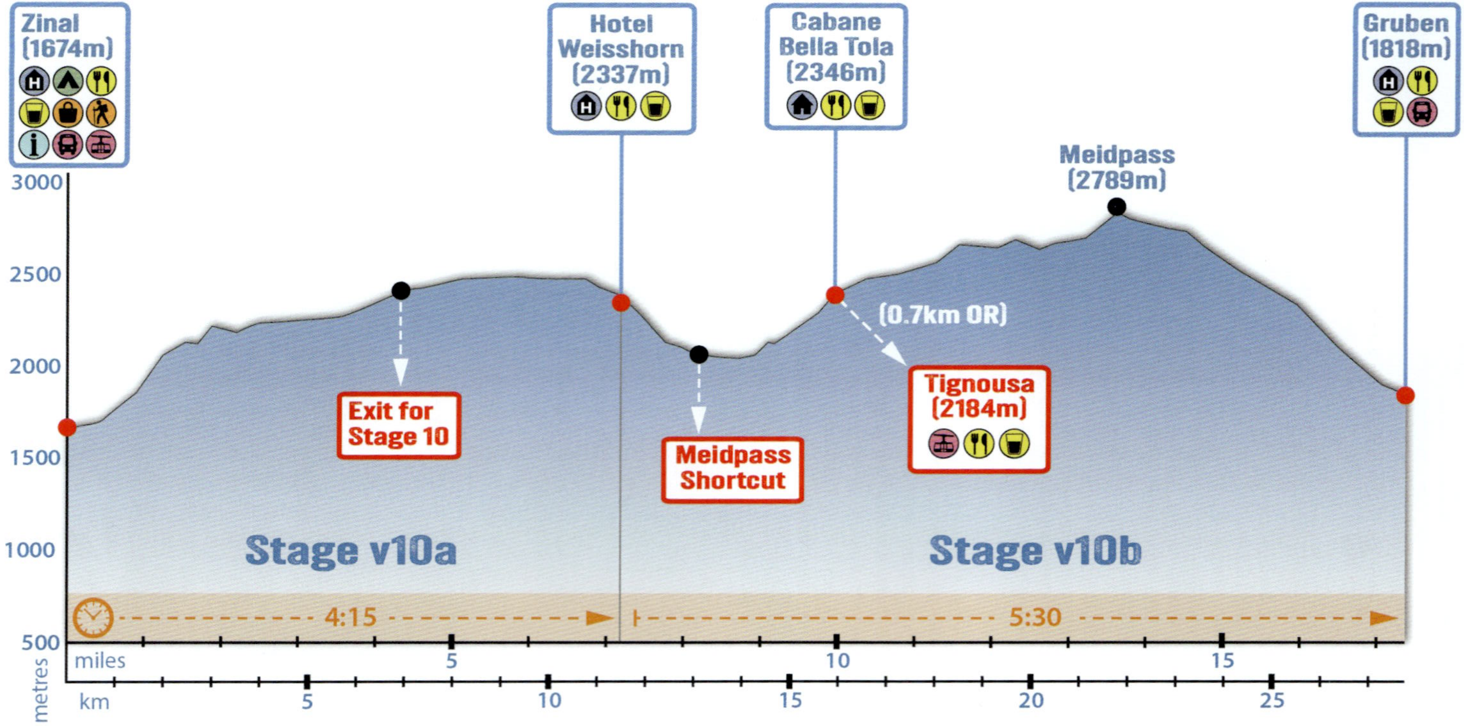

Zinal
(1674m)
Hotel
Weisshorn
(2337m)
Cabane
Bella Tola
(2346m)
Gruben
(1818m)
Meidpass
(2789m)
Exit for
Stage 10
Meidpass
Shortcut
(0.7km OR)
Tignousa
(2184m)
Stage v10a
Stage v10b
4:15
5:30
3000
2500
2000
1500
1000
500
metres
miles
5
10
15
km
5
10
15
20
25

Stage v10a: Zinal to Hôtel Weisshorn

See map on p131. Follow the Stage 10 directions to 94.

94 2:45: See map on p133. From the **junction (2340m)**, head N. After 20min, keep SH at another junction.

45 3:25: TL on a track. Just afterwards, TR on a path. 5min later, descend briefly on a track. Shortly afterwards, TR on a path.

46 4:05: Just after a strange sculpture called 'Haley's Comet', TL at a fork (no waymark) and descend towards the hotel.

47 4:15: Finally, a short climb brings you to **Hôtel Weisshorn (2337m)**.

Stage v10b: Hôtel Weisshorn to Gruben (via Cabane Bella Tola)

47 See map on p132. From the hotel, head initially NE on a path ('Gruben'). After a few minutes, TL at a fork ('Gruben'). After 20min, cross a bridge and TL at a junction ('Gruben').

48 0:25: 5min later, arrive at the buildings of **le Chiesso**: for the **Meidpass Short-cut**, TR and climb (see box below); otherwise, to continue on Stage v10b, TL on a track ('Chalet Blanc'). A few minutes later, TR at a fork ('Chalet Blanc').

49 0:35: TR on a path (no waymark). TR at the first fork.

50 0:45: From a junction just above **Chalet Blanc**, head N on a faint path ('Cabane Bella Tola'). After a few minutes, TL down a track. Just afterwards, TR onto another track heading N: ignore offshoots.

51 1:15: At a bench, follow the track around to the right: do not take the path beginning in front of the bench. Shortly afterwards, TL on a path heading uphill (NW). Shortly, keep SH across a faint track and climb on a path ('Cabane Bella Tola').

52 1:25: Arrive at **Cabane Bella Tola (2346m)**. Behind the cabane, pick-up a path heading initially NE ('Lac de la Bella Tola'). After 10min, keep SH across a track. After 10min, keep SH on a track. A few minutes later, TL on a path again. 10min later, pass some little lakes.

53 2:10: TL onto the track again ('Lac de la Bella Tola'). After 10min, TR at a fork. Shortly afterwards, TR at a junction ('Lac de l'Armina'). Soon, pass the little **Lac de la Bella Tola (2579m)**.

54 2:25: Just after a building, TL and climb on a path (easy to miss). Follow the path around the left side of the magnificent **Lac de l'Armina (2562m)**. Afterwards, continue upwards on the path. When the path disappears, follow waymarks. There are a few sections of boulders to cross.

55 3:15: Keep SH at a junction ('Gruben'): this is where the **Meidpass Short-cut** rejoins Stage v10b.

56 3:40: Cross the **Meidpass (2789m)** where the views are exquisite. Descend on a clear path. After 20min, pass **Meidsee (2661m)**, a beautiful lake.

57 4:55: See map on p146. Descend on a track through the hamlet of **Oberstafel (2334m)**. Just afterwards, at a signpost, keep SH on a path ('Gruben'). 5min later, cross a track and descend on a path ('Gruben'). Shortly afterwards, follow the path through the lovely hamlet of **Mittelstafel (2267m)**, following waymarks. As you approach the river, TL on a track ('Gruben'). Shortly, cross a bridge.

98 5:30: Immediately afterwards, TL and enter **Gruben (1818m)**.

Meidpass Short-cut

(1.25hr between 48 and 55)

See map on p133. At 48, TR and climb on a track. After 15min (2295m), TR onto a path. After 15min, TL at a fork: alternatively, TR for a short side-trip to **Lac de Combavert**. Keep heading NE and 45min later, arrive at 55.

Stage v10b
Stage 11
Stage 10
Gruben (1818m)
Gruben
Tschafil
Simmigu
Rotigu
Simmigrätji
Meidbach
Grüobbach
Grüobtälli
Grüobgrat
Niggelingt
Roti Rit
Ritzuegg 2975
Giigihoru 2748
Giigigrat
Furggwangjoch 3050
Furggwanghor 3161
Jungpass 2989
Hungerlitelli
Massstafel
Turtmänna
Brändji Oberstafil
Brändjispitz 2851
Hungerlihorli 3007
Hungerli Gl.
Rothorn 3277
Rothornjoch 3214
Värlooru Telli
Inner Rothorn 3257
Jungtaljoch 3219
Brändjitelli
Brändjihorn 3307
Brändjigletscher
Längi Egga 3028
Längi Egga
Pipjilicke 3048
Piipjitelli
Turtmaschafalpu
Ämser Schafalpu
Turtmannsee
Piipjigletscher
Gässijoch 3234
Gässispitz 3410
Barrjoch
Turtmannhütte SAC
Borthorn 2992
81
80
57
98
99
97

Schwarzhorn 2777
warzi Blatte 2974
Grosse See
Chumminilicke 2801
Niggelinglicke 2839
Borterhorn 2899
Rieberg
Driizänduhoru 3051
Augstbordgrat
Rieberg 2960
Rots Tällilicke 2936
Ginalspass 2909
Schwarzhoru 3200
Rots Tälli
102
Embdbach
103
Augstbordpass 2892
Inners Tälli
Wolftole
101
Steitalhorn 3162
Augstbord
Twära 2666
104
Horn 2891
Stage 11
Wyssegglicke 2991
Steitalgrat
Jungu/ Jungen (1954m)
Steital
105
Jungen (1954m)
Jungbach
Jungtal
106
Stage 11
Sparruhorn 2987
110
Sparruzug
St-Niklaus (1127m)
Sparrulicke 2881
107
Festihorn 3091
Wasulicke 3113
108
82
St. Niklaus
62
Wasmutälli
Birchmatten
83
Spisszug
Stock
Stahlen
Balmatten
Stage v12a
Wänguberg
Schwiedernen
63
Balacker

11 Gruben to St-Niklaus

On this wonderful stage, climb out of the Turtmanntal and over the Augstbordpass, the WHR's final col. Then descend into the Mattertal valley which will lead you triumphantly into Zermatt in a few days' time. The scenery throughout is fabulous and the highlight is one of the most beautiful viewpoints on the entire trek: from (104), you overlook the Mattertal, the Ried Glacier and a variety of peaks, including the Dom (4545m) and the Täschhorn (4491m); it is a great place for a picnic.

Afterwards, descend steeply to Jungen, a breathtaking hamlet, high above the Mattertal. Finally, a long, steep descent leads to the valley town of St-Niklaus: reserve accommodation in advance because it books up fast. If you cannot find a bed, then you could continue to Grächen (Stage v12b) or Herbriggen (Stage 12b/v12a): you can walk or take a bus/train.

Itinerary options: you can use the cable car from Jungen to avoid much of the descent into St-Niklaus.

	Start	Finish	Time	Distance	Ascent	Descent	Max Alt
11	Gruben	St-Niklaus	7:00	18.4km 11.4miles	1096km 3596ft	1787m 5863ft	2892m 9488ft

Approaching the Augstbordpass

Terrain	The climb to the Augstbordpass is long and tiring. Towards the top, there are sections of boulders to cross. The final approach to the pass is steep and unstable so watch your footing. Also, take care traversing boulders after 102 as it is easy to twist an ankle. Furthermore, the section between 102 and 103 is prone to rockfall after heavy rain. The descent from the viewpoint at 104 to St-Niklaus is long and steep.
Route-finding	Navigation can be tricky in low visibility, bad weather or snowy conditions. When the path disappears over boulders, follow waymarks carefully.
Transport	**Gruben:** see p138. **Jungen:** cable car to St-Niklaus (**www.jungeralp.ch** or **www.graechen.ch**). **St-Niklaus:** Train (S to Herbriggen, Randa, Täsch and Zermatt; N to Visp); Bus 551 to Niedergrächen and Grächen: to travel to Gasenried, change at Niedergrächen onto Bus 553; Bus 552 to Visp; Bus 554 to Mattsand and Herbriggen.

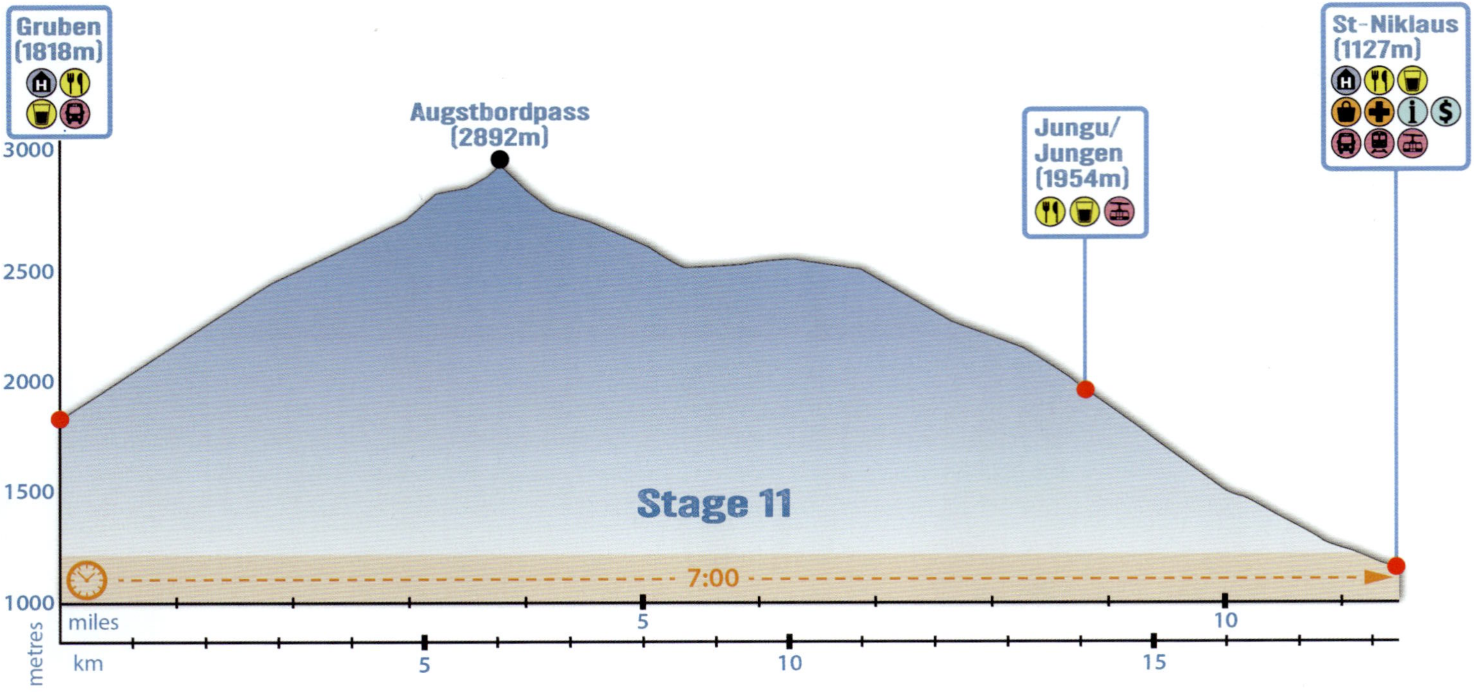

Gruben (1818m)
Augstbordpass (2892m)
Jungu/ Jungen (1954m)
St-Niklaus (1127m)
3000
2500
2000
1500
1000
metres
Stage 11
7:00
miles
5
10
km
5
10
15

Stage 11: Gruben to St-Niklaus

98 See map on p146. From **Hotel Schwarzhorn**, head E, steeply uphill on a path ('St-Niklaus'). After 10min, keep SH at a junction.

99 0:45: Keep SH at a junction ('Augstbordpass'). After 15min, TL at a junction ('St-Niklaus'). 15min later, pass some farm buildings. After 15min, keep SH at a junction, heading E.

100 2:00: Climb steeply up a rocky slope. At times, cross boulders (following waymarks). When the gradient eases again, you can see the col up ahead. Descend briefly and then climb across boulders, traversing the hillside (waymarks): it is easy to lose the route. After a few minutes, pick up a path again.

101 2:30: Cross the **Augstbordpass (2892m)** and descend on a path.

102 3:45: TR at a fork ('St-Niklaus'). Soon, the path crosses to the S side of the valley and then traverses E up its rocky flank: cross large sections of boulders (waymarks/cairns).

103 4:30: The path rounds a corner and contours SE around the slopes below the peak of **Twära (2666m)**.

104 4:45: Arrive at **one of the WHR's most beautiful viewpoints**. 5min later, TL at a junction ('Jungen'). After 15min, TL at another junction. A few minutes later, TR at a junction ('St-Niklaus'). After 10-15min, keep SH at a junction. When you can see Jungen just below, keep on the main path through trees, ignoring offshoots.

105 5:40: Arrive at the hamlet of **Jungen (1954m)**. Follow a path down through the incredible old buildings ('St-Niklaus'). TR at the chapel and continue descending. Now simply follow signs for 'St-Niklaus'.

106 6:25: Keep SH at a junction ('St Niklaus'). Shortly afterwards, cross a bridge. A few minutes later, TL at a fork, continuing downhill ('St-Niklaus').

107 6:55: TL at a junction ('Bahnhof'). Descend to the lower station of the Jungen cable car: then follow a road down to the train station. TL through a tunnel, under the tracks.

108 7:00: Arrive in **St-Niklaus (1127m)**.

Jungen

Routes between St-Niklaus and Zermatt

The Europaweg (Section 13)

There are two principal hiking routes between St-Niklaus and Zermatt: the famous Europaweg (the high route) and the valley route (the low route). However, because they converge mid-route (at the village of Herbriggen), it is possible to hike part of the way using the high route and part of the way using the low route (switching between the two at Herbriggen). You can also switch between the high and low routes further S, using the Stage v13b link route that runs between the village of Randa and the Charles Kuonen Suspension Bridge (CKSB). Accordingly, quite a few different itineraries are possible, each using a different combination of parts of the two main routes. We summarise the most popular options below.

When planning, bear in mind that the high paths of the Europaweg are more challenging than the low paths of the valley route. Accordingly, the valley is a good option if the weather is bad or you are short of time. If you are intending to hike any itineraries that incorporate parts of the Europaweg then, before leaving St-Niklaus, it is wise to check if the route is open: see **www.europaweg.ch**.

High High: the complete Europaweg (12a/12b/12c/13a/13b)

The Europaweg is the most famous hiking route between St-Niklaus and Zermatt and it has the reputation of being one of the finest hikes in Europe: there is no doubt that the original Europaweg was just that because, from start to finish, it was an exhilarating, high altitude balcony that was as beautiful as it was exposed. However, the route was prone to rockfalls and its N half (between Gasenried and the Europahütte), in particular, was frequently damaged by rocks, making it dangerous to negotiate: towards the end of its life, it seemed like the N half was shut more often than it was open. This was frustrating for WHR trekkers and expensive for the authorities (who regularly had to repair the path). Accordingly, the old route of the N half was closed permanently in 2018 and a new route was designed (which opened in 2021): in this book, the new route comprises Stages 12b and 12c.

Sadly, however, this new route for the N half is scenically inferior to its predecessor. Heading S from Gasenried, the challenging path undulates relentlessly (and seemingly interminably) through the forest with few fine views to take your mind off the not insignificant exertions.

Furthermore, while the old path kept you fairly high throughout, the new route leads you back down to the valley floor, depositing you at Herbriggen (1260m). This means that you then have a long climb back up again to reach the Europahütte (2264m) although, to be fair, this climb offers spectacular views (once you clear the tree-line). It makes for an exhausting day, especially if you hiked up from St-Niklaus that morning to start the Europaweg (at Gasenried).

Fortunately, the S half of the Europaweg (Section 13 between the Europahütte and Zermatt) has remained largely unchanged, and is as spectacular as ever, offering some of the finest views of the Matterhorn and providing a spectacular climax to the WHR. In fact, the S half has actually been enhanced by the addition of the staggering CKSB which was built across a rocky ravine where the path was regularly destroyed by rockfall (see p162).

Low Low: the complete valley route (v12a/v13a)

If the weather is bad or you are short of time, a series of paths and tracks travel all the way from St-Niklaus to Zermatt along the floor of the Mattertal valley. Although it lacks the majesty and drama of the Europaweg, the scenery is still lovely.

Low High 1:
St Niklaus-Herbriggen valley route (v12a) & Herbriggen-Zermatt Europaweg (12c/13a/13b)

This is a popular choice because it incorporates the finest sections of the Europaweg and avoids its least rewarding parts. Most significantly, you will not have to endure Stage 12a's stiff climb from St-Niklaus to Gasenried (to reach the start of the Europaweg) or Stage 12b's relentless undulations among the trees. Instead, you hike along the valley from St-Niklaus to Herbriggen (v12a) and, from there, climb to the Europahütte along a very beautiful part of the Europaweg (Stage 12c). From the Europahütte, you continue to follow the Europaweg all the way to Zermatt (Stages 13a/13b).

Low High 2:
St Niklaus-Randa valley route (v12a), Randa-Europahütte link route (v13b) & Europahütte-Zermatt Europaweg (13a/13b)

This option avoids all of the Section 12 Europaweg, following the valley all the way from St-Niklaus to Randa (Stage v12a). From Randa, you use the v13b link route to climb to the CKSB and the Europahütte (where you can sleep): the following morning, hike the Europaweg to Zermatt (13a/13b). Alternatively, you could overnight at Randa: the following morning, you would climb to the CKSB and start the Europaweg there; you do not need to climb all the way to the Europahütte unless you wish to sleep there.

High Low:
St-Niklaus-Europahütte Europaweg (12a/12b/12c), Europahütte-Randa link route (v13b) & Randa-Zermatt valley route (v13a)

Few plan to use this option because it misses the best of the Europaweg. However, it is a useful escape route if the weather is bad when you wake up at the Europahütte: it skips the Europaweg's high paths in favour of the safer valley route.

Transport between St-Niklaus and Zermatt

Regular trains travel between St-Niklaus and Zermatt (via Herbriggen and Randa), making it possible to skip both Sections 12 and 13. Alternatively, you can use the train simply to skip part of these sections: many trekkers travel by train from St-Niklaus to Herbriggen (missing the least enjoyable part of the Europaweg) and, from there, hike to Zermatt along the Europaweg. For timetables, see **www.matterhorngotthardbahn.ch**.

12 St-Niklaus to Europahütte

Section 12 incorporates the N half of the famous hiking path known as the Europaweg. The original Europaweg was a clear highlight of the WHR, however, constant rockfall made undertaking it a risky endeavour and the route was changed in 2021. Although the new route is safer than the original, unfortunately it is not as spectacular. The route to Gasenried (where the Europaweg starts) is unchanged and you begin the day with a stiff climb out of St-Niklaus: to avoid this, catch the bus to Gasenried or stay at Grächen the previous night instead (see Stage v12b on p164).

However, from Gasenried, the route has changed: instead of climbing high above the tree-line, the new Europaweg involves a tiring slog along an undulating path within the trees (where the views are largely concealed). Frustratingly, it eventually leads you back down to the valley floor (at the village of Herbriggen), ensuring that you lose most of the height that you gained during the climb from St-Niklaus to Gasenried. This means that you then have another long climb to reach the Europahütte from Herbriggen. However, the good news is that scenically this climb is a spectacular and worthy addition to the Europaweg: the path takes you high above the Mattertal valley with views of many famous Swiss peaks. To the E, the 4,000m summits include the Dom (4545m) and the Täschhorn (4491m). To the W, the views of the Weisshorn (4506m) and the Zinalrothorn (4221m) are incredible. And there are glaciers everywhere.

The Europahütte has a fabulous setting with staggering views from the terrace. Understandably, it books up quickly so reserve well in advance. If the Europahütte has no space, then alternatives include:

- **Randa:** from the Europahütte, use Stage v13b (in reverse) to descend to Randa (at the base of the valley) which has a few places to stay.

	Start	Finish	Time	Distance	Ascent	Descent	Max Alt
12a	St-Niklaus	Gasenried	2:00	3.9km 2.4miles	548m 1798ft	15m 49ft	1660m 5446ft
12b	Gasenried	Herbriggen	2:30	8.1km 5.0miles	265m 869ft	665m 2182ft	1713m 5620ft
12c	Herbriggen	Europahütte	3:50	7.2km 4.5miles	1094m 3589ft	90m 295ft	2345m 7694ft

The view W across the Mattertal

- **Domhütte:** with surplus energy, you could climb from the Europahütte to the Domhütte (which has exceptional views). Parts of the trail are exposed with fixed cables. From Europahütte to Domhütte: 1.25hr; 1.7km; ⬆655m.
- **Kinhütte:** from the Europahütte, start out on Stage 13a. After 3km, TL at a junction onto a signed path which climbs to the Kinhütte. From the junction to Kinhütte: 40min; 1km; ⬆310m.
- **Täschalp:** continue past the Europahütte and hike all of Stage 13a to Täschalp (where there is a comfortable lodge). Bear in mind that it is a very long way from St-Niklaus to Täschalp and few trekkers would be able to hike it all in one day: however, if you are starting to hike from Herbriggen, then hiking to Täschalp that day is feasible. If you had even more energy, you could take the trail from Täschalp to the Täschhütte and spend the night there (from Täschalp to Täschhütte: 1.25hr; 2.7km; ⬆520m).

Itinerary options: many people hike all of Section 12, from St-Niklaus to Europahütte, in one long day. However, to shorten the day, you could travel by bus from St-Niklaus to Gasenried and start hiking from there: take bus 551 to Niedergrächen and then change to bus 553 for Gasenried. Alternatively, the previous afternoon, you could walk Stage v12b to Grächen (or take the bus) and spend the night there (instead of St-Niklaus): from Grächen, it is an easy walk to the start of the Europaweg along Stage v12c.

Terrain	Stage 12a's paths are good. Although Stage 12b/12c is safer and less prone to rockfall than the original Europaweg, there are some steep and unstable sections which are quite challenging: you may have to use your hands to scramble up a few steep slopes; some exposed sections are protected by cables/ropes and steps bolted into the cliffs (which require a head for heights). Stage 12b also undulates relentlessly and paths within the forest can be muddy and slippery. Between Herbriggen and the Europahütte, the climb is long and tiring.
Route-finding	Generally straightforward. There are plenty of signs and waymarks.
Transport	**St-Niklaus:** see p149. **Gasenried:** Bus 553 to/from Niedergrächen. For St-Niklaus or Grächen, change at Niedergrächen onto Bus 551. **Herbriggen:** Train (S to Randa, Täsch and Zermatt; N to St-Niklaus and Visp); Bus 554 to St-Niklaus and Mattsand.

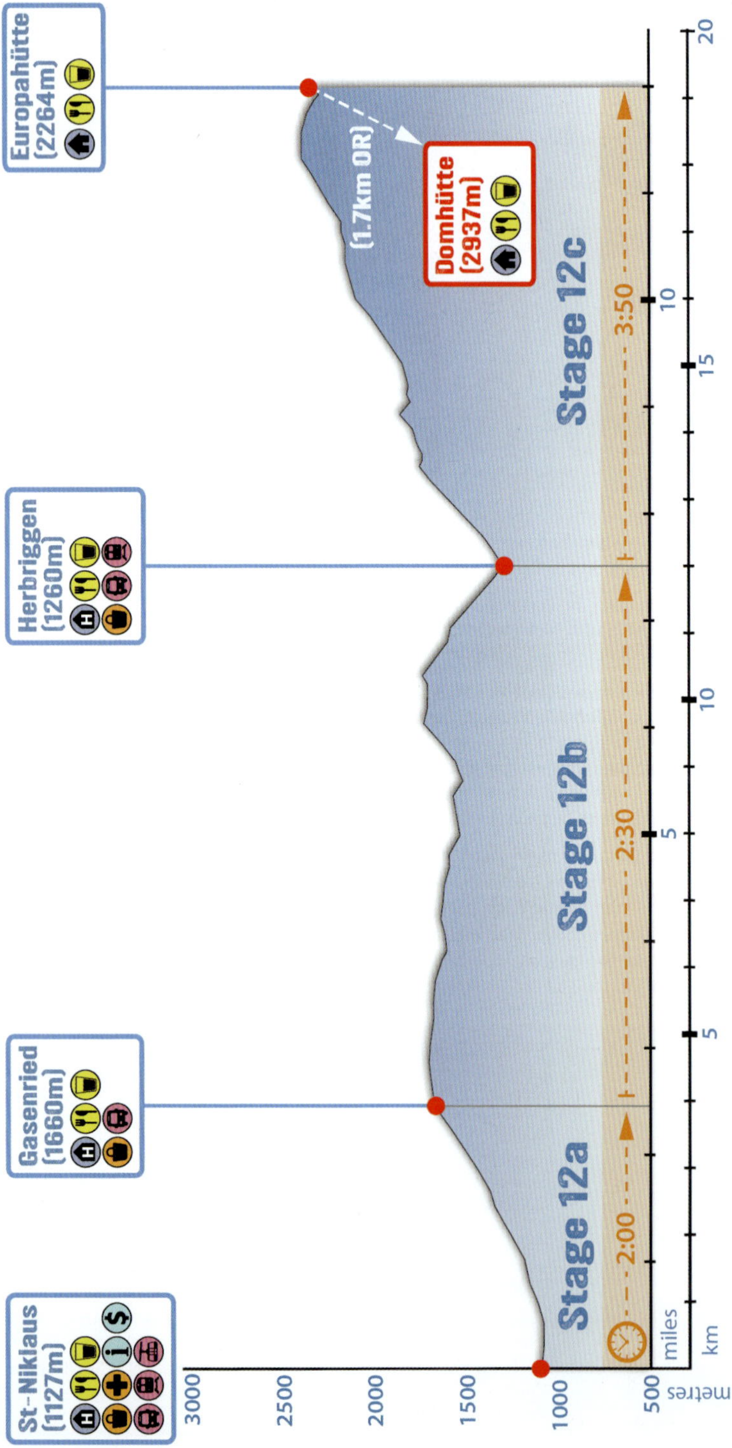
St-Niklaus
(1127m)
Gasenried
(1660m)
Herbriggen
(1260m)
Europahütte
(2264m)
Domhütte
(2937m)
(1.7km OR)
Stage 12a
Stage 12b
Stage 12c
2:00
2:30
3:50
metres
3000
2500
2000
1500
1000
500
miles
km
5
10
15
20

The Europahütte

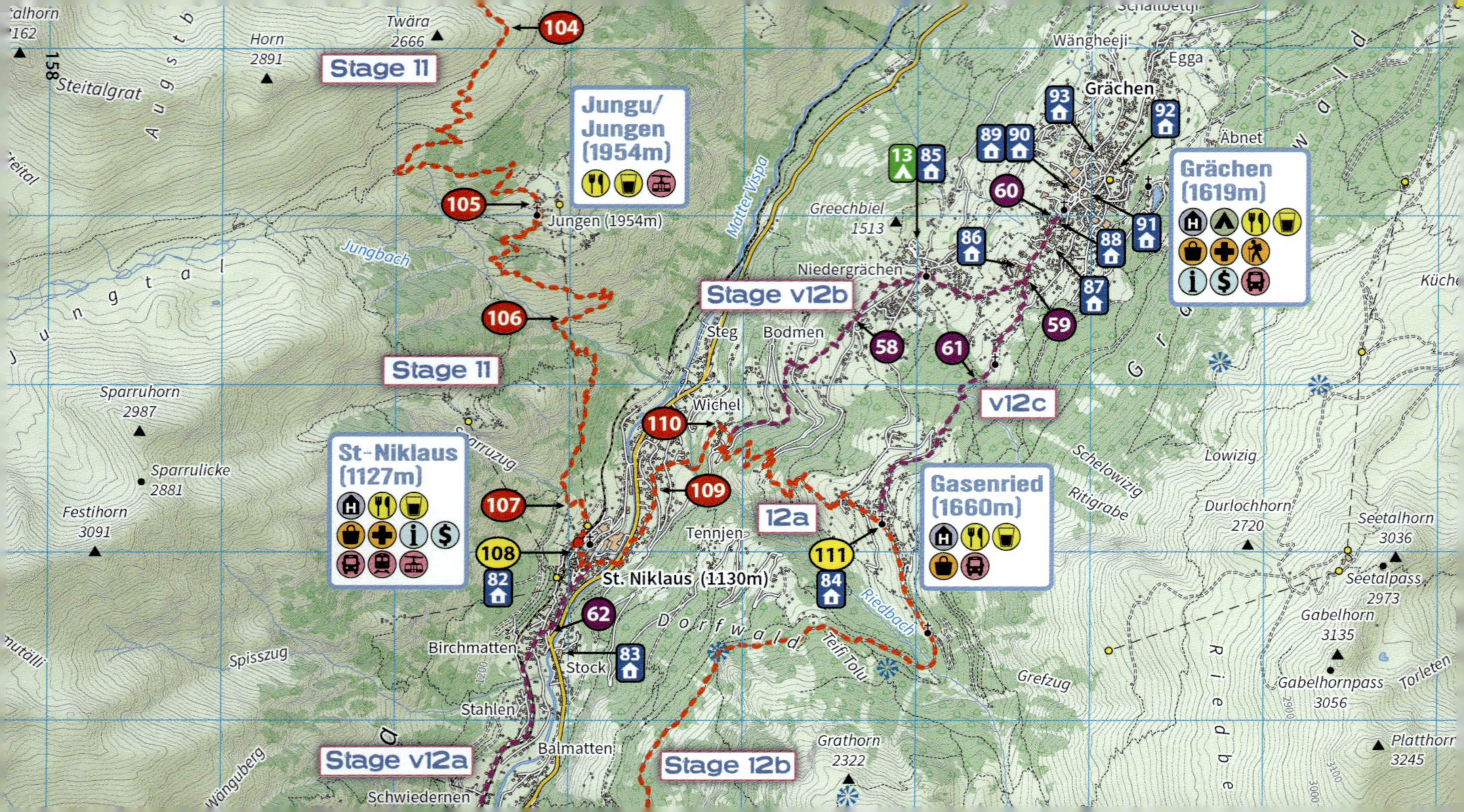
Stage 11
Twära 2666
Horn 2891
Steitalgrat
Jungu/ Jungen (1954m)
Jungen (1954m)
Jungbach
Matter Vispa
Greechbiel 1513
Niedergrächen
Stage v12b
Steg
Bodmen
Grächen
Wängheeji
Egga
Äbnet
Grächen (1619m)
Stage 11
Sparruhorn 2987
Sparrulicke 2881
Festihorn 3091
St-Niklaus (1127m)
Wichel
v12c
Schelowizig
Lowizig
Ritigrabe
Durlochhorn 2720
Gasenried (1660m)
12a
Tennjen
St. Niklaus (1130m)
Riedbach
Dorfwald
Teifi Tolu
Birchmatten
Stock
Spisszug
Stahlen
Balmatten
Stage v12a
Schwiedernen
Wänguberg
Stage 12b
Grathorn 2322
Grefzug
Seetalhorn 3036
Seetalpass 2973
Gabelhorn 3135
Gabelhornpass 3056
Torleten
Platthorn 3245
Riedbe
Jungtal
Augstb
104
105
106
107
108
109
110
111
58
59
60
61
62
13
82
83
84
85
86
87
88
89
90
91
92
93

Stage 12a: St-Niklaus to Gasenried

(108) See map on p158. From the **train station**, walk down a cobbled street past the post office. TR onto '**Dorfstrasse**'. Then take the first left, heading downhill on a narrow street. Cross a road onto '**Eyeweg**'. Soon, cross a bridge over the river. Immediately afterwards, TL on a small road.

(109) 0:15: Cross a main road and keep SH on a small road ('Grächen'). 5min later, TR. Immediately afterwards, TL and continue on another small road ('Grächen').

(110) 0:40: At the hamlet of **Wichel (1185m)**, bear right onto a small road. Shortly afterwards, TR at a junction. A few minutes later, TL and cross a road. Then pick up a path climbing into trees. 10-15min later, TR along a road: follow it around a bend. Shortly afterwards, TR and climb steeply on a track. Keep SH at a junction: ignore the path on the right which is also signed to Gasenried. 20min later, TL up a road. Shortly afterwards, TR on another road.

(111) 2:00: Enter **Gasenried (1660m)**.

Stage 12b: Gasenried to Herbriggen

(111) See map on p158. From the chapel in **Gasenried**, head S on a road. Pass a restaurant. TR at a fork, continuing on the road. Cross a bridge and then follow the path around to the right. Stay on the main path, heading W through the forest: later, the path bends left to head S.

(112) 1:15: See map on p163. TL at a junction and continue S. 10min later, TL at a junction. Just afterwards, cross a gully on a narrow, exposed path: there is a rope to assist. Soon, the path starts to climb steeply. After a viewpoint, descend steeply.

(113) 2:05: TL at a junction. Shortly afterwards, pass underneath a waterfall. Then continue descending steeply.

(114) 2:30: Reach a junction just above **Herbriggen**; descend on a path to enter the village (1260m); alternatively, climb S on a track for Stage 12c.

Stage 12c: Herbriggen to the Europahütte

(114) See map on p163. From the junction above **Herbriggen**, climb S on a track. Soon, continue climbing on a steep path through the trees. After 15-20min, TL at a junction, still climbing.

(115) 1:30: Cross a bridge across a torrent. Afterwards, climb a steep, exposed staircase. Then contour around the slopes. Soon the path climbs steeply again: ropes and steps to assist. Occasionally, there are signs warning of rockfall: move as quickly as safety allows. Eventually, emerge from the tree-line: the views are remarkable. After a steep climb, a superb balcony path contours around the hillside.

(116) 3:50: Arrive at the **Europahütte**.

This valley walk is useful if the Section 12 Europaweg is closed, the weather is bad or you are short of time. The route is pleasant but it is an anti-climax after the exquisite trekking of the previous days. Nevertheless, after Mattsand, there are superb views of the Breithorn (4164m).

Itinerary options: instead of travelling along the valley floor all the way to Randa, you could hike to Herbriggen and then leave Stage v12a by climbing out of the valley to the Europahütte on Stage 12c (Low High 1; see p153); if you have spent the night at St-Niklaus, you can do this in one go. Alternatively, if you were unable to find accommodation in St-Niklaus, you could spend the night at Herbriggen instead: strong hikers could tag Stage v12a's valley hike to Herbriggen onto Stage 11 (although this makes for a very long day); or you could take the train from St-Niklaus to Herbriggen instead.

Moving on from Randa: there are four options:

- Head directly to **Zermatt** along the valley floor (Stage v13a; p172): useful in bad weather or if the Section 13 Europaweg is closed.
- Climb to the **Europahütte** and spend the night there (Stage v13b; p173).
- Climb to the **Charles Kuonen Suspension Bridge** (Stage v13b; p173) and then switch to Stage 13a (avoiding the Europahütte): fit hikers could reach Zermatt that day.
- Take the **train** from Randa to Zermatt (p153).

Terrain	Good paths and tracks which are simple to follow. Short sections along quiet roads. Take care crossing the railway lines at Mattsand and Herbriggen.
Route-finding	Straightforward.
Transport	If short of time, consider taking public transport from St-Niklaus to Herbriggen/Randa. **St-Niklaus:** see p149. **Mattsand:** Bus 554 to St-Niklaus and Herbriggen. **Herbriggen:** Train (S to Randa, Täsch and Zermatt; N to St-Niklaus and Visp). Bus 554 to St-Niklaus and Mattsand. **Randa:** Train: (S to Täsch and Zermatt; N to Herbriggen, St-Niklaus and Visp).

	Start	Finish	Time	Distance	Ascent	Descent	Max Alt
v12a	St-Niklaus	Randa	2:40	9.6km 6.0miles	329m 1079ft	47m 154ft	1409m 4623ft

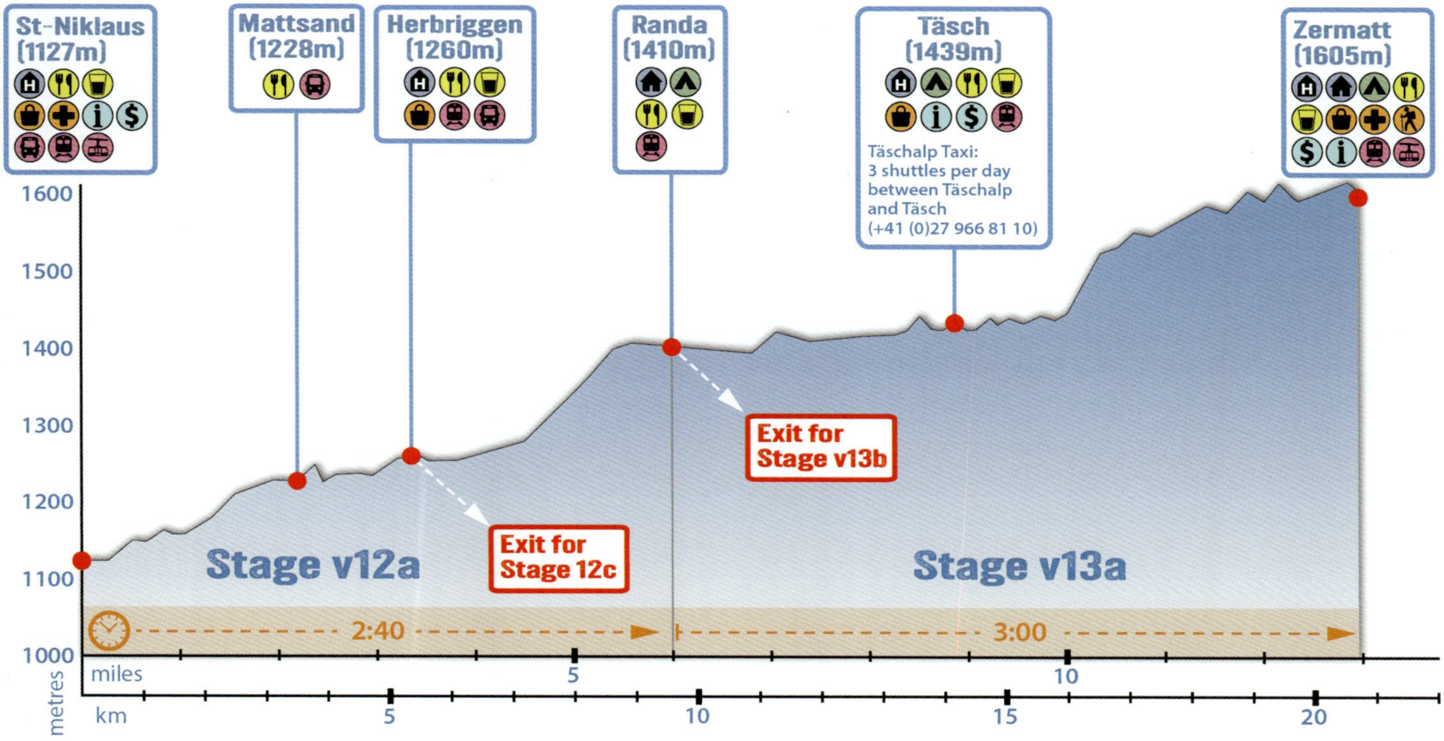
St-Niklaus
(1127m)
Mattsand
(1228m)
Herbriggen
(1260m)
Randa
(1410m)
Täsch
(1439m)
Täschalp Taxi:
3 shuttles per day
between Täschalp
and Täsch
(+41 (0)27 966 81 10)
Zermatt
(1605m)
Exit for
Stage 12c
Exit for
Stage v13b
Stage v12a
Stage v13a
2:40
3:00
metres
1600
1500
1400
1300
1200
1100
1000
miles
5
10
km
5
10
15
20

Stage v12a: St-Niklaus to Randa

(108) **See map on p158.** From the train station in **St-Niklaus**, walk down a cobbled street past the post office. TR onto **Dorfstrasse**. On arrival at the main road, TR ('Herbriggen').

(62) 0:10: TR up a road ('Herbriggen'). Soon, pass under the railway tracks.

(63) 0:25: **See map on p163.** Head through the hamlet of **Ze Schwidernu (1163m)**. Soon pass under the railway again. Immediately afterwards, TR on a small road running parallel to the tracks.

(64) 0:50: Arrive at the main road at **Mattsand (1228m)**. Before the chapel, cross the railway and continue on a small road ('Herbriggen'). Shortly afterwards, TR at a fork (yellow waymarks). After a reservoir, bear right on a track.

(65) 1:25: Arrive at a junction: if you wish to continue directly to Randa, keep SH and soon reach (66). To head into **Herbriggen (1260m)**, TL at (65), pass through a tunnel and then climb to the main street. From the **hotel** in Herbriggen, head S down the road. Soon, cross the main road and descend to the train station. Take care crossing the tracks and descend to the river. Cross a bridge.

(66) 1:35: Immediately afterwards, TL on a track ('Randa'). After 15min, TL at the hamlet of **Zenackern (1261m)** and cross a bridge over the river. Immediately afterwards, TR on a track alongside the railway. Keep SH when the track becomes a tarmac lane.

(67) 2:35: TR at a fork onto a road. Just after passing under the main road, TR.

(68) 2:40: Arrive at the station in **Randa (1410m)**.

The Charles Kuonen Suspension Bridge (Hängebrücke)

When the CKSB was built, it was the longest pedestrian suspension bridge in the world. Situated above Randa (at an altitude of 2070m), it is 494m long and 85m above the valley at its highest point. It takes about 10min to cross. It was constructed using 8 tonnes of cables and has a special system that prevents swinging. The bridge is part of the famous hiking path, the Europaweg, between Gasenried and Zermatt. It was built to replace the previous bridge, the shorter Europabrücke. The metal grating you walk upon allows you to see down to the valley floor: it is exhilarating but is perhaps best avoided if you have a fear of heights. If you do not wish to cross, you can descend to Randa, following Stage v13b in reverse (see p173).

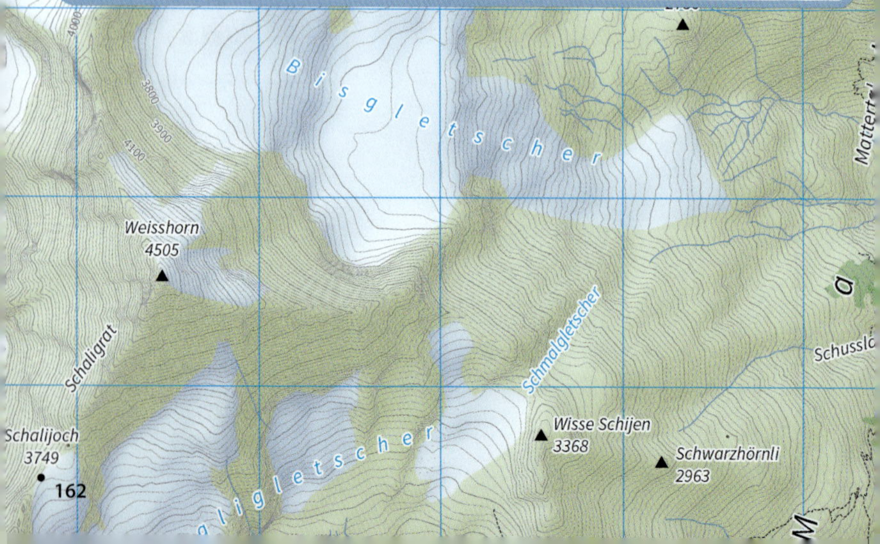

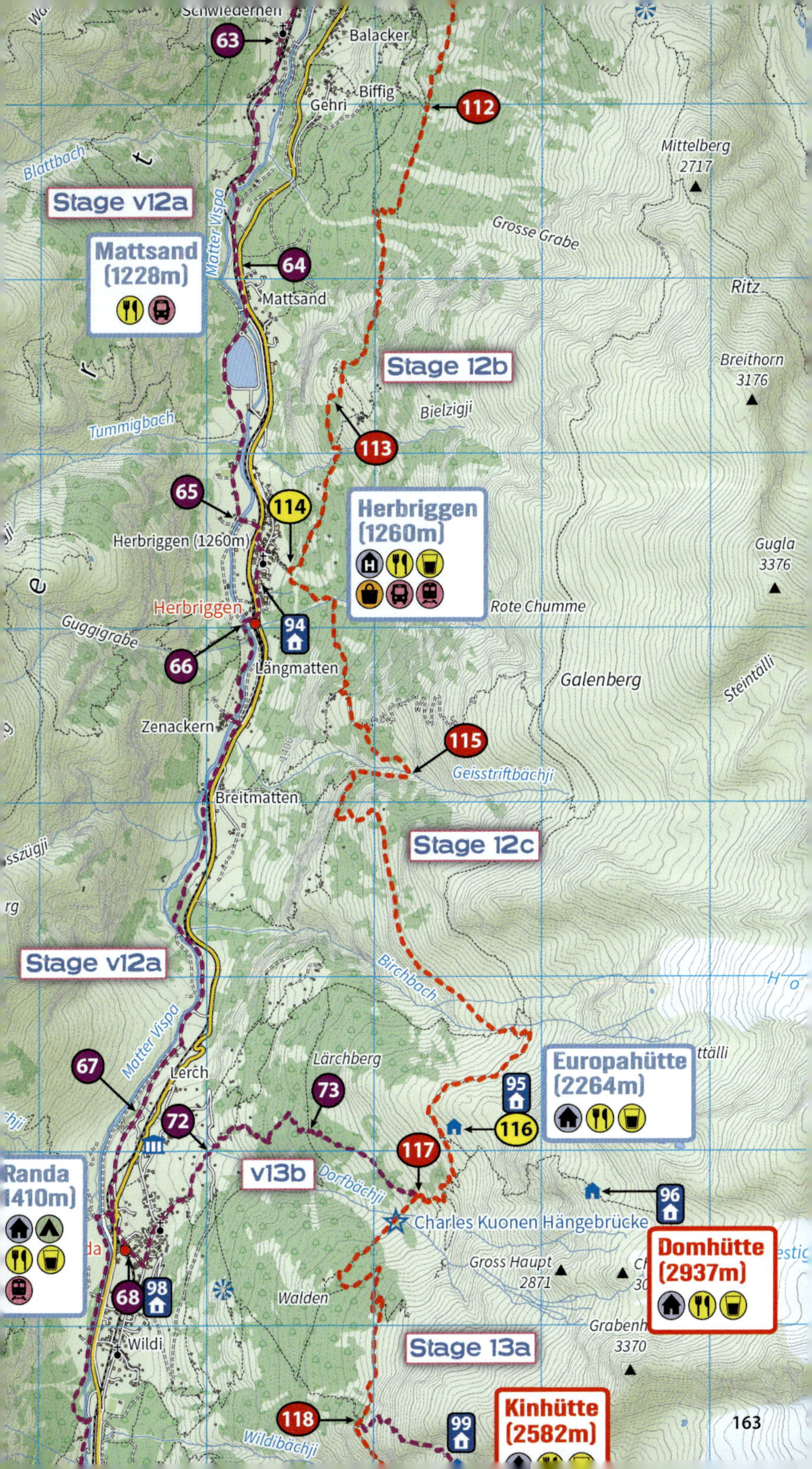

Schwiedernen
63
Balacker
Biffig
Gehri
112
Mittelberg 2717
Blattbach
Stage v12a
Mattsand (1228m)
Matter Vispa
64
Mattsand
Grosse Grabe
Ritz
Stage 12b
Breithorn 3176
Bielzigji
Tummigbach
113
65
114
Herbriggen (1260m)
Herbriggen (1260m)
Gugla 3376
Herbriggen
Rote Chumme
94
Guggigrabe
66
Längmatten
Galenberg
Steintälli
Zenackern
115
Geisstriftbächji
Breitmatten
Stage 12c
Birchbach
Stage v12a
Matter Vispa
Lärchberg
67
Lerch
73
95
Europahütte (2264m)
72
116
117
v13b
Dorfbächji
96
Randa (1410m)
Charles Kuonen Hängebrücke
Domhütte (2937m)
Gross Haupt 2871
68
98
Walden
Grabenh
3370
Wildi
Stage 13a
Kinhütte (2582m)
118
99
Wildibächji

v12b St-Niklaus to Grächen

Grächen

This pleasant climb leads to the relaxing village of Grächen. Accommodation in St-Niklaus is in short supply but there are plenty of options in Grächen. Spending the night in Grächen has the added advantage of substantially reducing the climbing on the following day's tough hike to the Europahütte.

Itinerary option: you could tag this stage onto Stage 11 although that makes for a long day. Alternatively, take the bus from St-Niklaus to Grächen.

Terrain	Good paths and tracks which are simple to follow. Short sections along quiet roads.
Route-finding	Straightforward.
Transport	**St-Niklaus:** see p149. **Grächen:** Bus 551 to/from Niedergrächen or St-Niklaus; for Gasenried, change at Niedergrächen onto Bus 553. Bus 552 (to Visp).

	Start	Finish	Time	Distance	Ascent	Descent	Max Alt
v12b	St-Niklaus	Grächen	2:00	4.6km 2.9miles	540m 1772ft	48m 157ft	1619m 5312ft

Stage v12b: St-Niklaus to Grächen

108 **See map on p158.** From the **train station** in **St-Niklaus**, walk down a cobbled street past the post office. TR onto **Dorfstrasse**. Then take the first left, heading downhill on a narrow street. Cross a road onto **Eyeweg**. Soon, cross a bridge over the river. Immediately afterwards, TL on a small road.

109 0:15: Cross a main road and keep SH on a small road ('Grächen'). 5min later, TR. Immediately afterwards, TL and continue on another small road ('Grächen').

110 0:40: At the hamlet of **Wichel (1185m)**, bear right onto a small road. Shortly afterwards, TL at a junction. After 5min, cross a road and climb on a narrow path. Cross the road again and continue uphill on a path. At the hamlet of **Bodmen (1358m)**, cross a road and continue on a tarmac lane. Shortly afterwards, TL ('Grächen').

58 1:20: Keep SH on a road. Shortly afterwards, TL on a tarmac lane (yellow sign). After a few minutes, keep SH to climb on a path (yellow signs). TL onto the road again. Shortly afterwards, TR on a path just before the little chapel at **Niedergrächen (1478m)**.

59 1:55: TL onto a street.

60 2:00: Arrive in **Grächen (1619m)**.

v12c Grächen to Gasenried

This short route to Gasenried is for those who stay overnight in Grächen. At Gasenried, you rejoin the main route (at the start of Stage 12b, which is the beginning of the Europaweg).

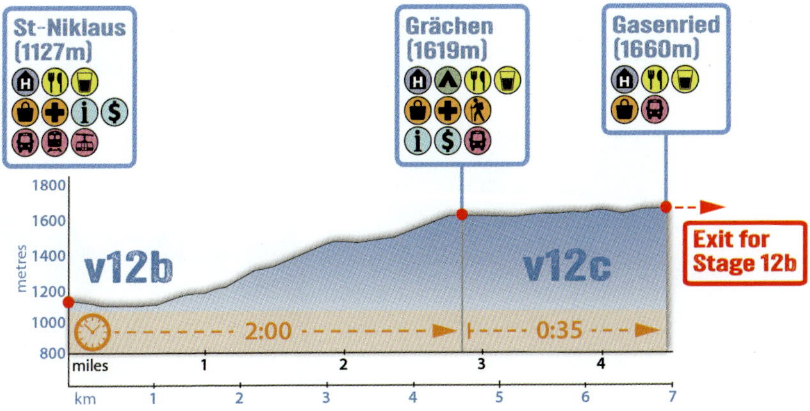

Terrain	Good paths and tracks which are simple to follow. Short sections along quiet roads.
Route-finding	Straightforward.
Transport	Instead of walking, you could take the bus from Grächen to Gasenried. **Grächen:** Bus 551 to/from Niedergrächen or St-Niklaus (for Gasenried, change at Niedergrächen onto Bus 553); Bus 552 to Visp. **Gasenried:** Bus 553 to/from Niedergrächen. For St-Niklaus or Grächen, change at Niedergrächen onto Bus 551.

	Start	Finish	Time	Distance	Ascent	Descent	Max Alt
v12c	Grächen	Gasenried	0:35	2.3km 1.4miles	67m 220ft	26m 85ft	1660m 5446ft

Stage v12c: Grächen to Gasenried

60 **See Map on p158.** From the chapel, walk SW down the main street of **Grächen**.

59 TL at a fork ('Gasenried').

61 Keep SH on a track. 5min later, near some buildings, TL at a fork onto a path ('Gasenried'). A few minutes later, TL onto a road.

111 0:35: Enter **Gasenried (1660m)**.

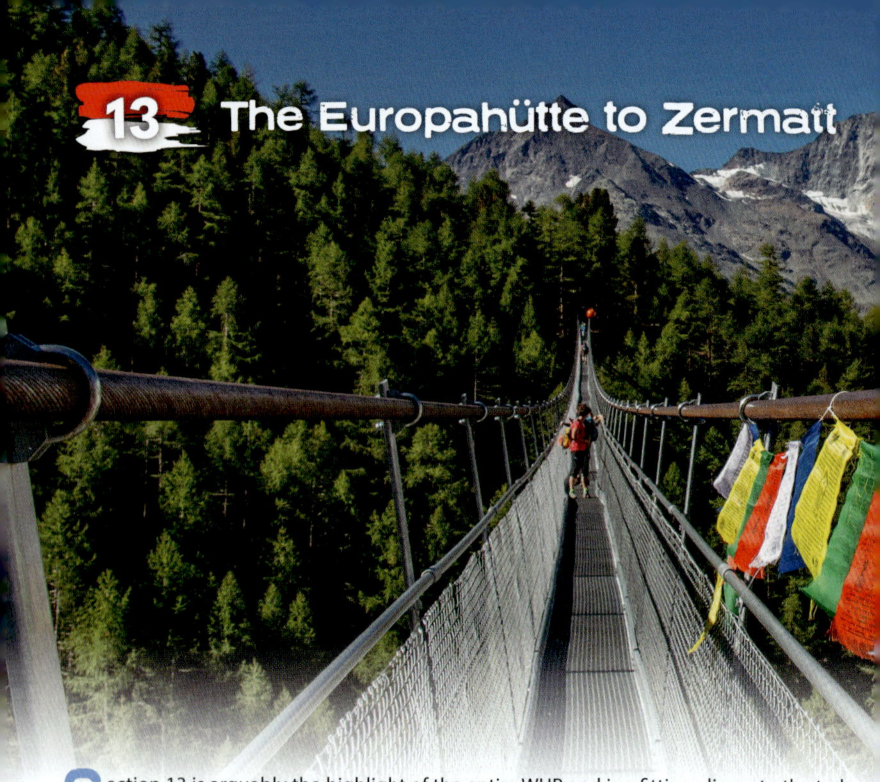

13 The Europahütte to Zermatt

Section 13 is arguably the highlight of the entire WHR and is a fitting climax to the trek. There are fabulous views of the Weisshorn (4506m) and the Zinalrothorn (4221m) on the W side of the valley. However, the Matterhorn (4478m) will soon command much of your attention: as you get closer to Zermatt, it changes shape before your eyes from a wedge to the iconic crooked form immortalized in a billion photos. Pray for good weather as these are the scenes that you have been dreaming about since Chamonix and the quality of the views is in no way exaggerated. Finally, after a long and magnificent balcony, descend into Zermatt to complete the WHR.

Mid-section there is accommodation at Täschalp, Kinhütte (OR) and Täschhütte (OR): see p155. It is worth noting that those who spend the night at Täschalp, and start Stage 13b early the following morning, often get the best photographs: by afternoon, the sun will be directly above the Matterhorn which can cause glare. However, most WHR trekkers do not stop at Täschalp, eager to reach Zermatt to celebrate the completion of the trek in the town's many bars and restaurants. Zermatt also has plenty of shops and attractions to keep you busy for a day or two, including the excellent Matterhorn Museum. For further information on Zermatt see p174.

	Start	Finish	Time	Distance	Ascent	Descent	Max Alt
13a	Europahütte	Täschalp	3:30	9.5km 5.9miles	512m 1680ft	619m 2031ft	2264m 7428ft
13b	Täschalp	Zermatt	3:45	12.4km 7.7miles	298m 978ft	850m 2789ft	2347m 7700ft

The Charles Kuonen Suspension Bridge

Itinerary options: because this is a high mountain route, in bad weather/low visibility, it can be sensible to switch to the valley route to Zermatt instead (Stage v13a; p172). To do this, use Stage 13a to descend from the Europahütte to the CKSB: instead of crossing the bridge, use Stage v13b (in reverse; p173) to descend to Randa. From Randa, follow Stage v13a to Zermatt.

Terrain	Paths and tracks are clear and well maintained. However, often the surface is rocky and uneven and gradients are steep. The Europaweg's lofty position, cut into the face of the cliffs, means that it is prone to landslides and rockfalls. Accordingly, the path is sometimes closed and the exact route can change as repairs are made or damaged sections are re-routed. As a result, the path on the ground may differ slightly from the directions below. There are many narrow and precipitous sections with steep drops: take care as a fall could be serious; some of the most exposed sections are protected with fixed chains/ropes. If you find that the route is blocked, then turn back. On narrow sections (particularly those with overhanging rocks), do not rest as it is possible that rocks could fall from above. There is also a long section of concrete overhangs/tunnels: move as quickly as safety permits and keep well underneath the overhangs for protection from falling rocks; at the time of writing, parts of the tunnels had collapsed and they were impassable. The descent from Sunnegga to Zermatt is another knee-jerker: you can avoid it by taking the funicular railway from Sunnegga right into the heart of Zermatt (see below).
Route-finding	Generally straightforward. Follow signs for 'Zermatt' throughout. However, on the descent from Sunnegga to Zermatt, there is a complicated labyrinth of paths: follow signposts particularly carefully.
Transport	**Täschalp:** Täschalp Taxis runs daily shuttles between Täschalp and Täsch (+41 (0)27 966 81 10; taesch@zermatt.swiss; www.zermatt.swiss). **Sunnegga:** funicular railway to Zermatt; **www.matterhornparadise.ch**. **Zermatt:** train to Täsch, Randa, Herbriggen, St-Niklaus and Visp.

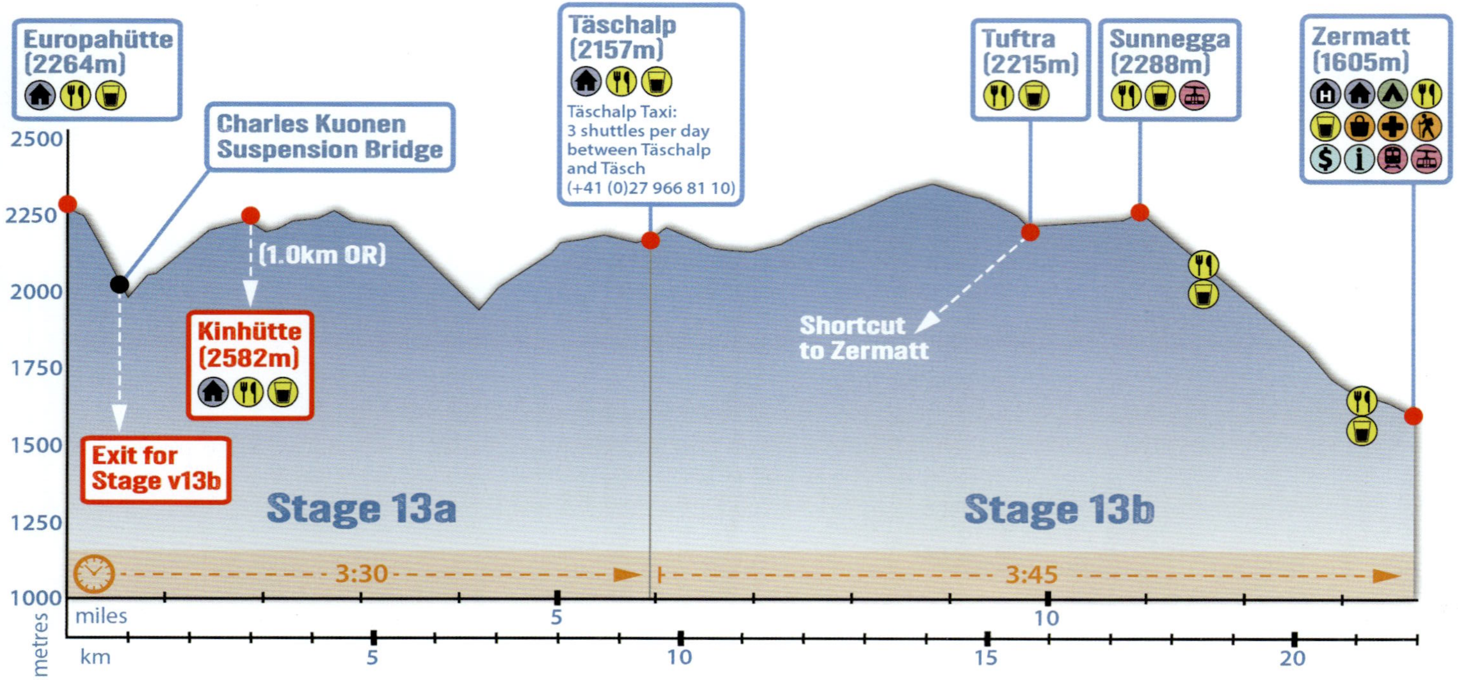

Europahütte
(2264m)
Charles Kuonen
Suspension Bridge
Täschalp
(2157m)
Täschalp Taxi:
3 shuttles per day
between Täschalp
and Täsch
(+41 (0)27 966 81 10)
Tuftra
(2215m)
Sunnegga
(2288m)
Zermatt
(1605m)
(1.0km OR)
Kinhütte
(2582m)
Exit for
Stage v13b
Shortcut
to Zermatt
Stage 13a
Stage 13b
3:30
3:45
2500
2250
2000
1750
1500
1250
1000
metres
miles
km
5
10
15
20

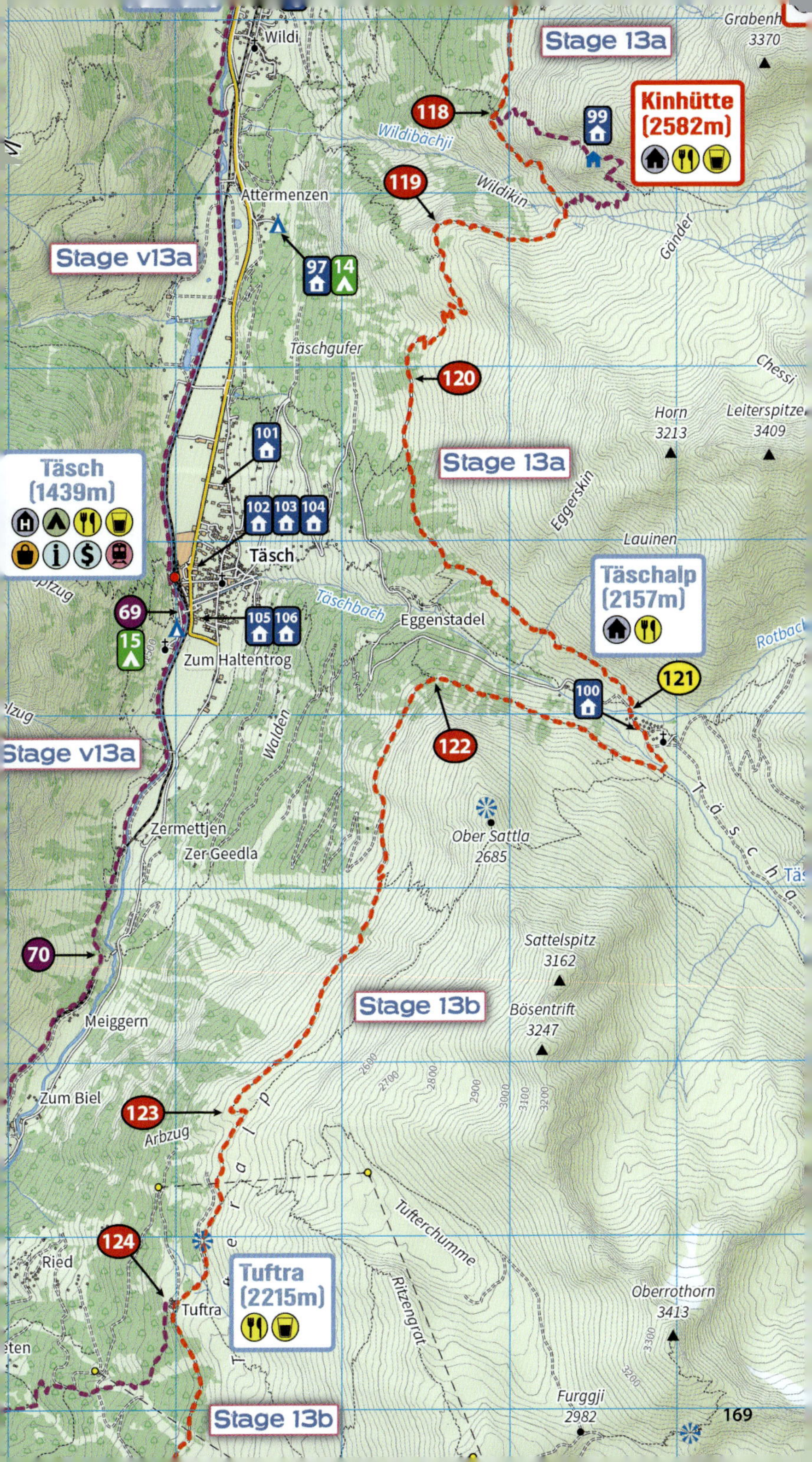
Stage 13a
Kinhütte (2582m)
Wildi
118
Wildibächji
99
119
Wildikin
Attermenzen
Stage v13a
97
14
Täschgufer
120
Horn 3213
Leiterspitze 3409
Chessi
Gänder
Stage 13a
101
Täsch (1439m)
102
103
104
Täsch
Eggerskin
Lauinen
Täschalp (2157m)
Täschbach
Eggenstadel
69
105
106
15
Zum Haltentrog
121
100
Rotbach
122
Stage v13a
Walden
Ober Sattla 2685
Zermettjen
Zer Geedla
70
Sattelspitz 3162
Stage 13b
Bösentrift 3247
Meiggern
Zum Biel
123
Arbzug
Tufterchumme
124
Ried
Tuftra
Tuftra (2215m)
Ritzengrat
Oberrothorn 3413
Furggji 2982
Stage 13b

Stage 13a: The Europahütte to Täschalp

116 **See map on p163.** From the **Europahütte**, take the path heading S and descend (initially over boulders). After 5min, TR at a junction.

117 0:20: Cross the **Charles Kuonen Suspension Bridge** (see p162). After the bridge, keep SH on a path. After a few minutes, TL at a junction and climb. A few minutes later, TR at another junction. The **Weisshorn (4506m)** is the huge peak to your right. Keep SH at another junction. Just afterwards, views become more expansive and the **Matterhorn** should appear to the SW. Soon, cross some boulders. Then take care on a narrow section protected with ropes.

118 1:10: **See map on p169.** TR at a fork (the path to the left goes to the Kinhütte). Immediately afterwards, TL at another fork. Shortly afterwards, descend steeply through a roped section. Then a precipitous path skirts the edge of the cliffs: take care. Pass through a tunnel: it is dark but there are light switches on timers.

119 1:55: Pass a grassy area (which is the first good place to stop since the Europahütte). Shortly afterwards, keep SH at a junction and cross some boulders. Soon, start to descend.

120 2:20: Walk underneath a section of concrete overhangs/tunnels (see p167). Just after the overhangs, start to climb again. A few minutes later, TL at a fork.

121 3:30: TL on a road. Then cross a bridge and enter the hamlet of **Täschalp (2157m)**. Keep SH to the **Täschalp Lodge**.

Stage 13b: Täschalp to Zermatt

121 **See map on p169.** TR on a path beside **Täschalp Lodge**. Soon, cross the torrent and climb on the other side.

122 0:30: Keep SH at a junction. 10min later, climb through a cabled section. Soon, TL at a fork, continuing to climb on a track: incredible views.

123 1:20: Head around a corner where there is a magnificent view of the **Matterhorn**. Then start to descend gently. After 20min, keep SH at a signpost. After a few minutes, TR at a fork.

124 1:55: **See map on p171.** A few minutes later, arrive at the hamlet of **Tuftra/Tufteren (2215m)** where there is a restaurant: if short of time, you can descend directly to Zermatt from there. However, to continue on the Europaweg, head S ('Sunnegga'). After 15min, TL at a fork.

125 2:20: TL at the ski station of **Sunnegga (2288m)** and descend on a track ('Zermatt'). Shortly afterwards, follow the track around to the right. Just afterwards, TL onto a path ('Findeln-eggen').

126 2:40: TR and head through the hamlet of **Findeln-eggen**. Now follow signs for 'Winkelmatten'. After 10min, in the hamlet of **Ze Gassu**, keep SH at a junction: do not TL (even though it is also signed to 'Winkelmatten'). At the next fork, TL ('Winkelmatten').

127 3:20: Cross the **Gornergrat railway** track and continue down a path. TR onto a lane and arrive at **Winkelmatten (1672m)**. TR by the chapel and descend on a small road: there are some footpaths you can use to cut corners.

128 3:40: Arrive at the river at the bottom of **Zermatt**. Congratulations: you have completed the WHR. For the centre of town, cross the bridge and climb.

Stage v13a
Zermatt (1605m)
Tuftra (2215m)
Stage 13b
Sunnegga (2288m)
Spiss
Eggen
Ried
Haueten
Tuftra
Wiesti
Matter Vispa
Herbrigg
Winkelmatten
Sunnegga
Blauherd
Leisee
Egge
Wildi
Findeln
Ze Gassu
Bord
Grindjesee
Mossjesee
Findelbach
Gornerschlucht
Blatten
Balmbrunne
Riffelalp
Mountain Lodge Ze Seewjinu
Grüensee
The Five Lakes (Walk no. 11)
Landtunnel
Schweigmatten
Augstchumme
Gugle 2720
Ritzengrat
Dossen 1954
Riffelberg
Hohtälli
Gornergratsee
Gagenhaupt 2568
Rotenboden
Gornergrat
Murischloch
Riffelsee
Riffelhorn 2930
Usser Gorner
Gornera
Gornergrat to Riffelalp (Walk no. 23)
Gorn
71
16
108
109
110
111
112
113
114
115
107
124
125
126
127
128

v13a Randa to Zermatt (valley route)

The valley route just outside Zermatt

This valley walk is useful if the Section 13 Europaweg is closed, the weather is bad or you are short of time. It is more enjoyable than the v12a valley walk (St-Niklaus to Randa).

Terrain	Good paths and tracks which are simple to follow. Short sections along quiet roads.
Route-finding	Straightforward. Follow signs for 'Zermatt' throughout.
Transport	If short of time, consider taking the train from Randa to Zermatt. **Randa:** Train: (S to Täsch and Zermatt; N to Herbriggen, St-Niklaus and Visp). **Täsch:** Trains; Täschalp Taxis runs daily shuttles between Täschalp and Täsch (+41 (0)27 966 81 10; taesch@zermatt.swiss; www.zermatt.swiss). **Zermatt:** Train to Täsch, Randa, Herbriggen, St-Niklaus and Visp.

	Start	Finish	Time	Distance	Ascent	Descent	Max Alt
v13a	Randa	Zermatt	3:00	11.1km 6.9miles	281m 922ft	85m 279ft	1645m 5397ft

Stage v13a: Randa to Zermatt

68 **See map on p163.** From **Randa train station**, head NW on a road. Soon, bear left and pass under the road. Shortly afterwards, TL to cross the train tracks and a bridge over the river. Immediately afterwards, TL on a path alongside the river. **See map on p169.** 20min from the start, cross a bridge over the river. Immediately afterwards, cross back again. Soon, the riverside path passes a golf course.

69 1:25: Keep SH past the **campsite** at **Täsch (1439m)**: alternatively, TL and cross the bridge if you need supplies. After 30min, TL onto another path and climb. 5min later, TR at a fork.

70 1:55: TR at a fork and climb. Soon Zermatt comes into view ahead.

71 2:35: **See map on p171.** Keep SH past a **heliport**. 5min later, keep SH at a junction to head to the centre of Zermatt: alternatively, TL for the train station. Keep SH on a road overlooking the rooftops of the town. When the road ends, TL down an alley.

3:00: Arrive at the main street of **Zermatt (1605m)**.

v13b Randa to the Europahütte (Link Route)

The Zinalrothorn

Even if the Section 12 Europaweg is closed, you may still be able to walk the Section 13 part of it: Low High 2 (p153). Use Stage v13b to climb to the Charles Kuonen Suspension Bridge and then TR onto Stage 13a (p170). Alternatively, from the CKSB, you could continue up to the Europahütte, overnight there and then walk Stages 13a and 13b the following day.

Terrain	Generally, paths are well maintained and simple to follow. However, they can be muddy and slippery after rain. The climb is long and steep.
Route-finding	Generally straightforward (signs and waymarks).
Transport	**Randa:** Train: (S to Täsch and Zermatt; N to Herbriggen, St-Niklaus and Visp).

	Start	Finish	Time	Distance	Ascent	Descent	Max Alt
v13b	Randa	Europahütte	2:30	4.1km 2.5miles	866m 2841ft	11m 36ft	2264m 7428ft

Stage v13b: Randa to the Europahütte

68 See map on p163. From **Randa train station**, head SE along a road. After a few minutes, TL up another road ('Europahütte'). TL after the chapel. Immediately afterwards, TR ('Europahütte') and climb on a cobbled street past some beautiful traditional buildings. 15min from the start, TL at a junction ('Europahütte'). Soon you will glimpse the famous CKSB up to the right.

72 0:30: After 5min, TL onto a tarmac lane and cross a bridge. Afterwards, bear right and pick up a path, initially heading NE ('Europahütte'). Head either left or right at the first fork. 5min later, TR ('Europahütte') and climb steeply.

73 1:15: TL at a junction. Just afterwards, keep SH at another junction ('Europahütte').

117 1:55: Arrive at a junction beside the **CKSB**: for the Europahütte, keep SH and climb (alternatively, for Täschalp/Zermatt, TR and cross the bridge). After 25min, TL at a junction ('Europahütte').

116 2:30: Arrive at the **Europahütte (2264m)**.

Zermatt Day Hikes

The Gornergrat railway

There are plenty of mountain towns in the Alps but there are none quite like Zermatt. Set in a bowl near the top of the Mattertal valley, it is surrounded by magnificent 4000m peaks including the queen of them all, the iconic Matterhorn (4478m). The unusual crooked shape of the Matterhorn and its position, standing regally apart from its peers, draw the eye as you walk around the town. The mountain is absolutely integral to the character and atmosphere of Zermatt: it is easy to see why many people leave the town completely unaware of the names of any of the other high summits such as the Breithorn (4164m), Monte Rosa (4553m), the Dent Blanche (4357m) or the Zinalrothorn (4221m). And, in fact, the Matterhorn is so famous that it has three names: Matterhorn (German), Monte Cervino (Italian) and Mont Cervin (French).

But the Matterhorn alone is not what makes a stay in Zermatt so special: just as important is the unparalleled network of trains and cable cars that whisk the visitor into the heart of the mountains. They are expensive but they make the most incredible walking available to all, without too much effort: exactly what you need after the rigours of the WHR.

The network of walking paths is exceptional and the routes are all numbered and displayed on the free map available at the tourist office in Zermatt. A day or two on these paths will be an incredible finale to an incredible trek. In fact, you could easily spend weeks exploring them. To make life simple for you, we feature three of the best in this section: see the text below and the map on p176. The walk numbers are those used on the tourist office map.

The Five Lakes (Walk no. 11)

An easy but magnificent walk around the tarns near Sunnegga. It passes many of the classic Matterhorn viewpoints with stunning reflections of the mountain in the lakes. The route can also be accessed directly from Stage 13b of the WHR: signposts to the lakes from Sunnegga.

Time: 2.5hr

Distance: 8km

Ascent/Descent: 160m/450m

Refreshments: Blauherd, Ze Seewjinen, Sunnegga

Start: Blauherd (funicular railway and cable car from Zermatt).

Finish: Sunnegga (funicular railway back to Zermatt)

Edelweissweg (Walk no. 30)

On a fine day, this route will be a highlight of your walking career: it is the equal of any hike in the Alps. A long climb to Trift leads to the awesomely long Höhbalmen balcony path, a stone's throw from the Matterhorn. Afterwards, descend to Zermatt via the lovely hamlet of Zmutt. Because the climb cannot be avoided using public transport, the route is less-trodden and is normally peaceful.

Time: 7-9hr (depending on route used to Trift)

Distance: 20.5-22.5km

Ascent/Descent: 1140m/1140m

Refreshments: Edelweiss Alterhaupt, Trift, Zmutt

Start/Finish: Zermatt

Gornergrat to Riffelalp (Walk no. 23)

This is a Zermatt 'must see' with some exceptional views of the Matterhorn and a host of glaciers. The ride to the start on the historic Gornergrat railway is a treat in itself: best views on the right side of the train. This walk is simply unforgettable and you can enjoy it at your leisure as the route is almost entirely downhill.

Time: 2.5hr

Distance: 6.2km

Ascent/Descent: 10m/890m

Refreshments: Gornergrat, Riffelberg, Riffelalp

Start: Gornergrat (Gornergrat railway from Zermatt).
Finish: Riffelalp (take Gornergrat railway back to Zermatt)

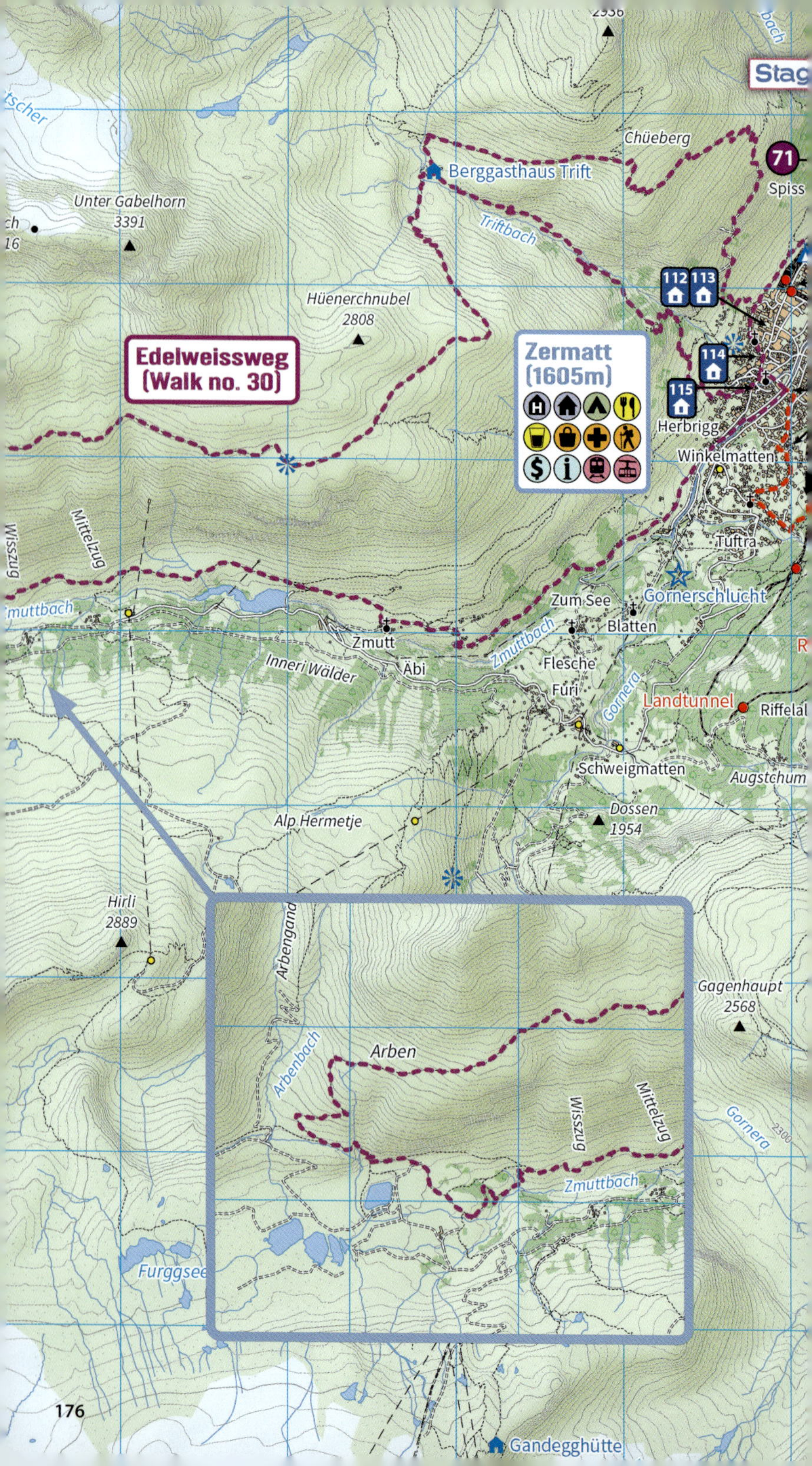
Stag
Chüeberg
Berggasthaus Trift
71
Spiss
Unter Gabelhorn
3391
Triftbach
Hüenerchnubel
2808
112
113
Edelweissweg
(Walk no. 30)
Zermatt
(1605m)
114
115
Herbrigg
Winkelmatten
Mittelzug
Wisszug
Tuftra
Gornerschlucht
Zmuttbach
Zum See
Blatten
Zmutt
Zmuttbach
Inneri Wälder
Äbi
Flesche
Furi
Gornera
Landtunnel
Riffelal
Schweigmatten
Augstchum
Alp Hermetje
Dossen
1954
Hirli
2889
Arbengand
Gagenhaupt
2568
Arbenbach
Arben
Wisszug
Mittelzug
Gornera
Zmuttbach
Furggsee
Gandegghütte

Tuftra (2215m)
Stage 13b
Sunnegga (2288m)
124
125
126
Tuftra
Ried
Eggen
Haueten
Wiesti
Matter Vispa
Sunnegga
Blauherd
Unterrothorn 3103
Oberrothorn 3413
Furggji 2982
Chessi
Tufterchumme
Ritzengrat
Leisee
Egge
Findeln
Wildi
Ze Gassu
Bord
Findelbach
Balmbrunne
Stellisee
Grindjesee
Fluhalp
Mossjesee
Grüensee
Mountain Lodge Ze Seewjinu
The Five Lakes (Walk no. 11)
Gugle 2720
Riffelberg
Hohtälli
Hohtälligrat
Gornergratsee
Rotenboden
Gornergrat
Murischloch
Riffelsee
Riffelhorn 2930
Usser Gornerli
Tuftgrat
Gornerglet
Gornergrat to Riffelalp (Walk no. 23)
110
111
107

Facilities along the route

Stage	Place	Hotel	Hut/Gîte/ Hostel	Campsite	Meals/ Drinks (non-residents)	Shops	ATM/Info	Transport
Start	Chamonix	Hotel	Hut	Campsite	Meals, Drinks	Grocery, Outdoor gear, Pharmacy	ATM, Info	Train, Bus, Cable car
1a	Les Praz de Chamonix	Hotel		Campsite	Meals, Drinks	Grocery, Outdoor gear		Train, Bus, Cable car
1a	Chalet du Paradis				Drinks			
1a	Les Tines	Hotel			Meals, Drinks			Train, Bus
1a	Argentière	Hotel		Campsite	Meals, Drinks	Grocery, Outdoor gear, Pharmacy	ATM, Info	Train, Bus
1b	Le Tour	Hotel	Hut		Meals, Drinks			Bus, Cable car
1c	Charamillon		Hut		Meals, Drinks			Cable car
1c	Refuge du Col de Balme		Hut		Meals, Drinks			Cable car OR
1d/v1e	Le Peuty		Hut	Campsite	Meals, Drinks			
1e/v1e	Trient	Hotel	Hut	Campsite	Meals, Drinks			Bus
v1d	Refuge les Grands		Hut					
2a	Col de la Forclaz	Hotel		Campsite	Meals, Drinks	Grocery Basic		Bus
2b	Chalet du Glacier				Meals, Drinks			
2b	Relais d'Arpette		Hut	Campsite	Meals, Drinks			
v2b	Bovine				Meals, Drinks			
v2b	Plan de l'Au				Drinks			
v2b	Champex-d'en-Haut		Hut		Meals, Drinks			
2c/v2b	Champex	Hotel	Hut	Campsite	Meals, Drinks	Grocery, Outdoor gear	ATM, Info	Bus
3	Sembrancher				Meals, Drinks	Grocery, Pharmacy		Train, Bus

Stage	Place	Hotel	Hut/Gîte/ Hostel	Campsite	Meals/ Drinks (non-residents)	Shops	ATM/Info	Transport
3	Le Châble							
4	Clambin							
4	Cabane du Mont Fort							OR
5	Cabane de Prafleuri							
v3a	Orsières							
v3b	Cabane de Mille							
v4a	Cabane Brunet							
v4b	Fionnay							
v4c	Cabane de Louvie							
6a	Cabane les Ecoulaies							
6a	Refuge de la Barmaz							
v6b	Cabane des Dix							
6b	Arolla							
7a	Le Louché							
7a	La Gouille							
7b	Les Haudères							
7c	La Sage							
8	le Tsaté							
8	Lac de Châteaupré							
8	Cabane de Moiry							

Stage	Place	Hotel	Hut/Gîte/ Hostel	Campsite	Meals/ Drinks (non-residents)	Shops	ATM/Info	Transport
9a/v8a	Barrage de Moiry							
v9a	Grimentz							
9b	Sorebois							
9b	Zinal							
10/v10b	Gruben							
v10a	Hôtel Weisshorn							
v10b	Cabane Bella Tola							OR
11	Jungen							
11	St-Niklaus							
12a/v12c	Gasenried							
v12b	Grächen							
v12a	Mattsand							
12b/v12a	Herbriggen							
12c/v13b	Europahütte							
v12a	Randa							
13a	Täschalp							Taxi to Täsch
13b	Tufteren/Tuftra							
13b	Sunnegga/Ze Gassu							
v13a	Täsch							Taxi (p172)
13b/v13a	Zermatt							

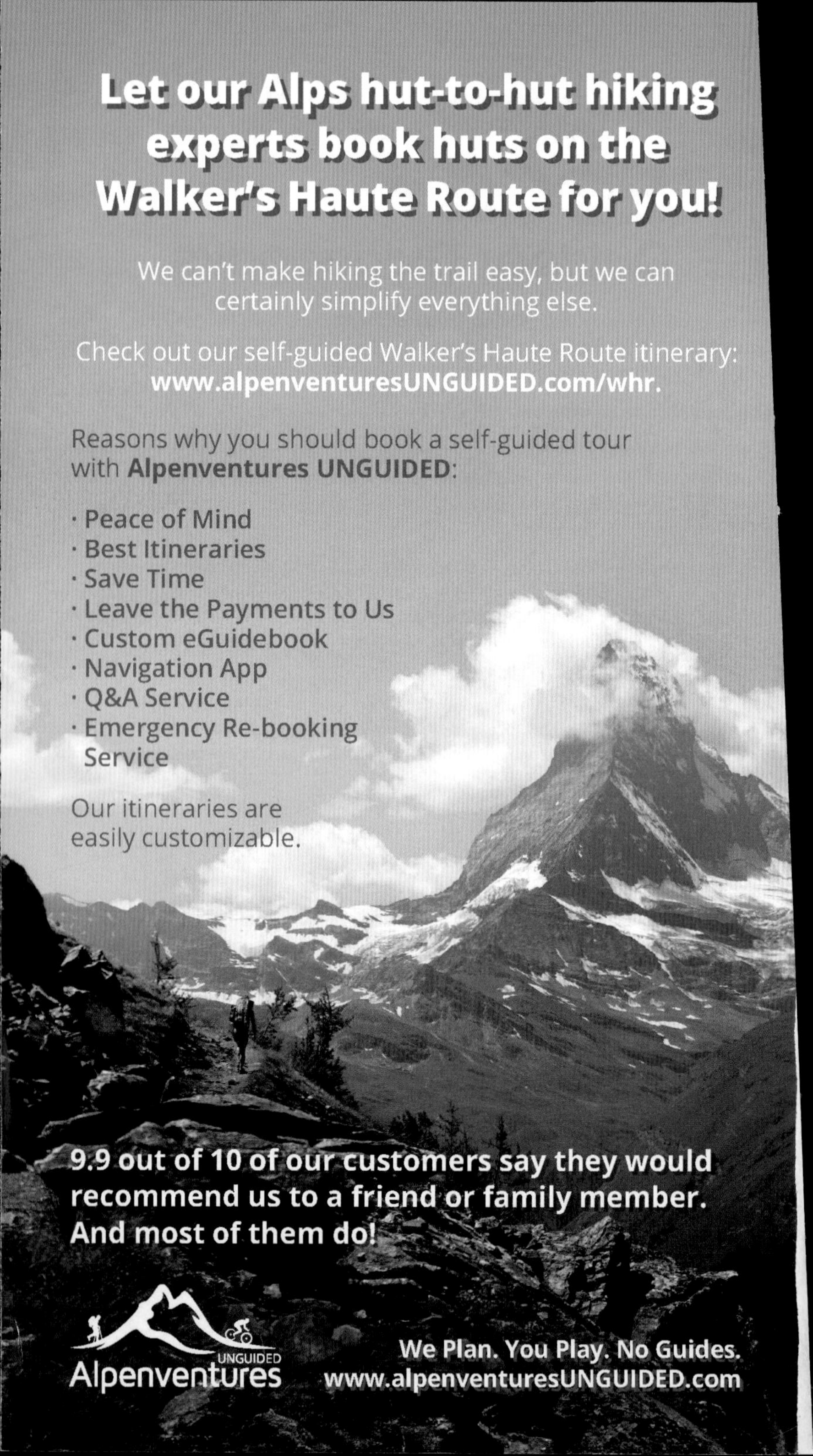
Let our Alps hut-to-hut hiking experts book huts on the Walker's Haute Route for you!
We can't make hiking the trail easy, but we can certainly simplify everything else.
Check out our self-guided Walker's Haute Route itinerary: www.alpenventuresUNGUIDED.com/whr.
Reasons why you should book a self-guided tour with Alpenventures UNGUIDED:
· Peace of Mind
· Best Itineraries
· Save Time
· Leave the Payments to Us
· Custom eGuidebook
· Navigation App
· Q&A Service
· Emergency Re-booking Service
Our itineraries are easily customizable.
9.9 out of 10 of our customers say they would recommend us to a friend or family member. And most of them do!
UNGUIDED
Alpenventures
We Plan. You Play. No Guides.
www.alpenventuresUNGUIDED.com